# CREATIVE EXPERIENCES
# FOR YOUNG CHILDREN

# CREATIVE EXPERIENCES FOR YOUNG CHILDREN

## Third Edition

Mimi Brodsky Chenfeld

*Foreword by Jane Wiechel*

HEINEMANN
Portsmouth, NH

27.00

**Heinemann**
A division of Reed Elsevier Inc.
361 Hanover Street
Portsmouth, NH 03801–3912
www.heinemann.com

*Offices and agents throughout the world*

© 2002 by Mimi Brodsky Chenfeld

The author and publisher wish to thank those who have generously given permission to reprint borrowed material:

Photograph top of p. 67 courtesy of Paul M. Bowers, © Paul M. Bowers.

Photograph on p. 89 courtesy of Henry T. Foster, First Impressions Photography.

Cover child—Mita McIntyre

Back cover children—Callie, Ryan, Chloe, Landen, Len, Dylan, and Noah

**Library of Congress Cataloging-in-Publication Data**
Chenfeld, Mimi Brodsky.
    Creative experiences for young children / Mimi Brodsky Chenfeld ; foreword by Jane Wiechel.—3rd ed.
        p.  cm.
    Includes bibliographical references.
    ISBN 0-325-00367-X
    1. Creative activities and seat work.  2. Education, Preschool—Curricula. 3. Education, Primary—Curricula.  4. Active learning.  5. Education, Preschool—Activity programs.  6. Education, Primary—Activity programs. I. Title

    LB1140.35.C74 C48 2002
    372.5–dc21
                                                                2002032811

*Editor:* Danny Miller
*Production editor:* Sonja S. Chapman
*Cover design:* Joni Doherty
*Cover photo:* Madeleine Farber
*Back cover photo:* Cara Chenfeld
*Manufacturing:* Steve Bernier
*Compositor:* PD & PS Typesetters

Printed in the United States of America on acid-free paper

06 05 04 03 02   RRD   1 2 3 4 5

For my mom, Iris Kaplan, who kept asking, "Is it finished yet?" (Mom, it's never finished!).

In memory of Joseph Kaplan, Rose and Charles Chenfeld, and those who went before us.

For my awesome children: Cliff and Chana, Cara and Jim, Dan and Kristi.

For my outasight grandchildren: Len, Callie, Dylan, Chloe, Ryan, Noah, and Landen.

For my anchor man, Howard.

For ALL the children and for those of you who love, care for, and teach them.

May we all walk together towards a world of peace.

# CONTENTS

# FOREWORD

Childhood wonder is an intelligence of the most profound and sincere variety. This intelligence, innate and immeasurable, is the hallmark of human zeal. If we strive to nurture this aptitude as a community, as parents and as educators, we can begin to fully harness its potential. This nurturing requires the ability to look beyond the perimeters of cut-and-dried adulthood and to empower children as facilitators of a brighter future.

Through providing children with an environment in which they are free to imagine, aspire, and create, we refine the tools that they will employ throughout adulthood. Through recognizing the value of the arts as a medium for creativity and aesthetic development, we promote the critical thinking skills that will aid them in problem solving. Through encouraging and expanding upon children's playtime activities and through supporting their caregivers and educators, we are reinforcing the foundations of achievement.

These efforts require patience, tolerance for the unconventional, and above all, vision. In our fast-food-ridden culture of immediate gratification, it is often difficult to resist the Band-Aid approach and to implement long-term strategies for resolution. Yet, if we are able as a community to invoke the collective vision essential to revolution, we will find that children themselves have long held, sometimes incognito, the attributes for success. After all, even the most esteemed biologist was once a child catching lightning bugs.

*Creative Experiences for Young Children* provides hundreds of teacher-developed ideas and strategies for creating learning communities in our classrooms—ways of celebrating the wonderments of learning and discovery. Mimi Chenfeld has offered us the opportunity to teach creatively and help our children and ourselves listen with hearts and minds through the beauty of poetry, literature, music, story, dance, drama, and play. The wide scope of Mimi's talents takes her from educator to artist, a friend of children and teachers whose personality sparkles like sand in the sun.

—Jane Wiechel, Associate Superintendent,
Ohio Department of Education, and
President, National Association for the
Education of Young Children (NAEYC)

# SOME ACKNOWLEDGMENTS

Writing acknowledgments is more challenging than writing this book itself! With time, space, and money enough, I would reprint Walt Whitman's entire text of "Song of Myself" in which he celebrates his relationships with every person and creature he knows or has passed by, singing to us that he is of the old and young, of the foolish and the wise, that he learns with the simplest and is a teacher of the thoughtfullest . . . (did I get away with that?). Then I would add my own lengthy (and alas, incomplete) continuation of Whitman's poem!

How lucky I am to spend so much of my time being with children, teachers, university students, families, and community members in extraordinary programs. Thanks to Ray Hanley, President of the Greater Columbus Arts Council; and Tim Katz, Terry Anderson, Jim Murray, and Jim Arter, who coordinate the GCAC's Artists in the School and Children of the Future programs; my wonderful family of artist/educators in our Days of Creation Arts for Kids; Irvin M. Lippman, Executive Director of the Columbus Museum of Art; Carole Genshaft and her Education Department Staff; my fellow poets—Terry Hermsen and Dionne Custer Brooks, working hand in hand and heart to heart with the Columbus Public Schools in our amazing collaborative arts enrichment program DepARTures; Barbara Topolosky, Director of the Early Childhood Program of the Leo Yassenoff Jewish Center, assisted by Sherie Wack and Taryn Terwilliger, and dear friends and colleagues on staff; Chairperson of Otterbein College's Education Department, Niki Fayne, and her super staff for welcoming my Arts Across the Curriculum course these many years; Kathy Shahbodaghi and her dedicated workers who coordinate the Columbus Metropolitan Library's outstanding summer programs for children; the fabulous OSU Hillel Folk Dancers who *always* open the circles to welcome all children.

These are some of my *constant* involvements. Because of the countless opportunities they offer me, everything, *everything* I believe is continually validated! With children of *all* ages and their teachers, we constantly explore ideas, experiment, discover, rediscover, and reaffirm. These are priceless gifts!

Brenda Stenberg, Tina Franks, and Jackie Brown of the Children's Department of the Bexley Library gave generously of their time and talents to help gather excellent examples of children's literature. Ditto Sally Oddi, Karen Kerchner, and Laura Jacobs of Columbus' premier children's bookstore, Cover to Cover.

So many friends, neighbors, family members, fellow educators, caring citizens shared photos and illustrations of children's works! I wish that each and every one could have been included in the book. *I live in dread of omitting any of their names. I apologize throughout these acknowledgments!*

Becky Love (she lives her name!), Director of Franklin County Board of Mental Retardation/Developmental Disabilities (MR/DD) Early Childhood Services spread the word of our book to Kathy Bernon, art teacher at the Early Childhood Learning Community at Marburn School and the ECE and Family Center at Johnstown Road, Columbus, Ohio. Kathy and staffs gathered dozens of photos of their beautiful children to share with readers of this book. Cathy Arment and her first graders at Etna Road School in Whitehall-Yearling Public Schools, Whitehall, Ohio, devoted time and creative energies to illustrating all of our themes; Mary Jane Walcher inspired Madeleine Farber of the Unitarian Cooperative Pre School, San Diego, California, to capture the beauty of her students and send their photos; Debbie Charna and Anita Candler photographed projects and bulletin boards from rooms and halls of the Columbus School for Girls. Kindergartners and squirrels were caught in images and shared by Jeanette Canyon, Devie Hiller, and Kate Zutell from the Columbus School for Girls. Carol Cruikshank and Chris Murray, super art teachers, sent slides of children's works from the Alpine School and Easthaven Schools, Columbus Public Schools; Joseph Cabalquinto took photos of Marlene Robbins' dance kids at Indianola School, Columbus, Ohio. Mark "Brad" Feinknopf, Cookie Zingarelli, Mindie Zisser, Leslie Rosen, Mary Warren, Golan Canaan, and Judy Romanello offered many photos and illustrations of the Leo Yassenoff Jewish Center Early Childhood kids. Kaye and Clarissa Boiarski and Leslie Zak helped me go through hundreds of photos from Days of Creation programs.

Every day envelopes full of treasured pictures and children's works arrived. Thanks to: Adit Granite, Jan Pettibone, Debbie Yoho, Rhoda Linder, Jennifer Lee, Alan Lee, Miriam Schulman, Ted and Lori Fireman, Dorothy and Cullen Daniel, Dennis Howard and Joanne Kadle, Caryn and John Falvey, Tom and Jean O'Brien, Ellen Half, Vesna and Guiseppe Mangano, Kristi Brodsky Chenfeld, Chana Gandal and Cara Chenfeld. Callie Rose Wilbat and Leah Miller contributed amazing numbers of excellent illustrations.

Tracy Napper and Jo Ann Weaver have been loyal friends of this book in all its journeys. I'm indebted to their love and caring.

Eileen Nelson and the Redleaf Publishing Company staff made it possible for me to continue writing this book by doing all the hard work of organizing and publishing my new collection, *Teaching by Heart*.

Extra special gratitude to Leslie Gelber and Mary Ausbrooks for salvaging our book from my typewriter into more millennium machines! Thanks, Sue Robinson, for pinch hitting.

Thanks to Marilyn Cohen, master teacher and sister-in-love; to Laura Walcher, my sister who edits me with tough love; to Herb and Bob and my bro, Mike and his Joy, who always root for me with humor; to all the families (Chenfelds, Gandals, Wilbats, Walchers, Cohens, Falveys, Jacobsons, Blooms, Selingers, Rappoports, Kaplans, Newmans, O'Briens) for lifelines of support. Thanks all our dear friends who didn't leave me through the years of this rewriting/revision process.

Thanks to the countless children, teachers, university students, community members who care about our kids for sharing your stories and ideas in our time together along the journey.

I'm indebted to all the organizations, schools, programs, festivals, conferences, inservice and staff development courses, and seminars in the Central Ohio area and throughout the country who have taught me invaluable lessons which I joyfully pass on to everyone along the way. We need each other and are there for each other. Thanks for the treasured experiences. Your names would comprise a Yellow Pages of fantastic resources! We may be scattered throughout the country and world but know that we are *one* family and all the children are *our* children.

Danny Miller, my editor at Heinemann, has been a total delight to work with. His humor, patience and wisdom are deeply appreciated. Thanks to the Heinemann staff for their invaluable help, including Production Editor Sonja Chapman and copywriter Charlene Morris.

And last and first, Howard.

Mimi

# PREFACE

The first draft of this book was written many months before publication. The following was the original beginning.

## PREFACE I

On February 16, 1993, about two hundred schoolchildren, many of them very young, were visiting the Twin Towers in New York City when explosions were heard, the lights went out, smoke filled the air, alarms and cries rang fear. Many were caught on the Observation Roof. About fifty-five young children, their teachers, and chaperones were trapped for six hours in a dark elevator hanging perilously between the forty-third and forty-second floors of one of the country's tallest buildings. When police and firefighters miraculously led them to safety, everyone was astonished at how calm and strong the children appeared after such a terrifying, life-threatening ordeal. How did those heroic teachers keep those children (and themselves) from completely (and understandably) panicking? Did they hand out worksheets? Assign silent seatwork? Prepare for tests? Or did they sing, tell stories, play games, talk together? What do you think?

Fortunately, we and our children are not caught in a darkened, smoky elevator suspended between high floors in a city skyscraper, but many teachers and children are caught in closed-in, test-driven, high-pressured, anxiety-ridden, alarming, topsy-turvy times. The earth under our feet quakes from geological and political shifts and the ground under the field of education shakes from upheavals of ideas, polarizing philosophies and opinions, criss-crossing decisions and directions. How to keep calm and strong through it all?

At the time that this was written (not so long ago), no one could have foretold the tragic events of September 11, 2001. Once again, the Twin Towers were the center of current events of momentous proportions.

## PREFACE II

In the daily barrage of heartbreaking images, words, and sounds of alarm that followed September 11, searing it forever on our collective and individual memories, little was written or told about the effect of the attacks and destruction on the thousands of children and teachers who attended schools and programs in the surrounding neighborhoods. Part of the countless accounts of heroism and courage are the stories of teachers who guided their students to faraway buildings in safer areas, kept spirits and motivation alive, cooperated with host staffs, and continued positive learning experiences. And heroic were the teachers who shared rooms, desks, materials, and time with the displaced children, offering reassuring welcomes to the traumatized migrants.

So the catastrophic events of September 11, 2001, must be added to that first memory written not so long ago and intended to begin this book. Our mandate to create and continue environments of warmth, safety, and trust, to share positive, joyful learning experiences, is more imperative than ever. In the increasingly troubled and dangerous world, the world we help build for our children must reflect our deepest values, our highest hopes, and our strongest efforts.

To repeat: *How to keep calm and strong through it all?*

The kids filled every seat on the preschool bus. One little guy wore cool sunglasses. When he stood up to exit, I saw that he was a thumbsucker. He jumped down from the bus—cool sunglasses, thumb in mouth, backpack on back. I asked him, "What's in your backpack?"

He told me, "Pampers."

As our toddlers carry their Pampers into an ever-widening offering of programs and on to kindergarten and up through the early grades, the air around them is sparked with discordant dialogue and dialectic. *Too much play? Start skills and drills earlier? Cut the arts? Developmentally Appropriate Practices? Whole Language? Phonics? Push first-grade curriculum down to kindergarten? Test toddlers? Get kids reading before kindergarten? Remove clay, sand, dress-up clothes from kindergarten? Too many frills? One reading method fits all? Strategies? Materials?* Which side are you on? Do we have to choose sides?

Through all these passionately felt and eloquently articulated issues whirling around them, children do what children *do*: play, wonder, interact, respond, manipulate, question, observe, laugh, doodle, talk, sing, dance, experiment, explore, discover, make connections, find where they belong in the ever more complicated scheme of things.

The old story goes like this: Long ago, two men had the same dream. They dreamt that the wheat everyone ate had something in it that drove people crazy. What to do?

"When everyone eats the wheat," one of the men suggested, "we won't. When everyone goes crazy, we won't."

They pondered the idea. Then the second man said, "But, if everyone goes crazy except us, they'll think *we're* crazy!"

Silence while they thought of a solution. Finally, one of the men said, "Look, when everyone eats the wheat, we'll eat the wheat. When everyone goes crazy, we'll go crazy. *But*, let's tie a knot in our belts. When we touch it, we'll remember who we really are and what we really believe."

Creative and loving teachers, no matter what pressures and problems surround them, invite their students into rooms where they are welcomed and regarded. Their time together is hallowed time. Harsh winds may be raging around them, even pounding the walls of their buildings, but in their rooms, children are safe, never humiliated, never alienated. They are "family." They are a community working together, sharing, helping, celebrating. Children feel free to ask questions, make mistakes, make discoveries, find ways to learn that give them the delicious taste of success.

It's not always easy to define creative teaching to those who wonder what it's all about! The late Herb Sandberg, beloved storyteller and kid lover from the University of Toledo, had a beautiful explanation. It's fitting to begin this book with his insight (needed now more than ever).

Herb remembered the tale of "The Emperor's Nightingale" by Hans Christian Andersen. In that story, the nightingale, with its sweet voice, is replaced in the Emperor's palace and heart by a shiny, bejeweled, artificial, mechanical bird of the brightest colors and a voice almost as lovely as that of the banished nightingale. Everything is fine until the Emperor gets sick. Nothing can cure him. He calls for the mechanical nightingale to sing for him, but it is broken. Death sits on the bed of the Emperor. Suddenly, the most beautiful, sweet, pure sound is heard. The real nightingale has flown back to sing to the dying Emperor. The song of the real nightingale is so pure and powerful that even Death is moved and leaves the Emperor. The Emperor is cured! The nightingale is never sent away again.

Herb shared this metaphor: "Most of our children hear only the sound of the mechanical bird. Too many of our kids have never heard the song of the *real* nightingale!"

Creative teaching means helping our children and ourselves listen with hearts and minds to the songs of the real nightingale, who sings of the beauty of poetry, literature, music, story, visual arts, dance, drama, delightful play. The nightingale sings of the excitement of learning and discovery. Its song is the song of wonder and enchantment.

The job description for creative teachers is a mix of metaphors. Creative teachers are Charlotte, spinning words in their webs to save the lives and spirits of their Wilburs. They are the eye in this storm—clear and calm in the center of the raging winds. They are Glenda the

Good Witch helping their Dorothies home to the safety of Kansas. Creative teachers are houses made of bricks so no wolves can blow them down. They are the home plate, Cities of Refuge, jumper cables, CPR for the spirits of their students, friends of the *real* nightingale.

When we listen to the song of the *real* nightingale, we will help our children develop lifelong love affairs with learning, gathering treasures to last for years to come that they will cherish and remember. If we listen only to the mechanical bird, we will become disoriented, enticed by the glitter of mechanical marvels and seduced by high-tech strategies and materials.

All of our children are waiting to learn in loving communities where the song of the real nightingale is the music in the air they breathe.

Tie a knot in your belt. Touch it and remember who you really are and what you really believe.

# SOME LETTERS, POSTCARDS, AND NOTES OF INTRODUCTION

Dear Reader,

Because I can't spend time with you, talking, laughing, remembering, planning together, I wrote this book. It's the closest I can get to being with you.

The following messages will help make some sense out of it all as we prepare for our adventures along the lifelong journey of learning, along the scenic route of creative teaching.

## LETTER ONE: IDEAS

This is a book of ideas, suggestions, shared experiences from *real* teachers and children.

A good idea is a good idea if *you* like it. If *you* like it, you will shape it to fit *your* students. Each of our classes or groups of children is a unique blend of individuals, never carbon copies of any other group.

Whether you are teaching in a special ed setting, an English as a second language program, a gifted and talented enrichment class, a multiage infant-toddler group, a traditional kindergarten—*whatever* your scene, the challenge is the same.

Find ideas *you* like. Change, adopt, adapt, arrange, rearrange, combine, connect, blend, mix and match the ideas to meet the needs of *your* specific setting and students.

Creativity is not a strategy or technique. It's not scheduled for Wednesdays after lunch if our dittos are finished! It's a *way* of being, thinking, and teaching. Teaching in the key of life means we're bright with enthusiasm, excitement, spontaneity, risk taking, open-mindedness, open-ended challenges, flexibility, divergent thinking, playfulness, imagination, and innovation.

Play with ideas! Make them your own!

*Postcard*

Please don't call me to ask permission to change any of the ideas offered. The ideas belong to you.

## LETTER TWO: MULTICULTURAL EDUCATION

My feelings about multicultural education for your children are similar to my philosophy about language. Just as our children need to learn and live in a language-rich, language-immersed (I like to say language-drenched!) environment in which language in all its components is happening all the time, so our children need to learn to value diversity and respect and appreciate the cultural richness of others *at all times*. Your curriculum and everyday life with your students should be saturated with the awareness and knowledge of the gifts contributed to the human story by all of its peoples. The challenge is to celebrate diversity as we strengthen unity.

As you read this book, train yourself to blend multicultural awareness with all ideas. Photos, pictures, books, music, games, vocabulary, designs, and food are all obvious and delightful ways to enhance familiarity with and sensitivity to diverse cultures. Don't limit your multicultural curriculum to things. A learning community of respect and appreciation for ourselves and others is the garden in which multicultural education takes root and flourishes.

Yes, with you, children will learn songs, stories, customs, and celebrations from cultures other than their own, but they will also learn a deeper lesson: that all the children of the human family make music, make stories, make art, make dances, share feelings and dreams. Common threads tie people together even as they weave different patterns.

Lori Rubin and Navaz Peshotan Bhavnagri wrote about the challenges of welcoming Chaldean immigrant children into our communities and schools. Their beliefs about this specific situation extend to all children in all settings.

"Schools have to be safe, pluralistic and inclusive environments where all students are genuinely accepted and respected. Ultimately, all students have to be prepared to live harmoniously in communities that are becoming increasingly multiethnic."[1]

## LETTER THREE: YOU ARE BILINGUAL!

One language for the spirit of the children, the joyous spirit of learning together in a loving environment, the spirit of the first syllable in FUNDAMENTALS—FUN! The other language for all those who challenge you to explain what you are doing, hold you accountable! *You* must *know what you're doing at all times and have the language to clarify your lessons*. When the worried parent stopped at the kindergarten room and found the children singing and dancing to their special good morning welcome song, she asked the teacher what was going on. The teacher responded: "Small and gross motor skills, sequential learning, language development, following directions, cooperation, patterning, vocabulary development, listening skills, reviewing information. . . ." Wow! The parent was immediately reassured. She needed that explanation.

Do *you* know what you're doing, and can you explain it? You *are* bilingual![2]

## LETTER FOUR: MAGIC VOCABULARY

Within our vocabulary of thousands of words, a few words take on special powers. They're the words representing our most fascinating areas of interest or the people, places, and things we feel most deeply about. I call these words our *Magic Vocabulary*. Even our youngest children have the start of their own Magic Vocabulary, and when we are tuned into their interests and "favorite" magnetic fields, we can connect to any curriculum in relevant ways. Be aware of Len's fascination with all kinds of *balls*, with Ryan's talent for mixing up *concoctions*, for Chole's love for *The Little Mermaid*. These are high on their Magic Vocabulary lists. Dante will stop anything to play with *blocks*. Sierra will always wake up from her snooze if you say, "Let's *sing*." Nathan will skim blurry pages of books but will hold the pages that feature *dogs*.

What's on *your* Magic Vocabulary list? What's on the Magic Vocabulary list of your students?[3]

## LETTER FIVE: MULTIPLE INTELLIGENCES

Howard Gardner's important contribution of the "multiple intelligences" encourages us to consider intelligence in more pluralistic ways. We humans are a complex mix of strengths, interests, and abilities. Gardner's basic intelligences, describing different spheres of learning, are verbal-linguistic, logical-mathematical, visual-spatial, bodily-kinesthetic, musical-rhythmic, interpersonal, intrapersonal, and naturalistic. Intelligences are still being added. When we are aware of these important differentiations in each individual, our teaching will be enriched by the great variety of learning opportunities we offer our students.[4]

### *Postcard*

No *one* method or material, however excellent, will be effective with *all* students.

## LETTER SIX: LETTERS HOME!

Communication with families is a high-priority component of success! Creative teachers have letters in the mail (some even before the first week of school) to the families of their students, welcoming them to the new year, inviting them to be actively involved in their children's school lives. What interests, hobbies, skills, stories, collections, careers can they share with the children? Leave room for write-in responses and be sure to schedule time for families to share their gifts with the children as valued and honored classroom visitors. Second, most of the things we toss out in the trash can be treasures in the classroom. List some of the items you ask families to bring in to your scrounge box or "junk" bag. Children learn that many "throwaway" things are wonderful resources for countless projects. Ask families to save such items as paper towel rolls, toilet paper rolls, plastic and Styrofoam fast-food containers, coffee and cereal boxes and cans, colorful wrapping paper, greeting card pictures, old magazines. . . . This is an ongoing collection of scrounge stuff that children help recycle into important and creative works of art, displays, constructions, and collections. Those of you who have been with young children know that many times they would rather play with the *box* a gift comes in than with the gift! Boxes of every size and design should always be welcomed into your space. Don't wait too long. This is a right-away writing assignment that sets the tone of closeness and cooperation between school and family. A most important link.[5]

### Postcard

Really mean it when you invite families to be an integral part of your program and classroom. Be responsive. Make room for their contributions and welcome them to your room! Encourage their meaningful participation.

## LETTER SEVEN: SOME COMMUNITY RESOURCES/ SUGGESTIONS FOR FIELD TRIPS AND CLASSROOM VISITORS

Sometimes, when author/illustrators like Michael Joel Rosen[6] visit a classroom or a school, preparations for that visit have gone on for weeks! Follow-up projects and activities inspired by his visit are expanded and enjoyed. Creative teachers value the importance of special visitors and field trips to generate a myriad of viable and exciting experiences (ends in themselves) that enrich and expand their students' level of involvement and learning. As you read lists of suggestions in the appendix, remember, they mean nothing in themselves! *It's what you do with them that gives them life, that turns the ordinary into the extraordinary.* A field trip to a nearby field with a creative and loving teacher sharing sensory awareness, conversation, observations, songs, stories, and ideas for illustrations, poems, and crafts projects will be more valuable and enjoyable to the children than a private jet whisking them to an African rain forest with a grim, superstructured, inflexible, unenthusiastic, unimaginative teacher. I'd rather have my child walk to the field around the corner. Wouldn't you?

Every community—rural, urban, suburban—has its own offerings. Often the best ideas are right in front of our eyes but we miss them (see the appendix for many suggestions).

## LETTER EIGHT: SIX LIFE THEMES

The six themes in this book flow along with the ever-expanding worlds of children as they move from their close-up focus on themselves— their bodies and their senses—out to their immediate surroundings, to their families and friends, and continuing outward-bound to the greater worlds around them.

Even as you read about each theme separately (this is a circular book written as it must be in a linear way!), know that each is intertwined with the others, inextricably connected. None exists in isolation. Each spills over to the others and enriches and is enriched. Read along but play with possibilities to integrate, connect, and combine. Surprise yourself and delight your students with your own original fusion.

| THEME ONE: | OUR FANTASTIC BODIES/OUR AMAZING SENSES |
|---|---|
| THEME TWO: | OUR FEELINGS |
| THEME THREE: | OUR UNIQUENESS |
| THEME FOUR: | OUR FAMILIES/OUR FRIENDS |
| THEME FIVE: | OTHERS WE MEET/OUR WORLDS WIDEN |
| THEME SIX: | OUR NATURAL WORLD/OUR ENVIRONMENT |

## LETTER NINE: SUBSECTIONS

Our six major life themes are sparked with subsections that highlight natural, accessible, delightful ways of approaching and enriching ideas. Keep making connections as you read.

### Think About It

A brief discussion of the theme. If *you* don't consider a concept or idea valuable, vital, or interesting, you certainly *can't* teach it with enthusiasm.

### Discovery Times/Wonder Times: Points of Interest

Plato said that all learning begins with wonder. In our manic world of dizzying machines and mechanical marvels, wonder too often and too early turns into a packaged bread; joy turns into a dishwashing liquid; bold becomes a detergent; and love turns into a cosmetic. The enchantment of wonder must be held in the forefront of our thinking, leaving room for the discoveries children make and share with you. This book is about the scenic route on our journey. We talk together, gather ideas, pay attention to the concepts and points of interest that most compel our students. These are meaningful, relevant launching pads for open-ended, never-ending adventures in learning. Any one of the items in this subsection can propel weeks and months of exploration. Oh, the wonder of it all![7]

### Suggested Vocabulary

Every idea inspires its own vocabulary. How natural and easy it is for children to enrich their vocabulary when words are connected to ideas that are meaningful to them! This subsection offers suggestions for just that connection—it's a starter list and needs the addition of ideas you and your students contribute. Words are worlds of possibilities in themselves. For example, the word *cat* can be illustrated, sculpted, turned into a puppet, a riddle, a game, a story, a poem, a chant, a mask, a costume, a song, a poster, a dream, a drama, a chart, a report. . . . Think about the potential activities inherent in our words.

### Talk/Listen/Read/Write: The Gifts of Language

How can children of the human family learn their language without countless daily experiences in talking and listening? Talking is the normal way people relate to each other as they work, play, plan, and problem solve. When talking is valued, the importance of listening is elevated. Words spoken lead to words written and read. In human history, oral language preceded written language by centuries! We know that children don't learn well in silence, in grim, overly structured, tense settings. When I visit schools and see our young students sitting in hushed rooms, heads bent over long periods of seatwork, scolded when there's a whisper to each other, I grieve for the spirit of joyful learning lost, perhaps never to be regained. One of my favorite proverbs is the African saying, "Talking together is loving one another."

In considering this subsection, a reminder: *Language is at the very core of human learning.* Too often, we (who should know better) separate the components of language, teaching them in isolation. Our children, who naturally make connections and see relationships, too often are taught in disjoined ways. So I use the term *gifts of language* to keep the power, mystery, and wonder of language in all its dimensions as we walk and talk with our young children along this path.

## Music Makers/Movers and Shakers

This subsection is *not* a frill! Many infants hum and sing before they talk. Babies in the womb move and bounce to rhythms played in "outside" rooms! Music, dance, song, and playfulness are very, very old in our collective history. Caves carbon-dated thirty thousand to seventy thousand years old preserve clear paintings on their stone walls depicting illustrations of people and animals in movement. Musical instruments, amulets, and masks are treasures found in those caves. I think of the caves as history's lessons to us to remember that from the earliest days of the human story, music and dance and the arts were basic core activities helping people express events and feelings, helping people communicate with each other.

Movement is a sign of life. When something stops moving for a long time, we say it's dead! Too many of our children *sit* passively, inactively for too long in too many programs and classrooms. Our newspapers headline warnings of overweight, underexercised, unhealthy young children growing up in this computer age of ours. All of our children need active, rhythmic, musical, playful, physically satisfying moments every day. They need to sing together, listen to music of diverse styles and cultures, move and dance and play together. They need the enrichment of the language of music and dance. The arts are the connective tissue of the human spirit. The kids are already moving and singing. Join them! Remember, education is a moving experience![8]

## All Ways Art

Along with music and dance, the visual arts are at the heart of our human heritage. We are always incredulous at the amazing discoveries of archeologists and anthropologists who continually find evidences of our ancestors' artistry on rocks, in sand, on skins, and on buried walls of lost villages and cities. Humans have always made their marks! We leave traces of ourselves, records of our lives, messages and rituals, celebrations and secrets, in our paintings, sculptures, mosaics, designs, symbols. Our youngest children will need no prodding from you to fill their papers with colors.

Their small hands hold pencils and brushes that write shapes and squiggles that look a lot like the ancient symbols on cave walls! When I hear stories of arts programs cut from school offerings and curricula, I cry for the children who will be deprived of these natural, joyful, creative ways of learning.[9]

## Kids Count

Just as we know our children learn best in a language-rich, active, interactive, inviting environment, so we must mix in the everyday awareness of math concepts and words. Even the youngest children will show you one tiny finger for the one-year-old birthday! From their earliest months, young children are already interested in math concepts as part of *everything* they do! Your vocabulary, meaningful questions, diverse hands-on materials, time for free play (when kids explore, experiment, and make discoveries!) are some of the ingredients in the blend. How many? How big? More? Less? How far? How heavy? Counting, measuring, comparing, collecting, and so on are aerobics for the mind happening throughout the day as children enjoy playing and working together. Keep connecting ideas![10]

### Field Trips and Visitors

In case you run out of ideas, flip directly to the appendix and enjoy the list of suggestions.

### It All Comes Together

Every idea shared in this book encourages you to see how it all comes together. If you think in an integrated, holistic way, you can't miss the point. But, some days may be more fatiguing and you might feel bogged down. This little subsection will help clarify how easily ideas come together.

## LETTER TEN: GETTING STARTED

In my hyper travels around the country, so many teachers and education students ask, "How do I get started?" To answer that challenge, there is a list in the appendix that should help you get going. But, any of the ideas on any page in the book can be used as a "starter" in any combination. You may decide to adapt a "starter" as a finale!

Always look to the children for immediate and relevant resources. Serendipity launched a fabulous week's concentration on rain forests when Jamal came into school wearing a T-shirt design of animals and trees.

Be alert! Be open to and aware of the gifts the children bring in each day. It could be a special object, a word, a shared experience, new glasses, a new baby, or a loose tooth!

Remember, we can start but we can't *finish*. Ideas can't be finished. Can we *finish* feelings, senses, colors, shapes, nature, animals? If you think ideas can be *finished*, that's the way you'll teach. As we believe, so we teach. And your students will say (as too many kids have told me), "We've *finished* the solar system!" "We've *finished* Ohio history!" When a group of children told me they'd "finished the four seasons," I had to respond, "Hey, we might as well die!" Our only limitation is *time*! Ideas do nothing but beget, beget, beget.

# LETTER ELEVEN: PLAY

Be playful. Encourage play. Play is children's work. Play is the way young children best learn. In our increasingly high-stakes, pushed-down curriculum, play is too often downplayed.

Two small incidents catch the sadness and resentment of young children disappointed in these new school adventures that seem to break promises of delight and excitement.

The first day a kindergartner ran eagerly to school. When his dad picked him up, the child was slumped in disillusionment, his initial joy of starting kindergarten totally gone.

"What happened?" the distraught parent asked, rushing to the downcast child.

"There are no blocks in kindergarten," he told his father. Then he added, "But, Dad, you said it would be fun!"

Almost the first day of kindergarten and the anxious and excited little girl couldn't sleep because of anticipation.

"Mom," she asked, "will we get to play in kindergarten?"

Her mom explained, "Well, honey. Probably not as much as in preschool."

The little girl put her hands on her hips and informed her mother, "Well, I'll tell you right now: I'm *not* going to do all that paperwork!"

Chalk it up. Two more children perhaps lost to the joy of learning. The next day, the healthy boy played sick. When children learn in active, interactive, stimulating, enjoyable ways, in open-ended, non-threatening, cooperative, loving environments, they play *healthy* when they should be staying home because they're sick. Who's the slow learner?

Are we ready for our journey? Touch the knot on your belt. Touch the knot and remember who you really are and what you really believe. Read on!

## NOTES

1. Rubin, L. and N. P. Bhavnagri. 2001. "Voices of Recent Chaldean Adolescent Immigrants." *Childhood Education* (Theme Issue: The Global Village—Migration and Education). pp. 308–312.

There are many excellent books and articles to help strengthen your commitment to creating an environment of respect and appreciation for the gifts of all peoples. Here are just a few samples:

Derman-Sparks, L. 1993. *Anti-Bias Curriculum: Tools for Empowering Young Children*. Washington, D.C.: NAEYC.

Neugebauer, B. (edition). 1992. *Alike and Different: Exploring Our Humanity with Young Children*. Washington, D.C.: NAEYC.

McCracken, J. B. 1993. *Valuing Diversity: The Primary Years*. Washington, D.C.: NAEYC.

York, S. 1992. *Developing Roots and Wings: A Trainer's Guide to Affirming Culture in Early Childhood Programs*. St. Paul, MN: Redleaf.

Carnes, J. (project director). 1997. *Starting Small: Teaching Tolerance in Preschool and the Early Grades*. Montgomery, AL: Southern Poverty Law Center.

2. Chenfeld, M. B. 1993. "There's a Wolf at Your Door." *Teaching in the Key of Life*. pp. 27–30. Washington, D.C.: NAEYC.

3. When children's Magic Vocabulary topics are hallowed at the center of learning, joy and success are practically guaranteed! Here are two books that will strengthen your commitment to honoring the interests of the children:

Katz, L. and S. Chard. 1989. *Engaging Children's Minds: The Project Approach*. (2nd ed.). Stamford, CT: Albex Publishing.

Helm, J. and L. Katz. 2000. *Young Investigators: The Project Approach in the Early Years*. New York: Teachers College Press.

Jones, E. and J. Nimmo. 1994. *Emergent Curriculum*. Washington, D.C.: NAEYC.

Levy, S. 1996. *Starting from Scratch: One Classroom Builds Its Own Curriculum*. Portsmouth, NH: Heinemann.

4. Gardner's work on multiple intelligences has been so influential in our rethinking curriculum, how children learn, and how we teach that a few of these readings would be very valuable to you:

Gardner, H. 1983. *Frames of Mind: The Theory of Multiple Intelligences*. New York: Basic Books.

Gardner, H. 1993. *Multiple Intelligences: The Theory in Practice*. New York: Basic Books.

Gardner, H. 1996. "Are There Additional Intelligences? The Case for Naturalist, Spiritual, and Existential Intelligences." *Education Information and Transformation*, ed. by J. Kane. Englewood Cliffs, NJ: Prentice Hall.

Armstrong, T. 1994. *Multiple Intelligences in the Classroom*. Alexandria, VA: Association for Supervision and Curriculum Development (ASCD).

5. The relationship between school and family is now considered a major component in effective schools and successful learning. Keep this vital connection clear in your mind, in your scheme of things. Keep informed. Examples of some of the excellent resources available are:

Edwards, P. A., A. Pleasants, and S. Franklin. 1999. *A Path to Follow: Learning to Listen to Parents*. Portsmouth, NH: Heinemann.

Gordon, A. M. and K. Williams-Browne. 2000. *Beginnings and Beyond*. (5th ed.). Albany, NY: Delmar.

Boone, E. and K. Barclay. 1995. *Building a Three Way Partnership: The Leader's Role in Linking School, Family and Community*. New York: Scholastic.

Berger, E. H. 1995. *Parents as Partners in Education: Families and Schools Working Together*. Englewood Cliffs, NJ: Prentice Hall.

6. Among Michael Joel Rosen's outstanding books for children are:

*All Eyes on the Pond*. illus. Leonard, T. 1993. New York: Hyperion.

*Bonesy and Isabel*. illus. Robinson, A. B. L. 1992. San Diego, CA: Harcourt Brace.

*Elijah's Angel*. illus. Shively, W. 1996. New York: Workman.

*Fishing with Dad*. photos Shivley, W. 1996. New York: Workman.

*The Dog Who Walked with God*. illus. Fellows, S. 1998. Cambridge, MA: Candlewick.

7. Sylvia Ashton-Warner said, "Before I teach others, I must teach myself." We can't expect our children to learn to think deeply, to wonder, to find fascination in life's countless powerful themes; we can't expect children to become enchanted with an idea or topic unless we've learned to turn the ordinary into the extraordinary. Until we are in touch with our deeper feelings about life and learning. Two books will help us in our quest:

Kessler, R. 2000. *The Soul of Education*. Alexandria, VA: Association for Supervision and Curriculum Development (ASCD).

Sornson, R. and J. Scott. (editors). 1997. *Teaching and Joy*. Alexandria, VA: ASCD.

8. The arts, especially music, dance, and drama, have been tragically neglected in the history of American education. We are just beginning to realize and appreciate their importance as basic ways many people learn. Resources like the following will help you in this understanding.

Armstrong, T. 1994. *Multiple Intelligences in the Classroom*. Alexandria, VA: ASCD.

Benzwie, T. 1998. *A Moving Experience: Dance for Lovers of Children and the Child Within*. Tucson, AZ: Zephyr Press.

Chen, J. (editor). H. Gardner, D. H. Feldman, and M. Kreschevsky. (series editors). 1998. *Project Spectrum: Early Learning Activities*. Washington, D.C.: NAEYC.

Gallas, K. 1994. *The Language of Learning: How Children Talk, Write, Dance, Draw and Sing Their Understanding of the World*. New York: Teachers College Press.

9. For inspiration in encouraging the visual arts as part of all curriculum areas, enjoy books such as these:

Blecher, S. and K. Jaffee. 1998. *Weaving in the Arts: Widening the Learning Circle*. Portsmouth, NH: Heinemann.

Edwards, C., L. Gandini, and G. Forman, (editors). 1993. *The Hundred Languages of Children: The Reggio Emilia Approach to Early Childhood Education*. Norwood, NJ: Ablex.

10. American educators are rethinking our approaches to teaching mathematics awareness and concepts to young children. Examples of a few resources with helpful insights and ideas are:

Copley, J. V. 2000. *The Young Child and Mathematics*. Washington, D.C.: NAEYC.

Carpenter, T. P. and E. Fennema. 1999. *Children's Mathematics: Cognitively Guided Instruction*. Portsmouth, NH: Heinemann.

# CREATIVE EXPERIENCES
# FOR YOUNG CHILDREN

# THEME 1 | OUR FANTASTIC BODIES/OUR AMAZING SENSES

*Four-year-old Kimani and eleven-year-old Beth sat together watching the summer scene. Beth looked lovingly at Kimani and touched his curly black hair. "You have cute hair, Kimani," she said. "What about the rest of my body?" Kimani replied.*

*"Where are you going, children?" the visitor asked the preschoolers. "To Removement with Mim," they explained.*

*"I can't see," a VIP (very important person) who is visually impaired, age 6, announced. "But," he continued before I could respond, "I can hear double!"*

## THINK ABOUT IT

Our bodies! Our first, most immediate curriculum. Our senses! Magical gateways to our world.

From our six-week-old infants kicking, squealing, blinking, and wiggling into our childcare programs; crawling, stretching, reaching their way toward toddlerhood; standing, stumbling, falling, walking, jumping, running to early start, Head Start, pre-K and kindergarten, then moving, moving, always moving up through the grades, we know that *bodies* are high on their Magic Vocabulary lists.

At every age and stage, at their own individual paces and rhythms, young children astonish us with their knowledge and skills. They are eager to show us their muscles, how tall they are, how strong, how fast. They urge us to give them opportunities to flex, to exercise, to demonstrate what they can do. They haven't yet learned to inhibit feelings, to repress their joy in accomplishments. They're always ready to celebrate their mighty feats!

Watch young children enjoying playground time. Observe the balance, coordination, courage of the kids sliding, swinging, climbing, hopping.

FIGURE 1–1 *Is anything more fun than demonstrating our mighty feats?*

Their senses are keen. Smell that flower. See the rabbit no one noticed. Listen! Was that the far-off ring of an ice cream truck? They want to bite into their world—devouring its taste, smelling its sweetness, touching its core, hearing its crunch in their mouths!

Some of the earliest words of very young children are body words. Ask sixteen-month-old Landen, "Where are your eyes?" and two tiny fingers will poke at two tiny eyes. Babies understand. They learn about identification, location, comparison, recognition, differentiation, numbers, comprehension through activities that highlight body awareness.

When our children have many opportunities to enjoy experiences centered on bodies and senses, they feel good about themselves and others. In loving, safe, noncompetitive environments, where healthy physical development is promoted, they become more self-confident, more respectful toward their friends and classmates. Together, they discover and rediscover the power of mind-body harmony.[1]

Now for the bad news. With all we know about the vital importance of active learning for young children (for all of us), with all our research supporting and encouraging physical fitness for the well-being of human growth and development, our kids are considered the most out-of-shape, most physically unfit in history! Our children sit a lot! "Couch potatoes" doesn't refer to vegetables! Tom Hunter writes in his article "Some Thoughts About Sitting Still,"[2] "if we want smarter and stronger kids, we should shut off the machines and go play in the park with our children." Our pressure-cooker, pushed-down, test-driven curricula have too often cut time for free play, for outdoor play, for daily exercise, for hang-loose time to enjoy the fun of stretching minds and bodies. It's shocking to me, in this new millennium, to see countless children sitting passively in silent, worksheet-centered, joyless rooms with no room for the celebration of our first world—the world of the human body! How many children filling the dots of dittoed worksheets *about* the body are told to "sit still"? What is the lesson here?

There's always a good reason and it's always the right time and season to enjoy a rich variety of body-mind-building experiences. Blend in the senses and you'll find connections to every subject area.

If you keep your activities flexible and open-ended, every child in your group will find meaningful and delightful ways to participate. In the case of children with special physical or emotional needs, focus on the things they *can* do. You'll be surprised at the variety of ways humans *can* express themselves through movement. Although some children have special challenges, they are *whole* persons who are both aware of their limitations and capable of enormous compensations. Most of these children can teach us about courage, faith, and humor!

Let's get moving!

## DISCOVERY TIMES/WONDER TIMES: POINTS OF INTEREST

- Our bodies are made up of so many interesting, specific parts. They help us move in different ways. Aren't we lucky to be human beings and not jelly beans or baked beans?
- Each of our body parts has a name and more than one function (for example, fingers can do so many things, hands can move in so many ways).
- Most people have ten toes, ten fingers, two feet, two hands, and so on. But even though we all have thumbs, our thumbprints are unique.
- Some people, through accident or circumstances of birth or illness, do not have the usual number or function of body parts.
- People with physical disabilities can do extraordinary things with their bodies: blind people read through their fingers with Braille; deaf people use sign language and read lips; people with no hands learn to type, write, paint, and draw with their toes and even their mouths.
- The human spirit is full of courage and determination!
- Our bodies can do so many amazing things—is there any end to the list? We can keep adding ideas every day of ordinary, marvelous body-works!

- Through practice, we teach our bodies to accomplish more complicated, challenging movement patterns.
- It is so important to take good care of our bodies by exercising, eating nutritious foods, and practicing safety and good health habits.
- Our brain is in charge. Our brain is the boss. Our brain is in our head—that's why we call it "headquarters"!
- Our amazing senses—seeing, hearing, tasting, touching, and smelling—help us learn about everything around us. Every day, we should practice using our sensory powers.

## SUGGESTED VOCABULARY

This theme lends itself naturally to clusters of ideas and the words that express them. These are only starter lists to remind you of the richness of language and comprehension inherent in all the themes. Even if our young children are not yet ready to read or write them, they hear, say, and comprehend numerous words that are very relevant to their lives. Add words as you continue exploring together, making discoveries, sharing the excitement of expanding knowledge and imagination.

### Body Parts

| | | | |
|---|---|---|---|
| head | lips | fingers | ankles |
| hair | chin | fingernails | feet |
| eyebrows | face | wrists | toes |
| eyes | cheeks | heart | toenails |
| eyelashes | ears | chest | rear/bottom/tush/butt |
| nose | neck | stomach | bones |
| nostrils | shoulders | belly button | blood |
| mouth | back | hips | muscles |
| tongue | arms | legs | brain |
| teeth | hands | knees | skin |

### Bodies in Motion

| | | | |
|---|---|---|---|
| big | loose | shake | slow |
| little | tight | wiggle | skip |
| large | straight | flop | march |
| small | crooked | gallop | push |
| tall | grow | leap | pull |
| short | shrink | hop | spin |
| heavy | curl | trot | turn |
| light | stretch | jump | lift |
| weak | fall | crawl | forward |
| strong | rise | walk | backward |
| reach | run | fast | sideways |

## Bodies Coming to Their Senses

| | | | |
|---|---|---|---|
| sight | sharp | dark | loud |
| feel | taste | spicy | shout |
| sweet | listen | sound | plain |
| rough | bitter | notice | crunchy |
| bumpy | soft | cold | see |
| decorated | colorful | whisper | watch |
| smell | dull | light | quiet |
| look | touch | gooey | lively |
| sour | hear | noisy | peaceful |
| smooth | hot | observe | flowery |
| liquid | hard | | |

## Some Exercises

| | | | |
|---|---|---|---|
| sit-ups | jumping jacks | squats | stretches |
| push-ups | leg lifts | spin-arounds | arm twirls |
| touch toes | twists | skips | rolls |
| jog | kicks | jumps | bends |
| somersaults | cartwheels | | |

## TALK/LISTEN/READ/WRITE: THE GIFTS OF LANGUAGE

Body parts, bodies in motion, amazing senses are high on lists of favorite discussion topics in the lives of young children.

Children have important things to say about their bodies because they already have experiences and information to share. They are interested in all aspects of their bodies and show you every scratch and scraggly Band-Aid, their toenail and fingernail polish, bruises and splinters, new haircuts, and strong muscles. They make observations, ask questions, share their wonder. Leave time in your talks for appreciation and curiosity. You may not always have the answer; sometimes the answer is still unknown. But because you encourage questioning and wondering (the most important components of the learning process), your young students may grow up to find the answers.

Every spoken word is a word that can be written and read. Even the youngest children, who are years away from "reading," will begin to realize that the words they speak and hear have shapes that can be written. As often as possible, connect those relationships. Fun charts can be immediately created. For example, I listened to a group of children eager to show and tell each other if they had long hair or short hair! The teacher playfully jotted down their names on a flip chart and their hair lengths next to their names as they went around the circle dictating "short," "long," or "medium." They all felt fine having their ideas shared and went back to the chart during the day, looking at the words, finding their names, reviewing the discussion.

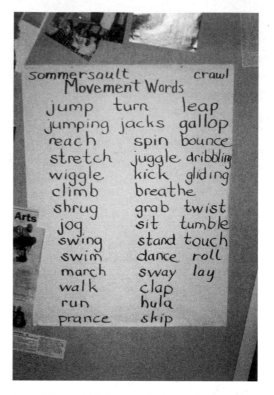

FIGURE 1–2    *Kids love words that get them moving!*

The names of body parts—bodies in motion and senses and sense images—are among the first vocabulary words of *all* children! Here are opportunities to honor the languages of children in your group who may not speak English. As you say the name of, for instance, a body part like arms, ask the children who speak other languages to share *arms* in their language. It's easy, it's natural, and it will enrich the comprehension and appreciation of *all* the children. This is ongoing! Not confined to a specific time slot.

### Open-Ended Questions

Such questions spur lively talk sessions. Examples of this kind of question are:

- "What do your eyes see right now?"
- "What do you hear with your ears right now?"
- "What are your favorite ways to move?"
- One group of kindergartners responding to the question, "How many ways can you move your eyes?" had some interesting observations:

"Eyelashes are like little bugs' feet"; "When you sleep, your eyes are closed"; "If I close one eye and open one other eye, it winks."

The question, "What are some things *hands* can do?" triggered an outpouring of ideas from a lively group of pre-kindergartners. Here are some of the comments that were written on the chalkboard:

**Hands can:**

| | | |
|---|---|---|
| touch things | take pictures | tickle |
| scratch itches | shut doors | clap |
| pinch | pick up things | put socks on |
| write | paint | play with blocks |
| pick up the phone | pick apples | cut, comb, brush, and |
| pet animals | play the piano | wash hair |

That discussion, integrating sense awareness with body parts, provided resource material for activities in art, music, movement, pantomime, and games. The children turned the ideas into riddles, poems, and charts.

Imagine the possibilities of extending and enriching the suggestions a group of four-year-olds gathered in response to the question, "How about our *feet*? What's so great about feet?"

Here are some of their answers that we turned into a chant and a dance:

Feet jump / feet hop / feet hop backwards / feet stamp / feet dance / feet kick / feet smell / feet walk / feet run / feet trip / feet slip / feet take little steps / feet take big steps / feet jump high / feet jump like frogs / feet jump like rabbits / feet draw pictures / feet wiggle / feet slide / feet leap / feet gallop / feet leap / feet turn / feet tiptoe / feet are neat

Easy to follow the choreography of the "text"!

## Shared Experiences

Children are fascinated by their bodies. Such universal events as loose teeth are topics that can intrigue kids for hours. Loose teeth, lost teeth, old teeth, new teeth—what stories the children can tell! Here we can encourage imaginative thinking by enjoying *real* accounts of how and where we lost our teeth and extending to fictional/fantasy dramas! This is another example of writing and reading connected to the talking and listening! Experience charts, chalkboard stories, individual stories with illustrations are natural extensions.

Always leave time for *humor*! A child was asked, "Who put the quarter under your pillow?" He answered, "The *truth* fairy!" After our laughter subsided, we brainstormed what the tooth fairy and the truth fairy looked like. Great illustrations and titles for pictures!

# OUR BODIES

Our eyes see friends and trees.

Our ears hear singing and wind blowing.

Our noses smell flowers and pizza.

Our tongues taste oatmeal cookies- Yum.

Our fingers touch our bear puppet's furry
                                        face.

Our legs run fast.

Our feet stamp to the drum-

Our hands clap to the music

Our arms stretch us high

FIGURE 1–3   *It's easy to gather ideas from lively class discussions.*

### Sense-full Talks

Delightful discussions center on favorite tastes, smells, sounds, textures, and sights. Highlight such conversations on seasons, weather, holidays, special events, and everyday, ordinary (extraordinary?) days. Look out the window—what do we see? Smell this lovely flower—what kind of smell is it to you? What's your favorite sound? Chart the answers, illustrate them, turn them into poems, games, surveys, and illustrations.

### Add the Senses

Add the dimension of sense-awareness to everything you do, every story, poem, or book you read, every idea you explore. Train yourself to challenge the children's imaginations with such questions as: "I wonder what the Three Bears saw out in the woods? Any suggestions?" or "That Winnie the Pooh sure likes honey. Let's taste some. How does honey taste to you?" or "Imagine the sounds the Wild Things are making! Anybody want to tell us about them or try out an idea about them?"

Including sensory images in your daily talks enriches vocabulary and expands appreciation for the power of language. Encourage all of the children to respond, but don't force them if they are shy or reluctant. Good teachers are like the Native American trickster, Coyote, who tricks people into learning! Look up your sleeve for loving and playful ways to welcome children into participation. When they know you value their opinions, experiences, and questions, they develop good listening habits and respect for others as they practice language skills.

*Let's look out the window. What do we see? Hear? Smell?*

*Let's look at this beautiful picture. What kinds of sounds can you imagine from the animals in the picture? Can you smell the field in the picture? What does it smell like to you?*

Remember, every word spoken is a word to read and write! With your children, become a gatherer of *their* words! Title pictures, poems, and dances. Label exhibits!

## Surround the Kids with Print-Rich Images

Old and new books, magazines, signs, posters, charts are examples of stimulating, language-inspiring ideas for the children to enjoy and use. Figures in action, names of exercises, challenging questions, newspaper and magazine illustrations with time to discuss and experience are invaluable resources. I visited a first grade and listened to the kids talk about an interview with a local high school athlete who shared his warm-up exercises. After reading the sequence together (with a little help from their teacher), the children wanted to follow the warm-up, which included bends, stretches, and sit-ups. They felt very proud of themselves and their teacher told me that the warm-up became part of their choices for daily exercises. Amy Polovick, movement teacher at Duxberry Park Arts Impact School, always has signs, books, pictures in use as part of her movement classes. One of her students' favorite books is *Hop Jump*. An oldie but goodie! Amy's dancing kids love to close in on demonstrating hops and jumps, twists and turns and show how they are alike and different.[3] Fantastic bodies in motion!

## Nonverbal Language—The Signs of Caring

A fascinating new development in exploring the gifts of language is the teaching of simple sign language communication to young children. We know that infants and babies communicate and express themselves through body movement, sounds, and gestures. Our very young children have many thoughts, feelings, and questions. Their comprehension is astonishing but their verbal development lags behind. Across the country, programs for young children are exploring ways to help them access language and communication more efficiently through teaching the children simple signs. Michele Sanderson, director of the Sophie Rogers Lab School at Ohio State University, talks enthusiastically about her program's experiences with sign language.

"In young children, movement, motor development, sensory awareness is so huge that it just makes sense to help them with natural ways to communicate their ideas."

Dance Flexibility

I like to dance, and befor I dance we warm up. We do splits, butterfly, flex + reflex, and other streches. I love to dance!

FIGURES 1–4    *See me move! Read* my *story!*

Michele and the staff of Sophie Rogers pay attention to the language that's important to their children, the words that seem most meaningful to them. Phrases like "all finished," "I'm hungry," "I'm thirsty," "I have to go to the bathroom," "Stop," "More," and so on. They base their sign language vocabulary on the language needs of their community.

"These are words and phrases that we find ourselves saying or asking the children very frequently. These are the ideas we close in on," Michele explains. "We learn those simple basic songs and we say and sign simultaneously. The children learn the signs easily. We find less frustration in trying to communicate, more enjoyable interpersonal relationships, the kind of freeing that dance and movement achieve, and fewer conflicts. Sometimes families are concerned that using the sign language will delay verbal language, but we've found the opposite. From our observations, we've seen our children's vocabularies increasing, the transition to verbal language is easier and helped enormously by giving the children the gift of communicating basic needs immediately."[4]

*Note:* You may have a specific time designated for "talk/listen/read/write" sessions in your schedule. But know that children have a lot to say *all day* and will grow beautifully in language development if they know those "skills" are not limited or confined to, say, circle time or rug time! I knew a forlorn kindergartner who had run to school to tell about his grandfather's visit only to be told that it wasn't his turn to share at circle time that day!

The gifts of language are for all times!

## MUSIC MAKERS/MOVERS AND SHAKERS

Children already move, hum, sing, and make music. When people ask me how long I have been teaching dance, creative movement, and music to children, I answer, "I've never taught children to dance, move, and make music. They're already doing it! I just hang out with them!"[5]

You don't have to be an accomplished singer or a trained musician or a professional dancer to keep music, singing, and movement alive with your children. Many children will sing their lives, making up songs and chants all through the day. Some kids are hummers, humming as they work and play. Just about *all* children are wigglers, tappers, and bouncers, demonstrating constantly that movement is a sign of life! Greg and Steve's delightful song "I Can't Sit Still"[6] catches that spirit of action. Don't fight it. Join it! Be sure that your children have many, many opportunities to move about; integrate music, singing, and movement in *all* ideas and daily routines! You'll find fewer behavior problems, greater attention spans and language development, and more cheery, chirpy children! And a more cheery, chirpy *you*!

FIGURE 1–5  *Listen to the infectious laughter of our climbers and wigglers!*

### Body Parts Rhythm Band

Our bodies are our first instruments. Hearts beat a special rhythm. Lungs exhale, inhale their special breath rhythm. Feet jump their special jumping rhythm. Hands clap—fast, faster, fastest; slow, slower, slowest; louder, softer—their special rhythms. Feet tap their special tapping rhythms. Teeth click. Hands slap the floor. Hands slap thighs. Hair swishes.

Experiment with body parts that make sounds and keep rhythms. Clap, tap, stamp, jump, whistle, sing, beat, and shake out rhythms. Listen to the sounds the body parts make. Work together and discover the joy of fusing energies and ideas. Play different kinds of music. Recite favorite poems and sing favorite songs accompanied by the body parts rhythm band.[7]

Remember, musical instruments are extensions of body rhythms and sounds. We blow our breath into wind instruments. We pluck and strum string instruments. We tap, pound, and shake percussion instruments.

## Make Rhythm Instruments

The earliest instruments came from nature, for example, dried gourds with loose seeds, animal skins pulled tightly over shells or wood, and stones and sticks with holes in them.

Tubes, tubs, cans, canisters, rolls of plastic, Styrofoam, and metal are excellent materials for homemade instruments. Decorate coffee cans and oatmeal containers for drums. Fill tubs and tubes and rolls with pebbles, sand, and beads for rattlers, shakers, tambourines, and rainsticks.

Paper plates filled with jingling-sounding materials and stapled together, then painted with bright designs make wonderful instruments.

Experiment with objects that make sounds. *Listen.* Invent new instruments. Click spoons together. Tap sticks and branches on tabletops. Clap wooden blocks together. Make rhythms.

## Music for Body Relaxation

In our often frenetic world, we need the feeling of inner peace and calm when the body relaxes with soothing, beautiful music. This is a time to help young children realize how much our bodies can do and still be able to rest comfortably and calmly. Encourage the children to let their minds daydream, wander, float. Later, you may want to discuss some of their imaginative sensory images; turn the images into pictures and poems.

## Musical Movement Moments Make Sense

Create musical interpretations of sensory images. With rhythm instruments and voices, explore and enjoy ways to re-create such images as the sounds of the ocean, breezes in a forest, the excitement of people gathering for a festival, early morning on a farm, rush hour in a busy city, a house filled with people. Accompany the sounds with movement, stories, poems, and visual arts. Which comes first? You decide.

*Note:* When I asked a kindergarten teacher if the children had instruments, she proudly opened a locked closet and showed me a large box of new, shiny, expensive instruments.

"Do the children get to play the instruments much?" I asked.

"Since the music teacher is on maternity leave," she confessed, "we've hardly played them at all."

A box of homemade instruments enjoying a central place in the room, in the daily lives of the children, is more valuable than a great supply of expensive commercial instruments untouched by human hands.

### Tune Up Body Parts to Make Music

Music is the result of effort and practice. Musicians need nimble fingers, flexible wrists, powerful hands, and strong lungs to make music. As you listen to music and play your own, emphasize the importance of exercising special body parts and practicing for developing musical talents and skills. Invent such musical talents and skills. Invent such musical exercises as playing a piano, strumming a guitar, and blowing a wind instrument.

### *Improvise Body Songs*

Be playful! Mess around with old, simple songs easily extended to your theme! I like to greet kids with,

"Good morning, dear *eyes* (blink) . . ."

"Good morning, dear *noses* (wiggle) . . ."

"Good morning, dear *shoulders* (shrug) . . ."

Everyone succeeds. Delight and surprise accompany clear responses that demonstrate that the kids get it.

The popular "If you're happy and you know it, clap your hands . . ." can easily extend to "stamp your feet . . . tap your head . . . kick your legs. . . ."

I love kidding the children with, "If you're hoppy and you know it—hop, hop, hop!" Think of all the variations of "head, shoulders, knees, and toes" that are enjoyed. Add your own patterns.

### *Movement Responses*

Raising hands seems to be the most accepted movement pattern in American schools. So many opportunities are missed when we limit choice of movement. Here are a few different ways children can answer questions. "Children, if you have ever heard of Alaska, tap your feet." "If you think you know the answer to two and two, clap it." "How many people here brought in their permission slips? Shake ten fingers if you did." Aren't these ways more interesting and fun than always raising your hands?

### *Daily Warm-Ups*

Our kids (and ourselves) *need* physical exercise in daily doses. Correlate warm-ups with curriculum. Use a variety of musical selections, stories, and word prompts. Here are some ideas for easy warm-ups connected to *everything*.

#### *Follow the leader*

This universal game invites the children to lead an exercise or movement of their choice. If the leader does something difficult to follow, encourage the others to do their best. I always shout, "If you can't do it, fake it!" When warm-ups are a daily event, children have many exercises to choose from. I've seen kids spinning exercise wheels or choosing a movement idea from a chart listing many ideas. Music of every culture works beautifully as long as it features rhythms easy to move to.

So many books help these activities along. Zita Newcome's *Toddlerobics*, J. Hindley's *Eyes, Nose, Fingers, Toes*, and Ratner and Calcagnno's *Body Book* are examples of favorite materials to inspire movement.[8]

### Exercises and numbers

"It's January sixth today. Let's do six exercises in honor of the number six." Write the exercises on the board and follow them in sequence. Or, "Today we're celebrating the number eight. Let's do eight exercises. Which shall they be?"

Another aspect of numbers and exercises is to assign numbers to each warm-up. "How many jumping jacks shall we do?" Write the number on the board. "How many windmills?"

Another variation of numbers and exercises is for the birthday child to choose the exercise of the day to correspond to his or her new age. "Five years old today? Jackie, choose five birthday exercises! We'll all do them with you!" (Check out the "Kids Count" section.)

### Animal exercises

Consider the movements of animals that can be used in exercises: *hopping* (grasshoppers, frogs, rabbits, kangaroos); *running* (dogs, foxes, squirrels, wolves); *galloping* (horses, donkeys, zebras); and *crawling* (snakes, caterpillars, lizards, salamanders). Do them. Talk about them. Extend them into art projects, games, stories, charts.

Eric Carle's delightful *From Head to Toe* challenges the kids to demonstrate that they can arch their backs like cats, wave their arms like monkeys, and bend like giraffes. Add their own animal movement ideas to the mix.[9]

### Exercises for seasons and special occasions

On a cold winter day, make up a few exercises based on seasonal activities such as snowball throwing, pulling on boots, and forming snow angels.

Turn the exercises into chants, into action stories. Illustrate. Don't forget the other seasons!

Celebrate field trips by highlighting movement ideas. For example, following a trip to a local library to see a play based on *Jack and the Beanstalk*, some kindergartners returned to create their own "exercises" for Jack *walking*, the beanstalk *growing*, the giant *stamping*.

FIGURE 1–6   *The children are always ready to move!*

### Exercise change game

This is one of my favorite ways to enjoy exercises. Talk about all the exercises the children know. Encourage them to make up their own for different parts of their bodies (for example, shoulder exercise, knee exercise). Carefully explain. When the music goes on, each child may choose any exercise to do. Everyone will be different. When you give the signal (for example, shake a tambourine, clap your hands), everyone changes to another exercise. Minds and bodies work very fast. Children have the opportunity to choose their favorite movement and to enjoy a unique warm-up. Use any lively, rhythmical music you like. I have used everything from Arabic belly-dance music to Appalachian round dances. The only rule is that the children must stay in their own spaces. If they jog or kick, they must stay in their own "self space." There are so many movement possibilities in our own "self spaces."

## Taking Inventory

The most universally loved game of early childhood is "Show me . . ." or "Where is your . . . ?" For example: "Show me your belly button."

"Where is your nose?" Here is an opportunity for every child to feel success and delight. A silly variation of this game is to point to the wrong place. Pretend absent-mindedness. Young children find great delight in these "mistakes" and will correct you with glee.

"Show me" can be extended from location to movement. For example: "What can your shoulders do? Show me." "How many things can your hands do? Show me." "What can you do with your eyebrows? Show me."

Many songs and poems take inventory. As the children sing or recite, they move and point to the appropriate parts. (Challenge the children to show you as the poem is read.)

### Changing Body Shapes

"Everyone keep your shape. As the tambourine shakes, find a *new shape* and hold it. Change again. Keep changing shapes and holding the new one for a few seconds." This activity is so successful and enjoyable that children ask for it again and again.

### How Many Ways?

Open-ended, safe-at-any-speed challenges are most beloved by the children. Rigid, absolute rights/wrongs discourage participation and joy. Creativity flows when children are asked, "How many ways can you

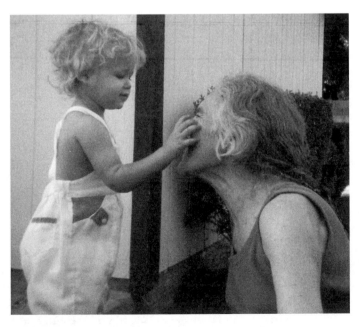

FIGURE 1–7    *"Where are my eyes? Show me!"*

jump . . . hop . . . walk . . . run . . . ?" You'll be amazed at the movement variations children will demonstrate.

### Be More Sense-Full

Children are natural mimes and mimics. They will *show* you faster than they will *tell* you. Using the magic words "show me," combined with sensory awareness, play such simple but enjoyable games as "Show me your expression tasting something delicious!" (After the improvisation, ask the children to tell you what the delicious food they were tasting was, or turn it into a guessing game.) "Show me how you look smelling a beautiful flower." "Show me a loud noise." After the movement interpretation, children can draw it, write it, or sing it. Or just go on to another challenge!

Close in on those sense-related body parts for the text or captions accompanying sense-full pictures. Enjoy these few example notes from the wall of a second-grade classroom decorated with delightful sense posters:

"My fingers touch a shiny icicle." "My ears hear my brother's drumming." "My nose smells pizza. Yum." "My tongue tastes a green lollipop."

Be sure to celebrate the works of your students by sharing, appreciating, and displaying them in many imaginative ways.

### See What I Can Do!

Thomas Moore's delightful song "Look at Me!"[10] is an example of songs that invite children to show off their accomplishments like touching their toes, stretching, jumping. We always add onto the song, asking the children to keep demonstrating more and more things they can *do*. These gatherings make excellent colorful "See What I Can Do" charts— either group or individual charts highlighted with colorful words and illustrations. They make great choreography!

### Bodies Around the Clock, Around the Room, Around the School, Around the World

Consider *morning* exercises: Wake up! Stretch! Bend! Brush!

Consider *around the room* exercises: When you get to the back wall, do five hops. When you look out the window, do seven jumping jacks. . . .

Consider *around the school* exercises: Playground dance. Swing. Climb. Jump rope. Hopscotch. Choreograph these to any rhythmic music.

Consider movement from *around the world*. Use the music of the world. All children hop, skip, kick, twirl, slide, clap, jump, and bounce. Invite your students to "move to the music." You'll be amazed at how closely they come to the movement of ethnic and cultural dances! So

FIGURE 1–8   *Debbie Clement warms up the kids before her singing program.*

often we drain the life out of folk dances by overemphasizing the *right* steps, the *right* position, and the children tense up. Teach in the key of life—be open to original interpretations to music and ideas. Create patterns. Enjoy!

One of my favorite books guaranteed to start the kids moving and dancing, celebrating the cultures of the world, is George Ancona's *Let's Dance*.[11] We humans are inspired by words, visuals, and imagination. Keep adding layers of comprehension and enjoyment!

### Be Aware of the Choreography of Stories, Poems, Songs, and Chants

It's hard to imagine a children's story, poem, or song that *doesn't* lend itself (even one line, refrain, or stanza) to playful movement possibilities. If we just *do* what the text describes, we're on a roll! We *can't* go wrong! From "Hokey Pokey" to the Little Gingerbread Boy running as fast as he can to Wee Willie Winkie running through the town to Jack jumping over a candlestick—no end of ideas—children love to show the action of the text. Be open to all their ideas. If you teach in the key of life, children will feel safe to offer and demonstrate their interpretations. If you teach in the key of death, you'll allow only an official pattern taught with rigidity and accompanied with tension ("No, Patrick, that's *not* how Hickory Dickory Dock ran up the clock!"). Be flexible and playful. Invite children to "shake out" their stiff muscles, "take a wiggly break," "run to a story."

They will always be learning vocabulary, sequential patterning, listening skills, comprehension, spatial awareness, cooperative learning, appreciation for music and literature, counting, problem solving, and differentiation (among other lessons)!

## ALL WAYS ART

Arts projects, activities, experiences are so plentiful for celebrating our fantastic bodies/our amazing senses that only a small sampling is possible in our limited space! Add your own ideas.

### Handprints and Footprints

Children dip their hands or feet in finger paint or watercolors, then press them on a large piece of butcher paper. Write their names below their prints if they cannot write themselves. A variation of this idea is to outline each child's hand or foot on the paper and have the children color and decorate their own prints. Tape the paper to the wall to create an attractive mural. Add words! Make designs and patterns.

### Thumbprints, Heel Prints, and More

Think of the fun of discovering the variety of designs possible when thumbprints, heel prints, fingerprints, and toe prints are used.[12]

### Helping Hands

Children trace their hands on separate papers, color them, and cut them out. Write their names on the hands. Hands can be used as indicators of daily chores or helpers of the day or just delightful decorations.

Ask the children what kinds of things hands and fingers can do. Write (or have the children write) some of the those ideas *on* the hands, on the fingers.

### Friendship Hands

Fold a piece of construction paper in half. On one half of the paper, handprint or outline a child's hand. On the other half, print the hand of a friend. Write the names below. This activity is an excellent way to introduce the concepts of likeness and difference.

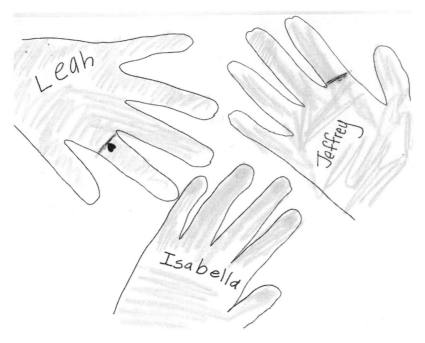

FIGURE 1–9   *Handprints are among our oldest designs.*

### Lei of Hands

I visited a kindergarten class and was welcomed with a lovely wreath of
friendly hands. The children had outlined and cut their hands out of
brightly colored construction paper. They decorated the hands and
wrote their names on them. The hands were stapled together in a long
chain. When visitors came to the room, the children welcomed them by
putting the chain of hands around their shoulders.

### Handouts

Children trace their hands, cut them out, and use them for the cover of
a hand-shaped book that they will fill with original pictures and stories.
These kinds of projects work with feet as well.

The kids love the inspiration of such delightful books as Paul's
*Hello Toes! Hello Feet!* or Rosen's *Freckly Feet and Itchy Knees.*[13]

Books, posters, poems, magazines aplenty enrich these experiences.

### Left and Right Hands

An enjoyable way to learn right from left is to do something with the
hand you want to focus attention on. Design a bracelet or ring, paint a

design on that hand, or dot that hand with a chosen color to set it off. All day direct attention to the decorated hand and help the children learn that the hand is, for example, their right hand. After a few days, decorate the left hand and focus attention on it.

### Finger and Hand Puppets

These simple, popular little puppets can be made out of a variety of scrounge materials—paper, cotton, flannel, or even scrounge from nature. A group of five-year-olds had the best time taping little leaves and branches to their fingers to use as hats for finger puppets. An innovative teacher asked parents to send in old, torn gloves rather than throw them out. She and her students cut the fingers off the gloves and had enough fingers for each member of the class to decorate an original finger puppet. Be sure to go beyond the making of the puppets and *give children plenty of time to play with their puppets*. Improvisation is the most important element of the experience. De-emphasize formal performances and encourage informal interaction among the children.

### Lollipop Face Puppets

Use lollipop sticks or tongue depressors. Cut out cardboard circles and have the children draw eyes, noses, mouths, and hair to make faces. Tape or glue the puppet's face to the stick. When the face is added, a puppet is born, complete with name, voice, story, and song.

### Paper Bag or Sock Puppets

Of the easy-to-make puppets, my favorites are paper bag and sock puppets. Again, with plenty of scrounge material at hand, children can make puppets with distinctive features. Scraps of wool or material can be used for hair, buttons for eyes, cotton balls for beards and mustaches, and cardboard or felt for hats. With your children, make up names, stories, and songs for the puppets.

Eyes are probably our most distinguishing feature. Add eyes to anything and you have a creature or character. Draw a circle, dot two eyes, and you have a face. Gather small stones, pinecones, and wood chunks. Paint eyes on them and you have little characters with their own names and personalities. Blow up balloons. Paint eyes on them and they become special characters. Add other parts, but start with eyes. What do these eyes see?

### Shoe Boxes of Eyes, Ears, Noses, and Mouths

Children like to cut up magazines. From your plentiful supply of old magazines, children cut out eyes, ears, noses, and mouths and put each part in its own shoe box. After a while, you will have a shoe box full of eyes or noses. Create original faces on paper circles or paper plates using parts from each of the boxes. (Maybe this is how Picasso got his start!)

## Collages and Montages

Body parts are the oldest, most popular artistic designs in human history. Here are two basic kinds of projects involving body parts. The children select one body part to cut out of magazines or draw. They compose an arrangement of, for example, eyes, and fill their papers with eyes of different colors, shapes, and sizes. Be sure to display all the children's work.

The other project involves a collage or montage of different body parts. The children cut out or draw body parts and arrange them in an interesting pattern on either their own paper or a large bulletin board to which all contribute.

## Body Silhouettes

Spread butcher paper, or any other inexpensive paper, across the floor. The children lie down on the paper in any position they choose. Outline their shapes with colored markers. Their body shapes are cut out and ready to be decorated with features, colors, clothes, and designs, or to be colored or painted with one color to make a silhouette. Add words!

I visited a first grade where the children's silhouettes were hung across the room on a clothesline. Another kindergarten class tacked their silhouettes on the four walls of the room.

## Body-Works Collage

The children cut pictures out of magazines and newspapers that show bodies doing things such as playing, working, and resting. They create their own collages or together create a class collage. Both are exciting projects. Close in on dancers, athletes, or people in action doing everyday activities.

## Scrounge Bodies

Your supply of scrounge materials should always be ample. Give the children many opportunities to participate in the highest form of creative activity: "making something out of nothing." The children use whatever materials they find; they glue, paste, tape, or clip odds and ends together to make body shapes.

## Favorite Body-Works Books

Here is a chance for children to gather pictures and designs of their favorite kind of body-works and create their own books. (Staple the pages together; make it simple.) The first graders' body-works books featured joggers, mountain climbers, and construction workers. Add words. Turn them into poems and songs.

### Pipe Cleaner Bodies

Pipe cleaners bend and twist and make wonderful bodies in motion. Give the children lots of time to experiment.

### Stick Figures

Use Popsicle sticks, straws, toothpicks, wires, or tongue depressors. Glue or tie various lengths of material to shape a variety of figures.

### Clay Figures

Roll, push, pull, twist, pat, clap, pinch—experiment with clay and encourage the children to find ways they most enjoy working with clay. "How many different body shapes can we sculpt today?" Display and celebrate all the works.

### Body Poses

The children take turns modeling for their classmates. Encourage the children to sketch, paint, or color the model's position quickly, because it is a challenge for the model to hold a shape for more than a few minutes.

### Exercise Chart

Devote a special place in the room—a board or portion of a wall—to pictures and diagrams of physical exercises. Children cut out pictures of exercises from magazines and newspapers. Label the exercises so that

FIGURE 1–10 *On a beautiful day, we sketch our friends dancing.*

the name is prominently displayed next to the diagram or picture. Exercise "leaders" refer to the chart as different warm-up exercises are featured each day.

### Exercise Wheel

Paint a large cardboard circle a bright color. Divide it into sections. Have children paste an illustration of a clearly defined exercise on each section. Be sure the exercises they choose for the wheel are familiar and easy to do. Cut a pointer out of cardboard, paint it a different color, and clip it to the center of the wheel. Spin the pointer and where it stops is the exercise the children will do. Assign different children to spin the wheel each day and lead the exercises.

### Exercise Cards

Cut out or illustrate examples of exercises and paste one on each card. Design a special pocket or place for the exercise cards. Children choose a few cards each day to start their warm-ups.

### Shape-Up Poster

Divide the paper or a portion of a wall into columns such as:

I CAN DO SIT-UPS      I CAN DO PUSH-UPS      I CAN JOG

The children write their names in each column and draw or paint a design next to their names to show "they can." Keep adding exercise sections. Children have lots of practice writing their names, creating designs, and feeling good about themselves.

*Note:* Just as our children must learn in language-rich environments, so they must be enriched by arts-rich spaces! If you can't get to museums or galleries, invite prints, postcards, posters of great works of art featuring the beauty and power of the human body, faces, features, bodies in motion, and so on into your classroom. It's important for our young students to know and appreciate the diverse ways artists through the years and across the world have honored our fantastic bodies as favorite subjects. As often as possible, ask the children to paint, draw, sketch, sculpt their interpretations of great works of art! Most artists wish they still had the freedom of spirit and courage to create as do our young artists.

Children enjoy looking at, for example, Modigliani's faces or Renoir's hair and faces. They marvel at how Michelangelo carved such perfect hands for David and find inspiration to model their own clay hands and feet. Folk art from cultures the world over honors the human body in countless presentations.

### Celebration of the Senses

As with all ideas, there are endless variations. Here are just a few suggestions for highlighting our amazing senses. Following walks, talks, shared classroom experiences, games, books, or holidays (every topic is relevant!), children love to illustrate their ideas with paints, markers, crayons, scissors, and scrounge materials, creating murals, group pictures, posters, charts, cards, poems. . . .

Shower and Aliki's *Listening Walk*[14] is still high on the list of children's popular sense-full lists!

## KIDS COUNT

We just got an email from our nephew, about to be a first-time father. Guess the weight and height of our new any-minute-now baby! Guess the date and time of his birth. Friends and relatives are sending in their guesses. Measurements, dates, and time are but a few components of math awareness in the learning journey of humans. How old are you? How big? How many? are basic simple questions challenging our youngest children practically from birth. The Latin word for finger is *digit*. Think of numbers and fingers! Think of the rhythm of counting. Think of the everyday, always connecting ways that kids count. Add to these few examples! Subtract the ideas you don't like. Multiply the ways you can enrich comprehension.

### Count Heads

How many children are in the class? As you go around the room very gently touching every child's head, ask the kids to join you in counting. (Every person is important in this process.) Announce the grand total of children in the class. Write the number on a chart or on the board. How many boys? How many girls?

### Heights and Weights

Measuring the children's heights and weights is one of the first things many teachers do at the beginning of the school year. Even the youngest children know the meaning of a mark, number, or color next to their names. "That's how high I am," a four-year-old explained as he showed his statistics on a bright yellow chart.

When this delightful activity occurs early in the school year and is repeated every few months, the children learn a lot about their own development, and about measurements, numbers, and addition.

Enjoy experimenting with ways to measure. More measurement suggestions are provided in this guide.

### High Fives

Even American babies know high fives and gladly demonstrate their favorite way of communicating. With toddlers and older youngsters, add high threes, high fours, and so on. The children love high tens. Keep the playfulness!

### Ten Little Piggies and Other Body Parts That Count

Is there a baby around who hasn't had ten little toes counted as little piggies accompanied by a repetitive chant? We humans love repetition as long as it's fun, has rhythm, is playful! Caryn Falvey[15] encourages the teaching and learning of math concepts to be developmentally appropriate, meaningful, authentic, and enjoyable. She believes that kids have a natural sense of number, a natural sense of order about things. They see relationships, recognize patterns, solve problems. They have a nose for new ideas. Like counting noses and counting nostrils!

She challenged her students to answer, "How many nostrils are in this room at this moment?" The children's hands flew up in the air with suggestions like these, "Count each nostril." "Count by twos. It's faster!"

They did both and Caryn introduced the idea of multiplying the twenty-four children by two nostrils each, plus her own two nostrils. Fifty nostrils!

Count fingers, hands, feet, shoulders. Take inventories! Graph and chart your results.

### Moving Moments

How many seconds in a minute? Sixty. If I tap you sixty beats, can you keep wiggling for one minute? Don't stop! Can you keep hopping for sixty beats? How many hops did you get in that minute? Can we keep walking for one minute? How far did we get? Let's try *half* a minute. How many beats? Right! Thirty! Measure your time in jumps, jiggles, taps, and wiggles. How about . . . no one moves for sixty seconds? What a challenge!

### Giant Steps, Baby Steps

How many giant steps does it take to get you from your chair to the front of the room? How many giant steps do you need to cross the hall? How many giant steps from here to the office? How many giant steps take you around our room?

How many baby steps do you need to get from your chair to the front of the room? How many baby steps do you need to cross the hall? Experiment with half-giant steps. Correlate giant steps with whole notes and baby steps with quarter notes. This activity is a good way to help children discover interesting facts about numbers, fractions, movement, and rhythm.

### Birthday Exercises

How old is the birthday child? Seven! Seven-year-olds need movement gifts in sevens. What special things can we do seven times each for our birthday child? Here are some of the suggestions made by thousands of children over the years.

| | |
|---|---|
| 7 claps | 7 turnarounds |
| 7 stamps | 7 jumping jacks |
| 7 kisses (throw kisses) | 7 hops |
| 7 shoulder shrugs | 7 finger dances |
| 7 cheers | 7 jumps |
| 7 smiles | 7 blinks |
| 7 waves in the air | 7 kicks (kick legs out) |

Another of the many variations of birthday celebrations and numbers is to ask the birthday child to choose the birthday number of exercises to be featured that day. Last Friday, Molly was five. These are the exercises she chose for her class to perform:

1. run
2. touch toes
3. tiptoe and stretch arms
4. twists
5. turns

We practiced the five exercises in order. Soon the children remembered them by numbers, so when we played lively music we simply called out, "Number one," and the children ran, "Number two," and the children touched their toes. Be playful. Rearrange the number patterns!

Add movement ideas to the birthday chart or cards. Add numbers! A great way to learn sequences.

### Math Talk to Get Bodies Moving

Eavesdrop on Marlene Robbins as she organizes her movement classes from kindergarten to fifth grade. The language we use in our everyday lives is full of ideas that count! Here's an excerpt from one of Marlene's sessions:

> Let's divide into two groups. . . . Half of you work on a movement pattern that features full turns. The other half come up with a movement pattern that features half turns. We'll take about ten minutes. . . . Let's speed up this movement. Do it double time. . . . Can we connect part one and part two of your dances with a smoother transitional movement? . . . Let's cross the floor in a diagonal line, one at a time. . . . Partners! You only have five counts to be back in your space. . . . Well, let's see how we want these wonderful movement sequences to go. How many parts do we want in this dance? Which shall we do first? Is there a refrain or a chorus to repeat for extra emphasis? . . . Let's all get into First Position. . . . Notice the way group three came up with an interesting four-count right-left pattern. Let's all try it.

Stay with Marlene and the children for a while and you'll see one of their favorite movement games in action. The children sit in a large circle. One child dances in the center, then chooses another child to join the dance. Then they both move out to choose two other children. Now the four dancers choose four more children to join in. It continues from eight to sixteen dancers. The next round completes the inclusion of all the children dancing together in the circle. Hands held, they circle clockwise and counterclockwise. Twenty-seven kids, one adult. Twenty-eight pairs of hands and feet. Fifty-six tapping feet. Fifty-six clapping hands.[16]

As you enjoy the following suggestions, number the ways children demonstrate comprehension, language development, listening skills, problem-solving skills, risk taking, sequential learning patterns, and ownership.

### Cheers, Chants, Raps, and Rhymes Count and Keep Us Moving

Numbers and counting, sequences and patterns are the stuff of most rhymes, cheers, raps, and chants that children love. When we're shouting "Two, four, six, eight, who do we appreciate? Kenisha! Kenisha! Yaay!" Kenisha gets to perform her best movement trick. Bodies in motion can easily demonstrate movement interpretation of such familiar rhymes as "This Old Man," "Three Blind Mice," "Hickory Dickory Dock," "Five Little Monkeys Jumping on the Bed," and so on. The kids move and count! Add and subtract!

### By Ones, by Twos, by Teams, by Groups

Children easily understand the concept of one/solo/singular. One child moves. One body part moves. One and one make two. Now two people move. We move two body parts. Count them. One. Some. All. These are mathematical relationship ideas relevant to our young learners. In challenging books like Stuart Murphy's *Jump, Kangaroo, Jump!*[17] kids enjoy the story of a field day with many different team formations, teams coming in first, second, and third, teams performing in specific sequences. The story introduces fractions to the formations, which, for older students, is a meaningful way to begin those concepts. The language of math becomes more familiar as it's used in many relevant ways.

### Body Machines of Moving Parts

When you control all of your muscles and hold your bodies still, you are on zero. Now one part moves. Tap out a rhythm on a drum, tabletop, or tambourine. The children decide which part they want to move. Then two parts move. Each child has a different pattern. Then three parts move. Some children move two feet and one hand; Tarik moves two shoulders and one wiggly nose. Try to match the rhythm with the number of parts moving. Continue to five or six parts. Then turn on the body machines and move all the parts you can.

One at a time, each machine stops (gently touch each head) until no machine is moving.

Use any music with steady, strong rhythms as accompaniment. Watch the kids demonstrate that they understand these number concepts.

### Multilingual Number Words and Body Words

Throughout this book, you'll be reminded of how easy it is to include the vocabulary of children in your program who speak languages other than English. Your English-speaking kids will naturally learn basic words for body parts and movement as well as numbers. Put them together and your lessons will be multiplied in enrichment. Imaginative books such as Susan Middleton Elya's *Eight Animals on the Town*[18] combine colorfully illustrated animals, Spanish words interspersed with the English text, numbers, and lots of action that the children enjoy interpreting with body movement. Bird, Dog, Horse, and Pig are some of the animals in action. They wind up dancing all night. Eight animals bid the readers, "Good night," "Buenos Noches." As you're counting, ask the children who speak different languages to add their numbers! Imagine how *two eyes*, *one nose*, *one head*, *two arms* sound as they're chanted by your bi- or trilingual students!

In any language, the vocabulary and daily experiences in meaningful math concepts are plentiful. Your awareness of how easily these everyday connections can be made is of primary (there's a math concept!) importance. Keep ideas multiplying! You can count them on your fingers!

---

**Field Trips and Visitors**

Be sure you check out the numerous suggestions in the back of the book for enriching your children's lives with enjoyable and valuable classroom visitors and field trips. Dancers, athletes, musicians, physical therapists, computer programmers, construction workers, and so on are but a few of the resources children enjoy that communicate the importance of bodies in motion and sensory awareness. Celebrate these special events with preparation, appreciation, and follow-up activities.

---

## IT ALL COMES TOGETHER

Any single idea on these pages can become the hub of a wheel of multidimensional activities and experiences. As you read through the suggestions, know that none of them happens in isolation. They are *part of*,

FIGURE 1–11   *Eric "the Fish" blends body movements, rhythms, and drumming with kids of all ages.*

not *apart from*, many other ideas, as connections happen all the time, naturally, easily, and with excitement. In these "It All Comes Together" sections, I am merely highlighting such integration. I hope as you read through the themes, you will constantly find ways in which it all comes together. That's the magic!

Marilyn Cohen's kindergartners enjoyed learning about their fantastic bodies! Their hands could do so many things! Their feet could dance and walk and jump and hop. Their arms could wave and sway and reach. The children's understanding deepened when they began to close in on the marvelous connection of body parts to our amazing senses.

Inspired by Aliki's classic book *My Five Senses*, Marilyn and her students launched an expanding, joyful web of interwoven learning strands.[19]

Each of the five senses was celebrated in numerous ways. Working as a class, in small groups, and as individuals, the children drew, discussed, painted, wrote, experimented, sang, demonstrated, and dramatized their findings. Every sense triggered its own interpretations. For example, here are a few of the components of the children's *sound* activities: They heard with their ears; drew pictures and cut out pictures of ears; chose images of "sound makers"; talked about and illustrated the sound makers (animals, machines, natural objects, instruments). They drew their own sound pictures, dictating and using their own inventive spelling to caption the pictures, such as "tick-tock," or "clink," or "growl." They made rhythm instruments, listened to them, recorded them, and moved and played to them. They experimented with vibrations, from tuning forks to vibrations on their skin. They created a tape of sounds and turned it into a riddle game, turned it into a movement figure behind a screen, turned it into poems. They created books featuring each of the senses by using such challenging ideas to write and illustrate as "two smells I like," "two smells I dislike," and "I like to look at _____."

From books to riddles, from scientific experiments (comparing and contrasting textured materials, foods, and smells) to art projects, from charts to graphs to songs to more books and stories about the senses, Marilyn's kindergartners immersed themselves in learning. You can be sure that they will use their senses in everything they do. They will always appreciate their fantastic bodies and their amazing senses.[20]

## NOTES

1. See important research and information on physical fitness and body awareness in such studies as these:

Council on Physical Education for Children. 1994. *Developmentally Appropriate Physical Education Practices for Young Children*. Reston, VA: American Alliance for Health, Physical Education, Recreation and Dance.

Sullivan, M. 1996. *Feeling Strong, Feeling Free: Movement Exploration for Young Children*. (2d. ed.). Washington, D.C.: NAEYC.

2. Hunter, T. 5/2000. "Some Thoughts About Sitting Still." *Young Children*. Vol. 55 (3) p. 50.

3. Amy Polovick teaches movement at Duxberry Park Arts Impact School, Columbus Public Schools, Columbus, Ohio.

Walsh, E. S. 1993. *Hop Jump!* San Diego, CA: Harcourt.

4. Michele Sanderson directs the Sophie Rogers Lab School, Ohio State University, Columbus, Ohio. She recommends:

Acredolo, L. and S. Goodwyn. 1996. *Baby Signs*. Chicago, IL: Contemporary Books.

Garcia, J. 1999. *Sign with Your Baby* (book, video, and laminated signing card). Northlight Communications. <*www.handspeak.com*>

5. Three books full of loving, joyful ways to be with children are:

Chenfeld, M. B. 1993. *Teaching in the Key of Life*. Washington, D.C.: NAEYC.

Chenfeld, M. B. 2001. *Teaching by Heart*. St. Paul, MN: Redleaf Press.

Sornson, R. and J. Scott. (editors). 1997. *Teaching and Joy*. Alexandria, VA: ASCD.

6. Scelsa, G. and S. Millang. 1995. *Greg and Steve Rockin Down the Road*. Cypress, CA: Youngheart Music.

Check the list of some of our talented music makers in the appendix. All of them have songs highlighting bodies in motion!

7. Poems like "Orchestra" by Shel Silverstein celebrate our first musical instruments—our bodies. Just *do* what the poem says!

Silverstein, S. 1974. "Orchestra." *Where the Sidewalk Ends*. New York: Harper and Row. p. 23.

8. Newcome, Z. 1996. *Toddlerobics*. Cambridge, MA: Candlewick.

Hindley, J. illus. Grastrom, B. 1999. *Eyes, Nose, Fingers, Toes*. Cambridge, MA: Candlewick.

Ratner, S. and S. Calcagnno. 2000. *The Body Book*. New York: Orchard.

9. Carle, E. 1997. *From Head to Toe*. New York: HarperCollins.

10. Moore, T. 1980. *Thomas Moore Sings the Family*. Thomas Moore Enterprises, Inc. 3710 Monroe #2, Charlotte, NC 28205. 704-371-4077.

11. Ancona, G. 1998. *Let's Dance*. New York: Morrow Jr. Books.

12. Merriam, E. 1964. "Thumbprint." *It Doesn't Always Have to Rhyme*. New York: Atheneum. p. 63.

13. Paul, A. W. illus. Wescott, N. B. 1998. *Hello Toes! Hello Feet!* New York: DK Ink.

Rosen, M. illus. Sweeten, S. 1990. *Freckly Feet and Itchy Knees*. New York: Doubleday.

14. Shower, P. illus. Aliki. 1991. *The Listening Walk*. New York: HarperCollins.

15. Caryn Falvey, an expert in math curriculum, is principal of the Ann Antolini School, New Hartford, Connecticut.

16. Marlene Robbins is movement specialist at the Indianola Alternative Elementary School, Columbus Public School, Columbus, Ohio.

17. Murphy, Stuart J. illus. O'Malley, K. 1999. *Jump, Kangaroo, Jump!* New York: HarperCollins.

18. Elya, S. M. illus. Chapman, L. 2000. *Eight Animals on the Town*. New York: G. P. Putnam's Sons.

19. Aliki. 1989. *My Five Senses*. New York: Crowell.

20. Marilyn Cohen taught kindergarten at Bet Shraga Hebrew Academy of the Capitol District, Albany, New York. She was honored to be the recipient of the Kohl Award for Excellence in Teaching. Marilyn is featured in my collection *Teaching by Heart*, 2001, Redleaf Press.

# THEME 2 | OUR FEELINGS

*Dimitri was obviously down in the dumps. His teacher asked him what was the matter.*

*No answer.*

*"Do you feel sick?"*

*"No."*

*"Do you feel sleepy?"*

*"No."*

*"Well, Dimitri, what do you feel?"*

*Dimitri thought for a moment, then answered, "I feel my feelings."*

\*

*"When I was little I was shy.*

*I go to gymnastics. I decided not to be shy anymore.*

*I'm not afraid of anything—even worms—even bears—because I am smart."*

—Morgan (four and a half years old)

## THINK ABOUT IT

As you begin this theme, let me ask you, How are you feeling? How *are* you? Comfortable? Feeling safe and secure, energetic, interested, eager to begin reading? Or are you tense, distracted, fatigued, annoyed, resentful?

The way you feel at this minute will surely affect the reading, comprehension, attention, and enjoyment of this wonderful chapter!

Isn't it amazing that with all the complex mix of emotional levels and situations happening within us combined with the tumult and turmoil that often surrounds us, we still function, creating, achieving, and developing as unbelievably as we often do?

In recent years, our emotional selves have received great attention. David Goleman's popular work *Emotional Intelligence*[1] continues to generate important dialogue about the definition of our emotional makeup and needs in connection with education and our chances for success in life.

This important emphasis on emotions as a major component of learning, behavior, achievement—all aspects of our lives—should not be taken for granted.

When I began teaching in the fifties (I'm going to stay in education till I get it right!), one of my students had just come through a painfully tragic event a few months before school started at the end of the previous school year. His mother had taken his baby brother, left a note on the table, and disappeared. How could this child *not* demonstrate a behavior change in school after such an event? Believe it or not, his third-grade teacher had no response to his situation, tolerated no inattention or "acting out" by the child, and told me I was a mollycoddling, wimpy kind of person to reach out and recognize the child's still distressed condition and try to deal with his feelings.

"This is a tough world," she told me. "These children need to know there's no time for babying. He needs to get on with his work!"

Do you think anyone in the teaching profession today would ever express such a harsh view? I believe that if a teacher in today's world dismisses the deep feelings of a child over a stressful relationship or event, that person should definitely *change professions*. Theodore Roethke wrote, "Teaching is one of the few professions that permits love."[2] If you don't want to use the word *love* because you think it's corny, try *empathy*, try *compassion*, but don't try *indifference*, *apathy*, or *insensitivity*. Those words have no place on the spelling lists of teachers who care.

How effective will your lessons on *any* subject or topic be

if a child is a new child feeling unwelcome and alienated?
if a child is worrying about a home situation?
if a child is moving to another foster home? A new family arrangement?
if a child is a new big sibling?
if a child has nightmares from watching TV news images, violence, and fear?
if the child is a victim of teasing, prejudice, humiliation? (Worse, if it takes you a while to pick up on that?)
if a child is unsure of who is baby-sitting or carpooling?
if a parent is traveling and didn't get to say good-bye?

Isn't it obvious that your curriculum, your lesson plans and educational goals will be affected by those situations?

We, who spend our time with young children, know how real and valid their feelings are. Newborns and infants clearly express comfort, distress, fright, well-being, and curiosity. Toddlers demonstrate a wide

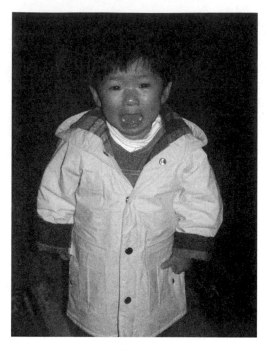

FIGURE 2–1    *How effective will your lessons be*
*if . . . ?*

range of deeply felt and clearly expressed emotions such as disappointment, frustration, grief, anger, joy, fear, possessiveness, and pride. We don't need post-graduate courses in communication to note that Jackie is happy today when she bounces cheerily into the room, flashes a brilliant smile, hugs her playmates, and kisses the puppets. Yesterday, she slumped into her daycare program, eyes downcast, lips pouty, blanket hugged to her body. We must *always* be alert, sensitive, and responsive to all of our children as we learn more about their behavioral patterns and understand more of their specific relationships and home situations. They have their own agendas! When we are tuned into the experiences and feelings of our young students, we know that Thursday is the day Jackie's mom visits her in the house she lives in with her grandparents. That weekly visit, often stressful and filled with feelings of loss and separation, is noted by our watchful eyes, by the ear inside of our *hearts*! We're lucky that our young children have not yet learned to repress their feelings, that they give us many opportunities to be immediately responsive to their needs. The older the children, the more subtle their expressions, the easier to fool adults who are not truly present and accounted for.

Life is not simple for young children (or for any age children!) in this complicated, highly mobile, often violent culture. Many of our kids experience numerous transitions: multiple households; childcare programs that in too many instances suffer from high turnover of staff; juggling before- and after-school care. Too many of our children feel lonely and alienated. Too many of our children have learned at very early ages to feel like failures, disappointments to their families. Our children are in search of companionship, community, and connections. As members of the human family, they have deep needs for the reassurance of safety, trust, constancy, and consistency—qualities difficult to promise in such anxious times. The urgent topic of the emotional health of our children has motivated serious dialogue in the educational field. The themes of many professional journals have been dedicated to such topics as "schools as safe havens" and "youth and caring."[3]

A kindergartner was weeping inconsolably in the school office while the secretary dialed his mother at work to come take him home.

"Is it the flu?" I asked sympathetically.

"Oh, no. Not the flu," the secretary explained. "His teacher is absent and he's so upset, he's sick over it."

Loving and caring teachers create safe havens for their children. In such sacred communities, children are welcomed, appreciated, and respected. Put-downs are not allowed! Children are not permitted to be humiliated. Such teachers are good listeners, asking gentle but important questions, opening doors for children to share. They realize the importance of verbal and nonverbal communication. They know the power of gestures and facial expressions. A smile goes a long way! Children are fortunate to have teachers who are reassuring, comforting, and understanding.[4]

But such teachers are not superheroes! They are human, too, with their own range of emotional needs and situations. Often they will share information with the children such as: "Friends, last night I didn't sleep so well. I was thinking about my grandmother coming home from the hospital. Would you forgive me if I seem a little tired today?"

This helps children understand that grown-ups have feelings, too. A greater concept is that this grown-up feels such safety and trust in the group that such information will be shared. Doesn't this invite children to feel safe in expressing their feelings?

No matter what the state of their emotional situations, caring teachers keep their focus on the children and their daily lives together. A friend teaching second grade through a bitter and nasty divorce year just held on for dear life through it all. After moving to a new city, a few years later, she received a letter from one of her former second graders, who wrote: "I was thinking about you last night when I saw the Little Dipper. I always think about you when I see the Little Dipper."

My friend was in shock. All she could remember of that year were sad events. Somehow, miraculously, through it all, she must have found times of inspiration and magical teaching.

*No matter the state of their emotional states, teachers keep their focus on the children and their daily lives together!*

No matter the state of their physical space, such teachers arrange areas in their rooms so children have opportunities to relieve stressful feelings in positive ways. A few examples are:

FIGURE 2–2    *In loving environments, children feel
safe in expressing their feelings.*

- puppets, stuffed animals, and dolls to talk to and through
- areas for peg pounding, block building, finger-painting, and clay squeezing
- quiet, safe "hiding places" for children who need and want a few minutes to sit alone and gather thoughts and feelings (I saw a large cardboard shipping box with a window cut out of it, a cheerful design by the children painted on it, and labeled "Alone House"—this was *not* a punishment but a place a child could choose to sit in quietly for a while.)
- cuddle-up corners with soft pillows, blankets, and huggable stuffed animals for children who need an extra snuggle to make it through the day
- listening chair/talking chair for children in conflict who need to sit with each other, listen and talk, and solve their problem
- peaceful place—an area of the room with soft colors, plants, gentle music, a journal and sketchbook to add peaceful images, photos, and pictures of beautiful, peaceful scenes[5]

Teachers who are tuned into the feelings of their students are realistic. They know that, despite their life-and-death presence in the lives of their students, their powers are limited. The children have experiences *outside* of the classroom that are not in the immediate range of influence of teachers. They come to school, to our programs, with emotional histories full of memories and life lessons that have shaped their worldview, their self-view. Yes, these teachers are realistic. They know that they can create caring environments that young children run to, feel safe in, where they can learn to accept their feelings and learn to understand and respect the feelings of others.

Because *children*, and not materials or methodologies, are at the central core of education, the doors of communication should swing open for families and teachers, home and school and community, to connect as often and as meaningfully as possible, cooperating, brainstorming, explaining, and advocating for the children. Many times a child's home and school situations improve because of the greater understanding made possible by the mutual concern and communication between teacher and family.

What can children learn from you? No matter what their home environment or family history may be, with *you* they can learn *safety*, *trust*, *respect*, *encouragement*, *acceptance*, *fairness*, *joy*, and *love*. Through your guidance and good common sense, children learn to deal with their feelings in healthy ways. Because you provide success-oriented experiences, your students will develop positive self-images, confidence, and the freedom and courage to *try* without worry, to *risk* without anxiety, to *explore* and *experiment* without fear of failure or humiliation.

FIGURE 2–3   *With caring adults, children learn trust, acceptance, and love.*

Because you are considerate of their feelings, sensitive to their moods, aware of and responsive to their special needs, you will help your children become stronger individuals, at peace with themselves and others and freer in spirit to learn and grow in the healthiest of ways. You are a role model!

---

*Note:* You will be continually reminded that all of the themes in this book are threads weaving through the daily fabric of our lives. None of these strands is more important than feelings. Even if you plan a special emphasis on feelings as a lesson for a designated time period, know that feelings can't be regulated to any limited curriculum schedule, because life doesn't permit airtight structures in the flowing, dynamic, challenging process of learning. The learning can't be separated from feelings, can it? What might you glean from this book if you read it feeling tense and uptight? The challenge for me as the author is to entice you, invite you, trap you in the magic of interesting and exciting learning experiences so . . . maybe . . . you forget for a while that you feel upset, angry, hurt. I catch you in my web! Isn't that part of what we need to do with our children? And don't you want to be Charlotte?

---

## DISCOVERY TIMES/WONDER TIMES: POINTS OF INTEREST

- Isn't it amazing that no matter what peoples' physical challenges, ages, languages, religions, cultures, countries, racial groups, customs, or regions, everyone has feelings? (Do animals have feelings?)
- Some feelings are positive and feel good, like happiness, friendliness, and love.
- Some feelings are negative and feel bad, like anger, jealousy, and fear.
- It is normal for people to have all kinds of feelings.
- It is important to be able to talk about our feelings with our families, friends, classmates, and teachers.
- We can express our feelings in many different ways.
- Our feelings are important, as are the feelings of others.
- Sometimes the way we express bad feelings hurts ourselves and others.
- We can learn healthy ways of expressing bad feelings.
- Everyone reacts differently to a situation. Each of us is unique.
- Even though we are different individuals, we share many feelings and can learn from, and help, each other.

| | | | |
|---|---|---|---|
| happy | eager | nice | kick |
| sad | impatient | stubborn | hit |
| glad | mischievous | ashamed | smile |
| mad | curious | divorced | hug |
| silly | brave | dead | died |
| serious | excited | sick | "feel good" |
| disappointed | nervous | hurt | "feel bad" |
| angry | calm | surprise | share |
| afraid | lonely | cry | give |
| shy | cuddly | laugh | love |
| scared | friendly | giggle | hate |
| jealous | affectionate | break | forgive |
| proud | mean | worried | care |
| pleased | help | sorry | listen |

You may be surprised at some of the words on the vocabulary list. Most children know many more words than we think they do. They are ardent TV viewers; they are part of many adult situations that children of earlier generations did not experience; they go to movies, fast-food restaurants, bowing alleys, and miniature golf courses; and they are readers of highway billboards, cereal boxes, magazine ads, TV program schedules, and video games. Nowadays they are learned in Pokemon, Digimon, and Harry Potter lexicons!

The astonished grandparents of a four-year-old boy related this incident to illustrate the rich vocabulary of young children. They were driving along, adults in the front of the car, the child in back, when an argument started over directions for their destination. Grandpa, the driver, grew exasperated with his wife's advice and became a little testy. From the back of the car, a child's voice asked, "Grandpa, why are you overreacting?"

Sometimes you can help your students change the way they feel by giving them a better word to describe their feelings. One of my young friends was worried about school. "I'm so depressed!" she moaned, "I'm so depressed!" I pointed out that "depressed" is a serious word describing a clinical mental state: "How about saying that you feel 'down in the dumps,' 'blue,' or 'yuk' instead of 'depressed'?" When she came to school the next day, she cheerfully announced: "I think I feel better. Feeling down in the dumps is a lot better than feeling depressed!"

## TALK/LISTEN/READ/WRITE: THE GIFTS OF LANGUAGE

Children should and must talk about their feelings. They talk about them through pictures, puppets, pantomime, songs, games, stories, and play times. They talk about them in large groups, small groups, and one-to-one conversations. Talking is valuable in itself. It gives children the chance not only to say how they feel but also to find others who share those feelings. Children are reassured that they are members of the human family and have common experiences. It helps them reach out to each other and develop sensitivity. It helps them become good listeners.

When children are eager to talk about something, they are telling you that it is a subject relevant and interesting to them. These kinds of meaningful interactive language celebrations lead naturally to art activities, books to share, songs to sing, improvisational plays, movement times, word gatherings, and more and more. Margie Goldach and Carol Highfield's group of pre-K kids turned their animated discussion about feelings into large, colorful charts that extended their talk sessions. The headlines on the charts read: "Things That Scare Me," "Things That Make Me Angry," "Things That Make Me Sad," "Things That Make Me Happy." The children listed their feelings for all the charts. They wrote their names next to the suggestions they dictated and were recorded by their teachers. The children were eager to point out the different items printed on every chart. They knew their contributions and those of their classmates.[6]

### Shared Experiences

Often, children going through rough times or down feelings won't or don't initiate conversation. Your watchful eyes and alert heart easily pick up on such occasions. Using words like "sometimes" or "once" to inspire group discussions is very effective.

"Sometimes I get so mad at my dog for chewing up my good new shoes. Did that ever happen to you? What gets you mad sometimes?" was the way a clever kindergarten teacher launched an important group talk that especially helped her with one grumpy student to work through his "bad mad day." The session led to a gathering of books that reflected a range of feelings. A favorite of children who are talking about their "grumpy" days is Molly Bang's *When Sophie Gets Angry—Really, Really Angry*. A delightful spin-off is to invite the children to create their own stories. (Be sure they are written down by themselves, or you, illustrated, and dramatized. Children are natural actors and storytellers.) For example: *When Melissa Gets Angry—Really, Really Angry*. One group of almost-five-year-olds crossed to the other side and followed their talk time and storybook time with their own spin-around: *When Tanisha Is Happy—Really, Really Happy* was one of these original creations. When books such as Bonnie Hausman's *A to Z—Do You Ever Feel Like Me?* or Hiawyn Oram and Susan Varley's *Badger's Bad Mood* are read and talked about, children find it easier to share their own feelings from A to Z or their own good or bad moods![7]

## Puppet Talk

If you have a special beloved classroom character who happens to be a puppet, magical things can happen. Your puppet can initiate group talks by telling or showing shyness, silliness, anger, joy, or disappointment (add all other emotions!). Often a bashful puppet can draw out the friendliness and caring of the children, who are encouraged to wave, sing, talk to, and reassure their special "friend." Remember, puppets have feelings, too![8]

## Stories Talk

A gem of advice comes from the Talmud: "Before you begin a lesson, start with a story." Sometimes it is not always best to direct a discussion to a specific incident or a child's particular situation. Let a story be a safe way to open the gates for trusting and respectful expressions of feelings. Teachers like Debbie Charna have shelves and bags and drawers overflowing with effective stories and books for every reason and occasion. When it's obvious that the children need to talk about feelings, she has three of her tried and always true favorite books on hand to inspire the children to share their own experiences and moods: Judith Viorst's *Alexander and the Terrible, Horrible, No Good, Very Bad Day*, Bernard Waber's *Ira Sleeps Over*, and Sandra Boynton's *A Is for Angry*. Through humor, trust, reassurance, and encouragement, the children sometimes make the whole journey and end up writing and illustrating storybooks that describe their wonderful days![9] Laskey's *Tantrums* helps young students recognize and deal with those terrible temper tantrums in more reasonable ways. McBratney's *I'm Sorry* really makes sense out of often troubling human relationships. Stories like these reassure children going through difficult times that they are not alone.

Being with children sometimes has unbearably painful challenges: how to deal with death? Here is another example of an excellent storybook that helps free children to talk about such topics when they are relevant and *must* be talked about: Mary Bahr's *If Nathan Were Here*.[10]

When I started teaching decades ago, there were virtually *no* books about *any* difficulties, "controversial" issues, topics of real meaning to young children. Now, the choices are incredibly plentiful. A variety of rich literature is part of the daily lives of young children.

## A Picture Is Worth . . .

Alert teachers are gatherers of the many excellent photos and pictures featured in magazines and catalogs and garage sales and wherever hidden treasures are found! Madison Avenue is gifted and talented in presenting images of people expressing a wide range of feelings. It's often easier to talk about the feelings expressed in a visual image (and *not* directed to any specific child who may be experiencing similar feelings).

"Children, I wonder what this person is feeling now? Any ideas?"

Sometimes, talking about the picture's feelings is safer than talking about one's own feelings. But the group talk about a photo or picture leads naturally to the sharing of personal feelings (*if* the children feel that this is a group of trust and respect). This easily encourages the children to create their own stories, pictures, and plays expressing strong feelings. I've seen colorful and creative children's art and writing with titles like "Happy Faces!" "Angry Faces!" "Sad Faces!" and words to read describing the pictures.

### *Playful Talks*

Probably more important than any adult-directed activity are the every-day at-play moments when children relate to each other: at the sand table, during block building, through dramatic play in dress up, in housekeeping areas, at art centers, and so on. The children's talking and being together is of immeasurable value. Eavesdrop on their conversations as they play house, play truck driver, play store, play school—play *whatever* is in their interest of the day to play. Feelings will be expressed and explored, language will grow, listening skills will be strengthened, and imagination will flourish. The importance of play in helping the children make sense out of the world, make meaning, cannot be emphasized enough.

To deepen your appreciation and respect for the stories of young children, read any book by Vivian Gussin Paley, an extraordinary teacher who documented the stories her students told her, the playing of those stories by the children, and the enormous wisdom and insight the stories provided for all. Many of the children's stories and "plays" deal with universal human feelings: loneliness, fear, love, loss. . . . Vivian inspires adults who spend time with young children to listen, to respect and honor the feelings of her students.[11]

FIGURE 2–4   *Children need opportunities to share their feelings in many ways.*

### Good Humor (Not Ice Cream, but . . .
### That's Not a Bad Idea, Is It?)

One too often overlooked way of dealing with deeply felt negative feelings like anger is through humor. Children are excellent at name calling and put-downs, so don't be surprised at the display of epithets expressed by even the youngest students when there are conflicts or hurt or angry feelings. The late Eve Merriam's poem "Mean Song" is a delightful example of changing insults and name calling to nonsense sounds and imaginative images.[12]

The words are silly. The point is clear. Even silly words can be hurtful. When we say things in mean ways, people's feelings can get hurt. As the kids are thinking up really wild and weird name-calling words like "purple pickle" or "frilly celery," my faithful little dog puppet, Snowball, listens to the kids tease. His furry head is downcast. He looks totally devastated.

"Friends, I don't think Snowball realizes you're just kidding around. I think his feelings are hurt because he hears you sounding like you're making fun of him!"

We talk about laughing with someone and at someone. We talk about how we feel if we think people are making fun of us.

We talk about how *really mean* words can make us feel sad and hurt, then we reassure Snowball that no one ever would want to hurt his feelings. He perks up and we think of other silly names that make us all laugh, like "purple pumpkin eater" or "munchy crunchy" or Eve Merriam's "snickles and podes. . . ."

> Children have so much to say about their experiences and feelings. Even shy children are reassured and encouraged through listening. Give your students many opportunities to talk—to you, to each other, to playthings and puppets. "There, I said it" is the kind of relief many children seem to feel after such sessions. The responses of teacher and classmates are also helpful in sorting out feelings. You are teaching children that expression is healthy, that sharing is better than hoarding, that communicating about feelings is better than developing a sense of isolation and loneliness.

## MUSIC MAKERS/MOVERS AND SHAKERS

Bodies don't lie! Look at the children! Posture? Energy? Facial expressions? What stories they tell about feelings!

Our children need many opportunities to *move* and to enjoy *active* experiences across the curriculum so bodies and spirits grow freer, so uptightness loosens, so nonparticipation becomes total participation.

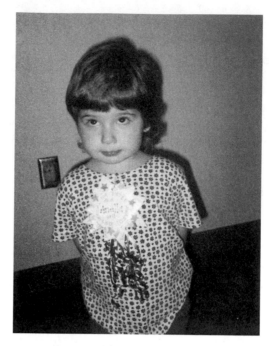

FIGURE 2–5    *Look at the children! Expressions don't lie.*

Music and movement times every day, connected to all subject areas, will help shake out negativity, hostility, and stress and will encourage natural energies to be expressed in healthy, lovingly directed ways. As I travel the country, many teachers complain that their children won't sit still for stories, are constantly in time-out for misbehavior, don't pay attention. I *beg* them to give the children time to warm up every day, stretch, jump, follow movement patterns (see Theme 1). If you sprinkle easy and healthy moving/musical moments throughout the day, you'll notice fewer arguments, discipline problems, hurt feelings, and conflicts. I asked teachers to send me postcards after they introduced more musical/moving moments into their daily schedules to let me know if it worked. I humbly admit to you, *it works!* Try it!

### Peekaboo Faces

Peekaboo is probably the most popular game of very young children. "Hide your face in your hands. One, two, three, peekaboo. Open your hands and show your face. Show your *happy* face. Show another *happy* face. Another! How about an *angry* face? Grr! Another!" Invite the children: "Hide your faces. Let's see some *sad* faces. Now some *happy* faces." Facial muscles, vocabulary, and awareness of the varieties of human expressions reflecting different emotions will be strengthened.

### Mirror, Mirror, on the Wall

This activity is similar to the previous one, but the children look in the mirror to see their own facial expressions. Then you can ask, "Which face do you like better, your happy face or your grouch face? Why?" Keep it loose and playful.

### Hands Show Feelings

Happy hands look different from mean hands. Sad hands look different from angry hands. Let hands show feelings. Give children the opportunity to try at least five variations of an idea. *They should never feel that one try at something is the total experience.*

### "Turn Yourself Into . . ."

Probably no three words in the English language can spur children into movement faster than these three words. The possibilities are limitless. Here are just a few to start your mind buzzing.

#### Statues

Angry statues, frightened statues, silly statues, happy statues . . . (remember, more than one version of each). Children love to move and *freeze*!

#### Present situations

A child who just lost a puppy or who just found a puppy, a child whose friend is moving away, a child whose favorite toy just broke, a child whose grandma is very sick. *Show the idea.*

#### The seven dwarfs

Bashful, Dopey, Grumpy, Sleepy, Sneezy, Doc, and Happy are excellent characters to help children express feelings. The children do shapes, walks, dances, pantomimes, and exercises for each dwarf. Bashful's dance, for example, contrasts greatly with Happy's dance. Expand the activity into art, music, drama, and creative writing. Create seven new dwarfs. Name them, describe them.

#### Move your shape

Ask questions to expand upon the statue exercise. For example: "How does your angry shape (or statue) want to move? Want to walk? How does your angry shape run? How does your silly shape want to stand? Want to sit? How does your bashful shape want to run? Can you do a grouch dance? What's your silliest walk?" End each idea by asking the children to "shake out," "melt down," or "wiggle out" their sad, silly, or disappointed shapes. Shake a tambourine to give them transition rhythm as they prepare for the next feeling.

#### Opposites

Important concepts, language development, and comprehension are but a few lessons learned in challenges such as "Turn yourself into the idea

FIGURE 2–6 *How does your friendly shape want to move?*

of brave! Show me brave." If the children understand the word, they will eagerly demonstrate it with strong, upright bodies. After experimenting with body movements and shapes for brave, shake out that idea and ask the kids to show you the opposite of brave. Try it with happy/sad, cheerful/grouchy, or friendly/unfriendly. Play music or rhythms that express these antonyms. The children learn to listen and respond to contrasts in music. Expand into songs, stories, poems, pictures, and sculptures.

### "When You're Angry, Jump!" and Other Advice to Get Things Moving

I visited a kindergarten class and saw a handmade poster showing a child having a temper tantrum and jumping in the air. The children had discussed their feelings and had suggested movements for the different emotions. "If you're angry, jump!" was one of the children's ideas. The teacher explained that the day a visitor was scheduled but did not appear, the children were angry. They decided to follow their own advice and jumped very hard for about two minutes. They felt much better afterward! Other suggestions the kindergartners made and followed were: "When you're silly, do a somersault"; "When you're sad, lie down on your tummy"; "When you're happy, skip"; and "When you're afraid, do jumping jacks and shout." I like to play with the kids and encourage them to have a "very jumpy or bouncy day"! Add music! Add original lyrics!

### Mood Music

It's easy to find music that evokes feelings. Every culture is rich with lullabies, exciting rhythms, mysterious chants, and so on. Accompany the previous activities with music that fits their movement. If it's a "hoppy day," and everyone's feeling pretty "hoppy," play hoppy music. What if you're "unhoppy"?

An enjoyable challenge is to ask the children to listen to specific music that expresses an emotion and follow the feelings of the music with their bodies. Unless you're focusing on a specific body part, encourage the children to use their whole bodies.

After listening to a portion of "Scheherazade" by Rimsky-Korsakoff, a group of five-year-olds decided that the music was scary and they did a powerful improvised dance showing all kinds of fright movements. After it was over, one little girl said, "I have lots of practice to dance about *frightened* now that my bedroom got moved upstairs!"

### Drumbeats and Heartbeats

Play a heartbeat rhythm on a tom-tom or a bongo drum, child-made or store-bought. If you do not have drums, cookie containers, coffee cans, or tabletops will do. Discuss the music of heartbeats with your students. Our hearts beat faster and louder when we are afraid, excited, angry, or full of energy. Our hearts beat slower and softer when we feel calm, safe, and loved. With your children, practice the different kinds of heartbeats.

Read or tell a story that expresses many different feelings. The children play the drums to accompany the feelings in the story—loud and fast for exciting and scary parts, soft and slow for peaceful, calm parts. Combine the drum rhythms of heartbeats with a round-robin story in which all of the children take turns adding words and movement to the action. Add other instruments to the basic drum rhythms. Encourage the children to tell or sing their own original stories and accompany them on the drums or other instruments.

Many Native American poems are drumbeat/heartbeat songs that evoke strong feelings. The repetition in such poems and chants helps children learn them easily. As you read them aloud, you cannot help chanting and feeling the pulse of the drumbeat/heartbeat.

### Listen to Music: Tell and Show a Story

This activity involves listening, imaging, and sharing ideas. Choose music that conveys a specific feeling. Ask the children to listen to the music carefully and try to picture what is happening. Make up a story that goes with the music. Expand the idea into movement. Listen, make up a story, and turn it into a dance. Write it! Illustrate it! Play it! Sing it!

### Familiar Songs That Evoke Feelings

Most young children love songs and singing, and they learn through rhyme, rhythm, and melody. You already know many songs that express feelings as well as provide springboards for further discussion and activities about feelings. Keep track of the songs you and your children enjoy. I visited a kindergarten class where a chart of songs and feelings was prominently displayed. Here are some of the items from that chart. Play with the songs—add your own lyrics and movement.

**Silly Songs**

"I Know an Old Lady That Swallowed a Fly"
"Pop Goes the Weasel"
"Boom Boom, Ain't It Great to Be Crazy"
"John Jacob Jingleheimer Schmidt"
"Zippity Doo Dah"

**Quiet, Sleepy Songs**

"Kum Ba Yah"
"Michael, Row the Boat Ashore"
"Rain, Rain Go Away"
"Twinkle, Twinkle, Little Star"

**Happy Songs**

"Here Comes the Sun"
"He's Got the Whole World in His Hands"
"My Favorite Things"
"Puff, the Magic Dragon"
"I Love You, You Love Me"

The songs of our lives have great meanings to us. We are comforted by familiar and beloved lullabies. We are cheered by favorite playful songs. There are songs for every emotion, every situation, every event! If your own treasure chest of music and songs runs low, turn to the appendix of this book and check out any of the excellent music makers for rich resources.

### Original Songs That Express Feelings

Young children make up songs as naturally as they speak. They are very much like Winnie the Pooh, who is always making up hums and songs to match his moods. For example, one of the children's favorite Winnie the Pooh hums, "Sing Ho! for the life of a Bear!"[13] begged to be adapted into their own songs. They "sang" their hum with a little singsong melody that followed the rhythm of the words. Here is the song that a group of young music makers created and danced to:

> Sing Ho! for the life of a girl!
> Sing Ho! for the life of a boy!
> I don't mind if I don't have toys.
> I don't mind if I don't make noise.
> We have lots of girls
> We have lots of boys
> Sing Ho! for the girls.
> Sing Ho! for the boys.

For weeks "Sing Ho" was the way those children expressed happiness.

### Animals and Movement

Young children truly enjoy animals, and almost any activity with an animal is guaranteed to succeed. "Let's change into cats. Are you a big cat? Little cat? What color are you? Are you sleeping? Rolling a ball of yarn? Sunning by the window? Let's see. How are you cats feeling today? Very shy? Let's see those shy cats. Very mischievous? Full of tricks? Show me what you're doing. Very sad? Why are the cats so sad? What could have happened?"

A group of six-year-olds changed into turtles. They crawled slowly. They were curious. They were frightened and hid in their shells. They slowly stuck out their heads to see if it was safe outside. They walked happily because there was no danger. "How do you feel now? Show me. Tell me." Once little boy-turtle lifted his head as he walked on all fours and expressed a feeling on his face that I had not seen before. "Very proud," he said, glowing. "My turtle isn't afraid of dogs anymore!" Mix with music and rhythm. Add dialogue and illustrations.

### Literature Is Full of Feelings

Literature offers poems, stories, books that highlight the whole gamut of feelings. Read, tell, improvise stories, dance to and accompany with rhythm and music as you celebrate such works. I remind the children that our bodies have to "tell" the story. We don't have to choreograph or move to every word. Highlight movement possibilities—the Gingerbread Man runs, runs, runs. The Three Little Kittens are sad because they lost their mittens. The Troll is angry listening to the Billy Goats trip-trap across his bridge. The Ugly Duckling feels lonely and unhappy when everyone ridicules him. Remember the magical powers of "Show me" as you encourage the children to move and make music.

"Show me the anger of Mr. McGregor when he saw Peter in the garden. What kind of music shall we use for our dance? Fast? Slow? Cheery? Loud?"

"Show me Little Miss Muffett frightened by the spider who sat down beside her. How does she move? What kind of music shall we choose? Do spiders frighten you?"

"Oh, my! The Tin Woodsman needs oil. He's so tight. Show me how he moves! He feels sad—why? What does he want?"

"Show me the Scarecrow going down the Yellow Brick Road! Loose, loose, loose! What does Scarecrow want?"

"Ooooh! That lion is scary! Listen to that growl! What's that? Show me how scared he is sometimes! . . . What does he want from the Wizard?" (A four-year-old child answered that question during a celebration of *The Wizard of Oz.* "Porridge!" he offered.)

We need a lot of porridge to challenge our music makers/movers and shakers!

(Remember, there is no finale to any idea! We just stop because of the limits of space and time!)

### *Welcome a New Day*

I saved this idea for the end of this section so you can see how beginnings and endings flow into one another and sometimes the beginning is really the ending and sometimes the ending is really the place to begin. We circular thinkers go with the flow!

Many of our students come to us with so many different home situations, so many painful experiences and memories. Even at very young ages, some of our children are already labeled "difficult," "behavior problems," or "underachievers." Too often, yesterday's events hang around their necks like albatrosses. I think it's important to begin each day in a fresh way. Even our youngest children understand the sacredness of that opportunity.

Hallow each day. Welcome the children to the new time together with special gestures, poems, songs, and ceremonies. Honor the new day and the new chance to do our best, to be our best selves.

With each class I teach, no matter the ages or grade levels, I begin with a special way to show appreciation and good wishes to everyone in the group, for the time we will share together. Maybe it's just a simple high five greeting. Maybe it's a song like Thomas Moore's "Good Morning to My Friends, Good Morning to My Teacher, Too." Maybe it's a poem like Shel Silverstein's "Invitation," which welcomes dreamers to come in. Maybe it's a special book like Byrd Baylor's *Way to Start a Day.* But, whatever the way, *your* way, the children begin with the magical feeling of being wanted and welcomed.[14]

## ALL WAYS ART

There is no theme that lends itself to a greater variety of enjoyable art activities and experiences than feelings. Feelings flow into colors, shapes, textures, and designs. Here are a few ideas to start you thinking of your own. Shapes, colors, textures, tones evoke emotional responses.

### *Paper Plate Faces*

Paper plates are just waiting for children to turn them into faces. Children draw features or arrange already-cutout eyes, eyebrows, lips, and noses. The letters C and U are excellent models for drawing eyebrows and lips; the children discover that Cs and Us facing up look happy and facing down look sad.

Add wool, carpet pieces, shredded paper, or cotton puffs for hair. Add ears and hats. Kids love glitter, sprinkles, and glue! Experiment with different facial expressions that illustrate feelings. Share ideas and observations. Add dialogue! Display all the faces on a bulletin board. Title the artworks and feel safe in their sharing.

### *Feelings Pictures*

If you are talking about a particular feeling, suggest that your students draw or paint a picture conveying that feeling. Another way to encourage this valuable expression is to ask the children to "Draw a picture about the way you feel right now." (Although you may not like the way some children feel, do not be critical or judgmental.) "Tell me about your picture" or "What is in your picture?" or "Why did you use these colors?" is the kind of response that invites children to interpret their artwork.

### *Happiness Board*

I know I am highlighting feelings of happiness, but I'm concerned about so many young children being so out of touch with any moments of happiness. These projects are offered in the spirit of inviting children to be aware of, remember, recognize, and appreciate the positive people, places, times, and events of their lives.

With your students, brainstorm images that evoke happiness to them. Write all their suggestions. Create a bright and colorful display of their words and ideas. Mix the words with the children's original illustrations. On a first-grade corridor bulletin board called the Happiness Board, I was particularly delighted by a bright yellow balloon with these words: "Balloons are always happy because they are like round pieces of the sky." (Samantha)

FIGURE 2–7   *Our feelings dictate their own design.*

## Happy Greeting Cards

"You feel good when you make someone else feel good!" was one of the ideas a kindergarten teacher wanted to convey to her students. They decided to make "happiness cards," put them in a grab bag, and let everyone pick one. The children enjoyed making the cards. They created designs that made them feel good and that would also cheer someone else.

A variation of this activity is to have the children pick the name of one of their classmates out of a grab bag (keep it a secret) and then make a card for that child. In addition to the happy design or picture, the card includes the recipient's name. The cards are collected by the teacher, who then calls on one child at a time to deliver the card to the child whose name is featured. Every child has a chance to deliver "good news." All the children receive a special card with their name on it. Include yourself! Add another delightful suggestion: "You can deliver the card any way you want to—by hopping, skipping, doing any happy movement!" Sing a happy song! Have a parade! Wave originally designed banners!

## Music to Paint Feelings To

Music inspires art. Feelings inspire music. Find music that expresses specific moods and feelings (lullabies evoke calm; shepherds' flute songs have a lonely sound; Spanish bullfighting music flashes the red cape of excitement). Offer the children paper and crayons, paints, markers, or finger paints, and instruct them to listen carefully to the music, picture it, and discover how it makes them feel. "Listen and let the music go into your brushes, markers, and paint and draw its feelings," one teacher instructed in a poetic way. When there is no fear of failure, no worry about getting something right or wrong, children are absorbed by the musical challenge and often create original and powerful works.

Leave time to ask the children afterward, "Tell me about your pictures. Do they have a story? What were your feelings?" Encourage them to write titles and stories for their works. One first grader filled a paper with a light blue color, hardly changing the shade or texture. He told his teacher, "The music made me feel like when I fall asleep and my room turns blue."

Vary the experience. Encourage the children to paint their responses to different kinds of music. None of their pictures will look the same. "Which did you like best? Did you have a favorite?" This question followed an art-music-feelings session in which the children interpreted three kinds of music: very noisy, dissonant, urban jazz; an instrumental rendition of a melancholy melody; and lively marching band music. "I liked the last one," Kent explained. "It made me happy to think I was in a parade. It was happy like a holiday."

"I liked them all," Annie said. "Even the very sad one. I like my sad picture the best, as a matter of fact."

After a long and intense discussion about good and bad feelings, a group of kindergartners suggested ideas for images that made them feel good. Flowers was the overwhelming choice! One of the kids said that raindrops made her feel sad because they looked like tears. The children loved the idea of flowers for happy feelings and teardrops for sad feelings.

Choosing their own materials, they created their own flowers (no dittos or worksheets here!). They taped their beautiful flowers to a green bulletin board, naming things that made them feel good, which they and their teacher wrote on the board. It looked like the flowers were talking! Raindrops of every size and style were created next, taped to the blue-gray sky of the board and dotted with written and dictated words evoking teary feelings.

Encourage the children to think of more images that inspire feelings. Always add words! Add movement and music.

## What Bugs You?

The children talked about things that bugged them, so their teacher, Lynn Thompson, suggested that the children design their own bugs and then write (with help from Lynn if needed) something that bugged them on their bugs. Their display was the hit of the school![15]

## Feelings Mobiles

Each child has a hanger and string on which to hang pictures, shapes, and objects expressing different feelings. Not only do they add life and vitality to your room, but they also make great conversation pieces! Use your scrounge materials.

## The Shapes of Feelings

"What kind of shapes say 'happiness'? Paint them. Draw them. Sculpt them in clay." These questions stimulate good thinking, good talks, and very creative artworks. One first grader responded, "Squiggly," painting colorful squiggly designs on her paper. "My happiness is squiggly like my room at home!" Think squiggly music and dance! Explore other emotions and know they take shape in the children's minds and artwork.

## Faces on Stones/Shells/Buttons

Very imaginative and delightful little "characters" emerge when children follow talks about feelings with opportunities to make faces showing different expressions on a variety of materials. Use your scrounge collection—scraps, beads, pom-poms, stickers—and invite the children to design happy/mad/sad/etc. faces on the materials of their choice.

FIGURE 2–8    *When you're feeling bugged, create a bug!*

### Collages (Group or Individual)

Children love to practice cutting, tearing, snipping. Spread a table full of old magazines, greeting cards, colored paper, scrounge materials, brushes, markers, crayons, and so on.

Invite the children to contribute examples of different kinds of feelings—expressed on faces, gestures, body postures—and as they select and create their images, ask them to paste their artwork on a large bulletin board. The excitement of easy-to-see feelings accumulating, building as more ideas are added, overlapping and interweaving, is very dramatic. The kids will want it to stay on the board for a long time, looking at it, talking, sharing their own feelings. Add words! Add movement! Make up stories about the images.

Children love colors. Expand your talks about colors to combine with feelings and the feelings colors evoke or the colors that represent different feelings. Remember, *all* answers are correct. This is not a closed-ended session with right/wrong answers. This is another important time for original thinking and freedom of expression.

Books like Dr. Seuss' *My Many Colored Days* beautifully demonstrate that combination and inspire children to create their own color moods on posters, pictures, books, cards, and collages. Expand into songs, dances, stories.[16]

## KIDS COUNT

In case you are wondering how math and feelings can be combined, do recall Elizabeth Barrett Browning, who counted the ways she loved Robert! Or listen to Paul Simon sing of fifty ways to leave a lover. I still laugh remembering the story my friend told about the fiftieth wedding anniversary of her in-laws. When she congratulated her father-in-law, he thanked her graciously. She then gushed to her mother-in-law, "How wonderful! Fifty years together! What a special anniversary!" Her mother-in-law bluntly remarked, "I can count the good years on one hand!"

Let's count the good years, the bad years, and the in between years.

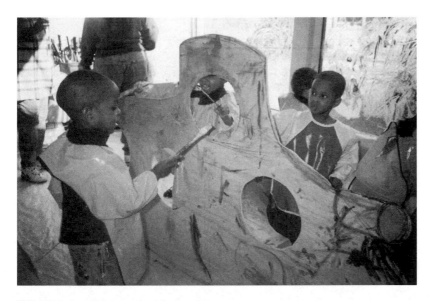

FIGURE 2–9   *Colors express feelings!*

## Lucky Numbers

Children are fascinated by numbers. They chant them, hum them, recite them, "show them." Even very young students have lucky numbers. They feel lucky when they think of those numbers. Feeling lucky is a great feeling! Names of children and their lucky numbers make great charts that are easy to graph, talk about, and tell stories about and illustrate. The first graders were discussing lucky numbers. They all agreed that when they were driving in a car, they looked for their lucky numbers on license plates. Every time they spotted their lucky numbers, they cheered.

### Find the lucky number in my picture!

Extending the idea of lucky numbers into delightful activities is as easy as 1-2-3! We asked the kids, "How many ways can you show the idea of your lucky number in your picture? We'll look at your picture and try to guess your lucky number. Write your number on the back of the picture." Among the second graders' drawings, I remember Jackie's very clearly. He drew a clown with four balloons in his hand and four bright buttons on his costume. In the corner of the picture, he drew a poster that read, "CIRCUS, MAY 4." The children guessed his number immediately. Jackie was delighted and said, "That's why it's my lucky number!" What a great feeling!

## Top Ten Lists

David Letterman isn't the only person who enjoys compiling lists. This is a favorite activity of young children, who collectively or individually gather numbered ideas. A natural link is to add numbers to those Feelings Charts we talked about before. Top Ten Things That Make Us Happy, Top Ten Things That Make Us Sad, Top Ten Things That Make Us Feel Peaceful, and so on. I passed a first-grade room and noted a chart that featured the Top Ten Things That Make Us Feel Silly. The first idea printed was:

1. When someone gets the giggles, we all get the giggles.

## Count to Ten!

The familiar advice of counting to ten before you have a temper tantrum is a delightful way to blend numbers and feelings. If you're really mad, count to twenty! And when we all count together, we help that child or those children who are upset get through the troubled period. Add movement. Read on.

## Count and Jump, Count and Clap

"We're so excited about our visitor coming soon and bringing a new puppy to meet us that we're going to jump and clap. How many times?

Twenty-five times! Wow! This is really exciting! Here we go!" (Add music and rhythms.)

### From Disappointment to Cheerfulness
### in Three Easy Steps

Many teachers of young children continue to look for ways to help their students experience the concept of ordinal numbers like first, second, and third. Every day we try to strengthen that understanding in a myriad of experiences. Here's an example of combining the concept with the theme of feelings. The kindergartners were deeply disappointed when their long-awaited and greatly anticipated field trip was canceled. A few of the children were crying. Their teacher gathered them together and asked them to wipe their tears and think of ways to wipe away the disappointment. She asked the kids to think of three fantastic ideas that would cheer them up. This is how they choreographed their newly reclaimed morning:

1. First, we are going to sing our funniest songs like "Down by the Bay."
2. Second, we are going outside for a really long playground time.
3. Third, we are having a big story and our snacks. (And they did.)

### One, Few, Many, All

When Oren was three, his mother stood at the window and gasped as she watched him pick all the flowers in the garden. He proudly carried them into the house and gave them to his mom. She thanked him but then said, "Oren, you didn't have to pick *all* the flowers *in* the garden. One flower would have been just fine."

Oren said, "Mommy, I love you too much for one flower. I love you enough for all the flowers."

I've always remembered this incident and the continuing challenge for young children to comprehend the mathematical concepts of one, few, many, and all.

This topic invites children to blend math concepts with wonder. Talking together, they share ideas about feelings and numbers.

"Can one beautiful rose make you feel as happy as a dozen roses?"

"One piece of candy makes you feel good. A few pieces are OK. But if you eat a whole bunch of candy, you might get sick!"

Oh my, the examples in the tip of this pencil are endless!

Can't one idea be enough?

### High Fives!

America's children greet, celebrate, honor, and cheer with our most common, digital gesture—high fives! Count em!

I challenged a three-and-a-half-year-old to count her high five fingers. She proudly did just that. I held up her other hand and asked her to continue counting. She repeated the count on her original high fives hand—1, 2, 3, 4, 5—and named her next number, thumb! Soon that thumb will turn into 6!

I love to play with the kids and invite them to show high threes or high sixes! When we're feeling really super, we show high tens!

*These are but a tiny fraction of the numerous ways math connects with everything, even feelings!* Can you think of three other ideas? Five? Ten? Infinity?

### Field Trips and Visitors

A reminder to check the extensive list of suggestions in the appendix of this book for ideas for those important, valuable experiences children enjoy when special classroom visitors are invited or when field trips are planned. Feelings of excitement, anticipation, and enthusiasm are heightened. Preparation for the event as well as creative follow-up activities are built into these situations. A variety of community resources, artists, and family members are very willing to celebrate the theme of feelings! You'll feel very good about the many opportunities waiting to be hallowed by you.

## IT ALL COMES TOGETHER

It always comes together when you connect ideas and see how naturally they overlap and intertwine.

Rose Stough's third graders followed group talks about feelings by listening attentively to Marilyn Sachs' *Bears' House*, a moving story about Fran Ellen, a lonely and alienated girl who finds comfort and a rich imaginary life playing with the Bears' House brought into school by her teacher. At the end of the story, the teacher gives the Bears' House to the child who accomplishes the most during the school year. Guess who does that?

The children acted, danced, improvised, interpreted scenes from the story as they read along, and after the story was finished, they designed Bears' Houses and showed the loneliness of Fran Ellen and her joyfulness playing with the Bears' House. They danced to the song "Waltzing with Bears" from the *Dr. Seuss Song Book* and memorized and recited Langston Hughes' beautiful poem "Hope," which ended the story. Inspired by Hughes' "Hope," they wrote their own poems about hope and illustrated them.

Role playing, dialogue exploration, movement variations, talk times were but a few of the spin-offs from the reading of the story. Significant insights about the importance of the feelings of others were discovered and shared. Because Rose's environment was a safe and loving place, her students made their own connections to the experiences of Fran Ellen's. Feelings were expressed and discussed. Letters, posters, pictures reflected the children's understanding of the people, places, and emotional situations of the story.

When children see relationships, make connections, and think in holistic ways, the learning is deep. It feels good![17]

## NOTES

1. Goleman, D. 1995. *Emotional Intelligence*. New York: Bantam Books.
   An interesting article discussing this topic is Cobb, S. D. and J. D. Mayer. 11/2000. "Emotional Intelligence: What the Research Says." *Educational Leadership*. 58 (3). pp. 14–18.

2. Roethke, T. 1974. *Straw for the Fire*. New York: Doubleday. p. 204.

3. Books like the following are helpful in understanding the feelings of young children:
   Denham, S. S. 1998. *Emotional Development in Young Children*. New York: Guilford.
   Snoufe, L. A. 1997. *Emotional Development: The Organization of Emotional Life in the Early Years*. Cambridge, UK: Cambridge University Press.

4. So many excellent articles are available about the climate we create for children. For example:
   The theme issue of *Educational Leadership*—"Schools as Safe Havens." 55 (2). 10/1997.
   The theme issue of *Kappan*—"Youth and Caring." *Phi Delta Kappan*. 76 (9). 5/1995.
   Leadershouse, J. N. "You Will Be Safe Here." 9/1998. *Educational Leadership*. 56 (1). pp. 51–54.
   Lundeberg, M. A. J. Emmett, P. A. Osland, and N. Lindquist. 10/1997. "Down with Put Downs!" *Educational Leadership*. 55 (2). pp. 36–37.

5. No matter how humble your surroundings, there's always room for comfortable rugs, cushions, easily reached materials, special cozy corners, beanbag chairs, and so on. All great teachers of young children are scavengers!

6. The Feelings Charts were created when Margie Goldach and Carol Highfield co-taught at the Leo Yassenoff Jewish Center Early Childhood Program, Columbus, Ohio.

7. Bang, M. 1999. *When Sophie Gets Angry—Really, Really Angry*. New York: Blue Sky Press.

Hausman, B. photos Fellman, S. 1999. *A to Z—Do You Ever Feel Like Me?* New York: Dutton.

Oram, H. and S. Varley. 1998. *Badger's Bad Mood*. New York: Arthur A. Levine.

8. I honored my beloved puppet, Snowball, in an essay:

Chenfeld, M. B. 2001. "Snowball." *Teaching by Heart*. St. Paul, MN: Redleaf Press. pp. 90–97, reprinted from *Early Childhood Journal* 27 (4) 2000, p. 205.

9. Debbie Charna celebrates books with children in the Columbus School for Girls, Columbus, Ohio. Three of her favorites are:

Viorst, J. 1972. *Alexander and the Terrible, Horrible, No Good, Very Bad Day*. New York: Atheneum.

Waber, B. 1972. *Ira Sleeps Over*. Boston: Houghton Mifflin.

Boynton, S. 1987. *A Is for Angry*. New York: Workman.

10. Laskey, K. illus. McCarthy, S. 1992. *The Tantrums*. New York: Macmillan.

McBratney, S. illus. Beachus, J. 2000. *I'm Sorry*. New York: Harper-Collins.

Bahr, M. illus. Jerome, K. 2000. *If Nathan Were Here*. Grand Rapids, MI: Wm. B. Erdmans.

11. Vivian Gussin Paley's highly recommended books are:

Paley, V. G. 1999. *The Kindness of Children*. Cambridge, MA: Harvard University Press.

Paley, V. G. 1986. *Mollie Is Three: Growing Up in School*. Chicago, IL: University of Chicago Press.

Paley, V. G. 1981. *Wally's Stories: Conversations in the Kindergarten*. Cambridge, MA: Harvard University Press.

12. Merriam, E. 1992. "Mean Song." *The Singing Green*. New York: Morrow.

13. Milne, A. A. 1957. "Expedition to the North Pole." *The World of Pooh*. New York: Dutton. p. 104.

14. For information on Thomas Moore's music, call:

704-371-4077
Fax: 704-371-4377

Silverstein, S. 1974. "Invitation." *Where the Sidewalk Ends*. New York: Harper and Row.

Baylor, B. 1978. *The Way to Start a Day*. New York: Scribners.

15. Lynn Thompson and her students delighted everyone with their bugs at the Avalon School, Columbus, Ohio.

16. Seuss, Dr. illus. Johnson, S. and L. Foucher. 1996. *My Many Colored Days*. New York: Alfred Knopf.

17.  Sachs, M. 1976. *The Bears' House*. New York: Dell-Yearling.

Hughes, L. 1987. "Hope." *Selected Poems of Langston Hughes*. New York: Vintage.

Rose Stough recently retired from a teaching career in the Columbus Public Schools, Columbus, Ohio.

I highlighted Rose's outstanding work with young children in such articles as:

Chenfeld, M. B. 1993. "Stuff." *Teaching in the Key of Life*. Washington, D.C.: NAEYC.

Chenfeld, M. B. 2001. "No Rx for Reading." *Teaching by Heart*. St. Paul, MN: Redleaf Press.

# THEME 3 | OUR UNIQUENESS

*We are sweet children.*
*We are kissable and lovable.*

—Wesley Brantford[1]

**See Me Beautiful**

See me beautiful
Look for the best
in me.
It's what I really am
and all I want
to be.
It may take some time.
It may be hard to find
but
see me beautiful.
See me beautiful
each and every day.
Could you take a chance?
Could you find a way
to see me shining through
in everything I do
and see me beautiful?

—Red and Kathy Grammer,
from *Teaching Peace*[2]

## THINK ABOUT IT

We are most unique and original when we are very young. Picasso told people that all his life he was trying to paint like a child. During our early years we have not yet learned what is "in" or what is trite, what are the norms of our culture, the expectations of our society. We're honest (blunt?) and direct. We see things in a fresh, new way. Thoreau believed that every child begins the world again. Most young children know that the foolish emperor is naked and they don't pretend to see his invisible clothes just to conform to the adults around them. Usually, they tell it like it is! They say what they see.

Nowhere in human evolution has there been another person exactly like *you*, with your special arrangements of qualities, traits, characteristics, likes, dislikes, talents, moods, interests, dreams, fears, and wishes. (Does the sum of all your parts equal *you*?)

Even identical twins who share identical genes are not identical! Big sister, Jackie, at six years old, described her three-year-old identical twin sisters, Annie and Michelle.

> Well, Michelle is easier to be with. Annie is sometimes grumpier. Michelle doesn't wear earrings, you know. Annie loves earrings. In the morning when she first wakes up, Annie doesn't like me right away but Michelle screams for me! Annie's favorite things are her cat and her Babar. Michelle's favorite thing is my "porcelain doll" (but I won't let her borrow it). Annie's softer, not as wild. Michelle is wiggly. A bouncy, wiggly girl. . . .

If we were lucky enough to be healthy and beloved children, our early years were years of enchantment, when we learned to love the

FIGURE 3–1    *Young children see things in a fresh new way.*

FIGURE 3–2    *Even when we wear the same shirts, we are completely unique originals!*

sound of our own names and to bask in the warmth of a friendly universe. Celebrations were not limited to a few set calendar days; they were daily occurrences. When we said a new word, the people in our lives smiled and clapped. When we took a new step, we were cheered on. Our talk turned to song; our walk, to dance. We were delighted with our drawings, our toys, our make-believe games. We were proud of our accomplishments and discoveries. We were full of courage and mighty strength. We were giants. We could see through closed doors, cause rain, and play with imaginary friends.

Because healthy and cherished children learn that they are special and wonderful, they can see beyond themselves and appreciate the unique qualities of others.

But what of our too many children who do *not* share such positive histories? Our world shrinks every day and grows more complex. The security and order provided by traditional institutions are lost as mobility intensifies, families are disrupted, and communities expand. Many of our young children are caught in these family, community, economic, and societal tangles. In too many instances, the safety nets are torn or have disappeared. Many come to our earliest programs lost from a sense of themselves, disconnected and already feeling rootless.

What are some things we need to remember as we meet the challenges of successfully teaching our diverse groups of unique learners?

Carol Ann Tomlinson offers some important suggestions.[3] She reminds us that teachers *must*:

FIGURE 3–3    *Loved babies learn that they are special and wonderful.*

- create healthy environments of respect and caring
- appreciate each child as an individual
- remember that we are teaching *whole* children
- always continue to develop experiences that link children and ideas
- keep our energy and humor
- strive for joyful learning

FIGURE 3–4    *Many of our children feel lost and lonely.*

If we are to teach in such a way that each child is recognized and regarded as an important, valued, unique individual with special gifts to be nurtured and shared, we must strengthen our *own* creativity. We must keep our own beliefs strong and unshakable. We must tie the knots in our belts.

It is easy to conclude that trying to teach the lessons of self-esteem, respect, wonder, joy in originality and creativity in such challenging times is too often like trying to grow flowers in cement. Rather than becoming discouraged, let us pledge greater commitment to welcoming and strengthening our children and their gifts. It is probably more important now than ever before in history that we learn to love and honor ourselves and others.[4]

Now, some thoughts about the C word! One of the most mysterious and elusive areas of the human story is that of *creativity*. In this high-tech, superpressured, speeded-up society, so many people are afraid of that word. *Do you think* you *are a creative person?* Don't narrow your response to remembering if you once took piano lessons or a class in sketching. We're not talking only about the *products* of the creative process but the amazing process itself. Because you are a member of this weird and wacky, wise and wonderful human family, you *are* creative!

Consider salad bars as examples of everyday creativity in action. Everyone is offered the same smorgasbord of items. The plates are the same size for all. But, as you look at the people going through the salad line, do all the plates look the same? Certainly not! Some folks pile on everything, others arrange their plates very neatly, everything in separate places ("Oh, no! My tomatoes touched my onions!"). Some people begin with fruits and come back for vegetables. Do you have a "buffet style"?

If the salad bar metaphor for creativity isn't working for you, consider gardens and apartment houses. How people design and plant their gardens is as diverse as the people themselves. Colors? Which flowers? Perennials or annuals? Herbs mixed with wildflowers? Rows or circles or random? The arrangement possibilities are immeasurable.

Check out the apartments in an apartment house. Each may have the same layout and floor plan, but is every apartment exactly the same once people move in? How people arrange and rearrange their spaces has everything to do with the creative process that pushes us to *select, choose, improvise, change around, combine, be playful, be open to new ideas, take risks, be flexible.* Every day that you make choices, mix and match, arrange a new pattern of *anything*, you are demonstrating the creative process!

The good news is that *human beings are creative*! The bad news is that creativity, though miraculously strong in the lives of people, is also fragile and, too often, can be crushed.

One of Harry Chapin's most poignant songs, "Flowers Are Red," sings the story of a little boy who, when told by the teacher to draw flowers, paints them with many different colors. She scolds him and tells him that flowers are red, grass is green, and that's that! He answers by reminding her about the beautiful colors in flowers, in the morning sun. This dialogue keeps on. The little boy still doesn't get it until he's punished for not following directions. He finally colors flowers red. Red *only*. When he moves to another school, his new teacher asks the children to paint a picture of flowers. He paints his flowers red. The new teacher repeats the boy's original feelings about the beautiful colors of flowers, of sunshine, and so on. It's too late. The little boy tells her, "No. Flowers are red." He learned his lesson! But what a lesson![5]

In this very uptight time in education, where everyone from state and federal legislators and politicians to community organizations is lobbying, criticizing, and legislating educational programs throughout the country, where high-stakes testing is prevalent and those tests are driving curriculum, it's easier for too many teachers to tell their young students that flowers are red, so put away all those other colors because they won't be on your test! It's too easy for our children to lose their joy in celebrating their own instinctive ways of seeing, expressing, and sharing because of rigidity, narrowness, overly strict structures and schedules, overemphasis on drilling for isolated skills.

Committed, courageous teachers who keep the morning sun shining, encourage the little boy and girl to be free to use all their colors if the colors are what they see, to joyfully experiment and explore, make discoveries, playfully use materials without fear of failure, criticism, or humiliation, are our unsung heroes! They throw lifelines to our children! Because they believe so deeply that we are all original, unique, and creative individuals, they find ways and time to help preserve the too often endangered spirits of our young children. Making time in their tightly organized schedules for playfulness, for free-spirited, open-ended activities, for divergent thinking, for problem solving, for humor (humor is one of the defining qualities of creativity), for lovingly sharing, these outstanding teachers keep the lights of learning burning. They're not burnt out! They're flaming with ideas and the knowledge that they are keeping faith with the children.

"Celebrating Our Uniqueness" is *not* a lesson plan or a worksheet! It's about a *way* of teaching that encourages children to know, at all times, that they are special human beings, individual and original.

Our potential talents are mind-boggling! Together with our children, let's inspire the greatest realization of those gifts waiting to be realized, waiting to be expressed.

My four little nudges for strengthening creativity (like aerobics for the mind and spirit) are:

1. *What else?* You'll always think of more, more, more and not get stuck in a rut, not feel smug, always be surprised at the unexpected connections you make.

FIGURE 3–5    *Creative, loving teachers encourage kids to use all their colors!*

2.  *What if?* The words of imagination—the words of magic—that can change an old weathered schoolroom into a rain forest, transform a hallway into an ocean of images, change those shoe boxes into a city. . . . "What if we could dance into the rainbow? What if we could understand the language of birds? What would they be saying?"

3.  *Show the idea!* We humans have *so* many ways to show ideas—in print, illustrations, symbols, posters, T-shirts, lunch boxes, masks, puppets, buttons, songs, riddles, games, maps, to list a few. When we offer minimal limited opportunities for children to *show* they understand ideas, we doom many of those children to failure. Expand possibilities for expression, communication, and comprehension.

4.  *Fake it! Try it!* Don't say, "I can't do it. I don't know how! I'm not good at this! Uh-uh!" Experiment, explore, take risks! Inspire the children to have "porridge" (courage!) with your own shining example! Touch the knot on your belt and remember![6]

In case you need reinforcement, choose any rendition of Paul Anka's popular song "My Way" and listen to it as you drive to school! Despite too often overly structured, scripted, easily limiting educational directives, remember you are not a carbon copy of anyone! You are a unique, original individual never before seen or known on the planet

Earth. Enjoy a bowl of porridge-for-courage (recall our preschooler's explanation of what the Cowardly Lion wanted from the Wizard!), touch the knot on your belt and do it *your* way!

## DISCOVERY TIMES/WONDER TIMES: POINTS OF INTEREST

- Our human family is very inventive and creative. Just think of all the different kinds of objects, tools, machines, musical instruments, designs, and arts that came about from people's imaginations!
- We are part of that fascinating human family.
- Each of us is a very important person with a unique personality, interests, habits, physical characteristics, talents, and wishes.
- Is there a limit to our learning and growing?
- Every day we learn something new about ourselves.
- We do things we have not done before: we learn new skills; we try different challenges. We keep practicing. (No one is perfect!)
- We are proud of our accomplishments and happy when our classmates share their interests and achievements with us.
- We are lucky to be able to enjoy our own imaginations, ideas, and questions. We have wonderful minds.
- We are capable of great learning and understanding.
- Every day we should celebrate our unique talents and appreciate and respect ourselves and others.
- We learn that through practice, difficult things become easier and obstacles can be overcome.
- It's exciting to exercise our special powers and gifts. Sometimes we surprise ourselves.

## SUGGESTED VOCABULARY

| | | | |
|---|---|---|---|
| me | magic | different | share |
| myself | special | strong | celebrate |
| I | terrific | proud | surprise |
| you | interesting | original | congratulate |
| we | good | smart | thank you |
| us | wonderful | clever | please |
| names | funny | curious | discover |
| idea | beautiful | learn | I can |
| imagination | handsome | make | see |
| boy | pretty | understand | hear |
| girl | adorable | grow | touch (feel) |

| | | | |
|---|---|---|---|
| people | cute | question | smell |
| person | great | wonder | taste |
| human being | important | respect | know |
| practice | paint | laugh | think |
| draw | memory | appreciate | read |
| write | talent | like | talk |
| birthday | skill | build | sing |

## Some Words About Words of Praise

The vocabulary list includes many words of encouragement because the words that children hear and see and live contribute to the climate of their environment. How we handle praise has become another area of dialogue in the education arena. Chick Moorman, in his always practical and helpful materials and sessions for teachers and families, breaks down our "words of praise" into three categories: evaluative, descriptive, and appreciative. He urges us to emphasize descriptive and appreciative words and de-emphasize evaluative (judgmental) kinds of statements like "That was good!" or "Your story/picture/project is nice!"

Alfie Kohn, widely known as a passionate and provocative educator, constantly encourages teachers and parents to evaluate the meanings and implications of self-esteem and praise. He challenges us to examine our beliefs about meaningful education. He stresses the value of children actively participating in their own learning, initiating and directing their energy, time, interests, and talents to significant activities and experiences. Kohn urges us to focus on helping our children grow into lifelong, creative, self-directed learners who become more competent and confident in the process and who don't rely on generic praise but value themselves and others.[7]

Even our youngest children believe us more and find our responses to their works and behavior more meaningful when we are specific in our appreciation.

"Ryan, you really went out of your way to help pick up all the paint brushes we dropped on the floor. Thanks!" or "Janete, I appreciate the way you kept your promise to Tina."

When it comes to creative works, sincerely asked questions are more valuable than evaluative comments like "Great picture!" Scholars warn us that those judgmental generic remarks are "feel-good" kinds of communications that could cause kids to become "feel-good" junkies. Train yourself to be specific; learn to speak descriptively: "Tell me about your unusual sky colors," or "How did you get your puppet to use such a squeaky voice? It made us laugh and was very cheerful."

Because your vocabulary is that of respect, acceptance, appreciation, and description, children learn to be respectful of others and appreciative of our diversity and individuality. Remember Michelangelo's motto: "I am still learning."

# TALK/LISTEN/READ/WRITE:
# THE GIFTS OF LANGUAGE

Often today it is more imperative than ever that time is set aside for talking, sharing, listening, reading, writing—all the gifts of language uniquely handed to the human family by life! How to juggle all these talents at once is the challenge to teachers of young children (and all children). Ideas, wonder, feelings, curiosity, Magic Vocabularies, information, experiences are the seeds in the core of learning and growing. The open-ended, divergent-thinking questions you ask, the taking of turns to speak, the attentive listening to each other, the writing of ideas as they are offered, the expanding of talk times into enriched projects, books, celebrations . . . these are the dynamics of an environment providing language immersion and emergent-language development for every child.

With you, from *day one*, children learn that their uniqueness, their special gifts, are welcomed and will be nurtured and regarded. How do the children learn such lessons? From *everything* you *do* and *everything* you *say*. The most ordinary activities become extraordinary in the magical hands of creative teachers.

## *What's in a Name?*

Our names are our most important first words. Pronounce them. Learn them. Recite them. Write them. Illustrate them.

FIGURE 3–6  *Talk! Listen! Share!*

FIGURE 3–7   *Young children love their names!*

I remember a first grader whose negative and frightening family experiences had taught him to fear even the saying of his name. At home, hearing his name called usually meant trouble. It took a few months for him to tell his teacher, "It's funny, at home I hate my name but in school I love my name!"

As often as possible, invite the children to write their names. Display them on charts, lists, posters connected to class and curriculum activities. Opinions, ideas, suggestions can be constantly in sight and referred to.

### Take Attendance in Special Ways

Even the most mundane activity, such as taking attendance, has possibilities for joyful components. Taking attendance can be a wake-up call if you play with such offerings as the following:

"Friends, when your name is called today, tell us your favorite color (or number, season, food, exercise, and so on)."

Jot down the children's responses and you have the makings of graphs, polls, and opinion charts and materials for stories, plays, songs, and pictures.

Include nonverbal prompts such as, "When your name is called, show us your muscles (or make a funny face or stand your tallest, and so on)."

In that simplest of moments, children will *really* listen, demonstrate comprehension, and begin the day knowing their teacher always has some surprises in store for them, always encourages their individuality.

## Sign In

From day one, teachers establish values and create positive learning environments in which children are taught that they are unique individuals whose ideas and experiences are highly regarded. I have seen many variations of what I call "sign-in" charts and posters. The older children have no trouble immediately spotting a poster with colorful printed instructions such as "Please sign your name," followed by informational categories such as "your lucky number," "your favorite animal," "your favorite holiday," or "ideas for field trips." The children sign their names and add their information or opinions under the indicated category space. By the end of the day, everyone has contributed. The chart is a resource for discussion, planning, art projects, creative writing, graphics, reporting, and decision making. Younger children need more explanation and directions for such responses, but they love to find their pictures on the chart, write the letters of their names next to their pictures (and printed names), and add samples of their favorite colors, shapes, designs, and animals.

## Taking Turns

Children are so hungry to share ideas that once they realize you value their opinions and experiences, they practically explode with excitement! Jumping, waving hands, and calling out are natural exuberant responses to such welcoming invitations. A few delightful ways to help children learn to take turns and be attentive and respectful to all their classmates follow.

### Talking sticks

Many native cultures use a variety of these artistic devices. Colorfully designed, often jingling with shells and bells, the stick is passed around. Whoever has the stick talks. Everyone else listens. The children know they will have their chance to hold the stick and be the talker. Keep the stick in a safe and special place.

### Talking hats

If you aren't comfortable with the ancient concept of the talking stick, create a special hat (feathers, plumes, colorful headband) and name it "talking hat." Whoever wears the hat has a turn to talk. All opinions and ideas are welcomed and heard.

*Round robins*

So many times *everyone* wants to say something. And not always about the same "subject"! When a group of children has a lot to say, it's easy to sit them down in your special circle, rug, or designated meeting place and go round the circle, giving *every* child a chance to share. Often, the children's contributions on such occasions offer excellent expandable themes and ideas. Expand as many of their shared suggestions and experiences into written language, art projects, music, constructions, and drama as possible. Children learn through such talking and listening times that every person's opinions and ideas have merit and must be treated with respect.

## A Picture Is Worth . . .

Criss-crossing the country, visiting all kinds of programs and schools, I am thrilled to see photographs of the children prominently displayed on bulletin boards, walls, cubby drawers, doors, and boxes. Caring teachers take time to highlight every child by photographing each one and celebrating the results. This activity is saying to the children, "You are an important and special person. Our class is composed of a unique group of individuals." For many children, this may be the first time they have ever been photographed. Talk about the pictures, add captions dictated by or written by the children. Cutting out paper in dialogue bubble shapes, inviting the children to write in them, then taping them above their photographs can be a very playful, thoughtful, or inspiring experience.

For example, if you are talking about things we wonder about, the children can write dialogue bubbles about their wonderings. Joseph wrote in his dialogue bubble, "I wonder about how sunflowers grow so tall." Imagine the delightful wall of photos, thoughts, dialogue. Remember, the contents of the bubbles *follow* the free flow of discussions. Talking together is the air that fills the bubbles!

## Special Child of the Week

Variations of this theme are countless. Every week, a child gets to be the Special Child. Simply described, it's a way of giving every child a day of special recognition and attention over and above daily awareness and appreciation. Conducting group talks, describing the ongoing celebrations, adding new ideas from the children, writing them down, communicating with families, making sure that if family support is not forthcoming, you find ways to celebrate that child . . . all are components of this project.

Here are a few samples of Special Child activities:

- A bulletin board is devoted to the child, who may bring in pictures, photos, and souvenirs.

FIGURE 3–8   *Children wonder about many things.*

- The child wears a hat, badge, name tag, shirt, or belt made especially for the occasion.
- The class interviews the child and asks prepared as well as spontaneous questions. Sometimes the teacher pulls together the information from the interview and creates a pictograph about the child. Sometimes the class makes a collage about the child, based on the interview conducted earlier.
- The child picks a game for the class to play, a song to sing, and a special recess activity.
- The child starts as leader in a game of follow the leader.
- The child picks the story to be read at story time.
- Children make up a song, dance, game, story, or poem about or for the child.
- The child shares meaningful objects or treasures.
- Classmates write special notes and letters and paint pictures for the child.

- Sometimes a party is given by the class to salute the child, and families and friends are invited. The child's bulletin board, collage, and crafts are featured. Songs, dances, and games are shared.
- The Special Child can be selected in several ways. Few of the teachers I spoke with chose children in alphabetical order. As one teacher explained, "Kids with last names that start with Ts and Ss are always last for life when you use alphabetical order." She used a grab bag of blank papers, except for one paper that had a beautiful design on it. The child who picked the paper with the design was the next Child of the Week.

*Note:* Save a week for yourself and join the many teachers who enjoy being the VIP of the day!

Reminder: Some children are shy or reluctant to be singled out for a variety of reasons. Because you are sensitive to each child's specific needs and feelings, you are flexible in this activity. In environments of trust and safety, children will feel free to confide in you. Take it from there.

## I'm Special Because . . .

(Remember, when children feel secure and cared about, they become avid talkers and attentive listeners.) "Our Uniqueness" is an always fascinating topic for young children, as each day reveals changes and growth, new accomplishments, new understandings. And don't just stop at talking and listening. Think across the curriculum of all the ways possible to enrich and expand ideas first articulated through talking.

Leave room in your plan book for surprises each day as the children walk (run?) into your room. Creative teachers are alert and observant: they notice a missing tooth, a new T-shirt, a shy smile, a mischievous twinkle, a defeated expression dimming the light in a child's eyes. *Children* always *need to be reminded about the ways in which they are special and unique.* Communicate in specific ways. Is Matt a good builder of blocks? Isn't Rachel ready with a song to share? Noah helps us notice birds' nests. Chloe likes to teach us her dances.

When children are constantly encouraged to honor their own special skills and interests, they are generous in regarding those of others. It's called mutuality. *"I'm special" blooms naturally into "we're special individuals"!*

## Open-Ended Questions

Even the best-intentioned teachers can squelch creativity by asking closed-in, convergent-thinking questions. I like to kid around (but I'm

FIGURE 3–9   *Our spirits are freed when we feel cared about and secure.*

deadly serious) with classes and inservice sessions by asking such stimulating questions for original responses as: "When was the War of 1812?" or "In what country was the Italian Renaissance?" Too many children spend too much time doing minimal original thinking or creative problem solving because the ways in which their teachers challenge them are very limited.

Along with required yes/no, right/wrong questions, we must offer children such questions as:

"What's your favorite kind of weather?"
"Do you remember when you were a baby? Tell us about it."
"Can you make up a story for the picture you're painting?"
"Let's think of all the things we want to notice when we go on our walk. What do *you* like to look at and think about when *you* go on a walk?"
"What do you wonder about?"

(Don't forget "What else?" "What if?" "Show the idea!" and "Fake it!")

### Story Talks

"Imagine, children, every story in every book in every library was made up by a human being! Don't we have wonderful imaginations? Our imagination is a *big* part of our uniqueness!"

FIGURE 3–10    *It's fun to use our imaginations!*

This is an example of one of the kinds of ways I like to talk to the children and fire them up about appreciating their ability to use imagination and original thinking.

Among my favorite books that highlight the theme of "Our Uniqueness" is *Frederick* by Leo Lionni, about the little mouse who gathers words and images to share during the dark winter months. Frederick is a poet! Friends, aren't we *all* Frederick? We have so many poems to say and write to keep us through the winter days!

*Bein' with You This Way* by W. Nikola-Lisa is a book to be bounced to, chanted, danced to, dramatized, illustrated, added to. Noses, hair color and length, eyes, legs, skin color—those characteristics we *all* have in common but are very individual, are illustrated in rhythmic, colorful poetry. Each page lovingly and exuberantly reminds us that no matter how different we are, how unique, we're happy to be with each other. This is a book to play with!

Michael J. Rosen's delightful book *With a Dog Like That, a Kid Like Me* sparks imaginative ideas as children see how the beautiful golden retriever moves like a pony whenever he's prancing around the yard or a lion when he growls. This reminds the "kid" to use his imagination and be anything he wants to be!

Alison Lester's beautiful book *Ernie Dances to the Didgeridoo* is set in Gunbalanya, Australia. A group of friends go through the seasons enjoying their own special activities and interests. The different kinds of happenings will inspire your children to think of (write about, talk about, illustrate, demonstrate) activities and interests that *they* enjoy! The children in the story are busy doing such things as listening to stories, going fishing, taking walks, learning dances, and painting.

William Steig's *Toby, What Are You?* encourages the children to use their imaginations and become any idea they enjoy, from a plate of spaghetti to a dangerous wild animal. Toby combines his playful make-believe games into guessing challenges. Your students will love to do the same! Guess what we're turning into?

Woodleigh Hubbard's touching book *All That You Are* inspires children to look more deeply at themselves and others. Are you a forgiving person? A good friend? A courageous person? Excellent qualities to think about![8]

Debbie Charna shares old favorites like *I'd Like to Be* and *I'm Terrific*[9] with her children. As they listen to and discuss the stories, they are inspired to think about their own special gifts, their own special strengths. They create a "We're Terrific" board—displaying creative writing, illustrations, charts, and symbols—that is a popular classroom gallery!

Inspired by literature-rich environments, encouraged to tell, write, illustrate, dramatize their *own* original stories, children will never let you down but will free themselves to honor their own individual ideas for stories and ways of sharing them as they learn to respect others. This is ongoing. A lifetime curriculum.

### Remember the Magic Vocabulary

Even our youngest children have their very favorite, beloved words that represent people, places, foods, fascinating areas of deep interest. I call these words and ideas the Magic Vocabulary. Because we are unique individuals, our vocabularies are very individual. We may share some topics of interest with others but the combinations are original, special

FIGURE 3–11 *Reading means talking and sharing.*

to each of us. Nothing generates more meaningful language celebrations than inviting children to contribute ideas from their Magic Vocabularies. Dylan will exuberantly talk about his love of cartoons and action figures. Len will mesmerize you with sports facts. Noah will tell you everything you want to know (and some things you don't want to know) about music and top ten CDs. Chloe will tell you about ladybugs. Ryan will explain his latest scientific experiment. Callie will talk about art and artists. Imagine the excitement of all these very meaningful topics! Soon, the children will learn that Landen loves Piglet and Maggie is crazy about pandas. Be sure to give the children many opportunities to talk, listen, read, write, sing, illustrate, demonstrate, share in any way they choose ideas from their unique Magic Vocabularies. Sandra Boynton's book *Yay, You! Moving Out, Moving Up, Moving On* expands the concept of individual choices and characteristics. Boyton talks about people who like to move fast, move slow; people who like cold weather or hot weather; people who are drawn to science; people who are moved by art. We have so many choices! Each person is a unique individual who makes choices. A good lesson for the children to talk about and ponder. Add your own questions.[10]

## MUSIC MAKERS/MOVERS AND SHAKERS

I had the great honor of being invited to present at the national conference of the Children's Music Network, a gathering of many of the nation's most beloved and talented music makers for children. Campfires blazed at night and groups gathered in different areas to talk and sing. Once again, as old, familiar songs were sung in very diverse ways, the amazing creativity of the human spirit was demonstrated over and over. Added to all the new variations of old songs were the marvelous newly composed songs shared, many for the first time. No limits on old or new songs! Another example of the uniqueness of the human family.[11]

Every culture that ever lived on the planet Earth made music and dance. Chants, songs, lullabies, ballads, play songs, love songs, war marches, mourning dirges, ceremonial songs—the songs of every aspect of life are sung and played by the nations and tribes of the world. The human voice is astonishing in the variety of tones and sounds it can express. Our culture shapes our voices. Listen to the high-pitched Japanese women's voices or the throbbing, exaggerated (to American ears) voices of the Chinese opera singers. Listen to mountain yodeling from Swiss villages, Macedonian women's voices loudly calling the community together, the mesmerizing blend of drumbeats and Native American chants made of vocables and phrases, the pulsating rhythms of African tribal songs . . . rap, madrigals, ditties, arias, spirituals, reggae, symphonic choirs—our planet throbs with musical rhythms, with songs, dances.

FIGURE 3–12    *Young children are natural gymnasts and dancers.*

Most of us have two legs and two feet but oh, what those legs and feet can do! I watched the National Cheerleading Competition on TV recently and was in awe at the amazing midair gymnastics accomplished by these collegiate acrobats. The movement abilities of the human body are immeasurable. If you doubt it, watch the Olympics! Or a folk festival! Or a ballet! Or a high school dance! Or a playground!

Unless they have been taught to fear music and dance, children will make music. Children will sing. Children will dance. They will make music, sing, and dance, be playful exploring and discovering new and old ways of expressing themselves if they are given numerous non-threatening, noncompetitive, hang-loose, enjoyable opportunities.

The following suggestions are only a few reminders of how easy it is for children to express their uniqueness through music, play, and dance. Add your own ideas!

### Our Names Are Songs and Dances!

Our names have rhythm. Chant them, clap them, turn them into songs and dances. Sit in a circle and invite the children to make rhythms out of their names: *Charley Anderson*—slow/slow/fast-fast-fast. Clap it, snap it, chant it! Shyer children need encouragement. Watch their expressions change when they hear their names turned into music and join their friends in dancing to their names! Add rhythm instruments. Create a symphony of names. Add movement. Choreograph the names! Put your whole self in!

Once you realize how much children enjoy hearing their own names called, you will get into the habit of using their names in almost every song you sing. A well-known song such as "Michael, Row the Boat Ashore" can be used to celebrate each child in your class: "Denzil, row the boat ashore, hallelujah"; "Stacey, help to stem the tide. . . ."

There is an old chant that goes like this:

> Hello everybody and clap your hands.
> Clap your hands. Clap your hands.
> Hello everybody and clap your hands.
> And clap your hands today.

There are many variations of its "melody," so feel free to improvise. A class of four- and five-year-olds had fun with the song when they and their teacher changed it to:

> Hello, Joe O'Brien, turn around.
> Turn around, turn around.
> Hello, Kira Kaplan, jump and clap.
> Jump and clap today.

One kindergarten teacher reported that after a workshop in which this idea was discussed, her entire morning had been changed by using the children's names in "Rockabye Baby."

"Just before our rest time," she said, "I thought I'd try the idea with one of our lullabies. We always sing a lullaby before we rest, so I thought I would take only a few minutes, but the children were so entranced and waited for their turn before they rested that it practically became our major morning activity! And today, as I came into the room, the children asked if we could do it again! By the way, we always change the lyrics around."

> Rock-a-bye Nicole, on the tree top.
> When the wind blows, the cradle will rock.
> When the bough breaks, the cradle won't fall.
> Go to sleep Nicole, cradle and all.

(The children sang with her, of course.)

Songs like "He's Got the Whole World in His Hands" can be easily modified to celebrate each child:

> He's got Brett and Neal in His hands,
> He's got Gabriella and Misha in His hands . . .

Or, "We've got Rashid and Megan in our hands. . . ."

A group of four-year-olds squealed with delight when we sang a special version of "The Bear Went Over the Mountain":

> The bear went over the mountain
> Who do you think he saw?
> He saw Rachel, Seth, and Billy
> He saw Laura, Bob, and Tiarra
> He saw Billy Ray and Iris
> And who else did he see?
> He saw . . .

## Our Own Original Songs

Most ancient poetry was originally sung. *Song* and *poem* are terms often used interchangeably by traditional cultures who honored all aspects of life with songs passed down through the ages.

Young children hum, sing, and chant their lives. They singsong their experiences, they compose their own symphonies of daily life. In my gatherings, I have collected the "songs" of thousands of children, who have given them titles, taught them to others, and added them to their own treasure chests of musical resources.

Encourage your children to make songs about many relevant topics. There is *no* boring topic! I even heard a first grader softly singing a song about using an eraser!

Is it too obvious to remind you to share *your* songs, *your* music with your students? Bring the instruments you play into the classroom and enrich learning across the curriculum as the spirit of learning is hallowed. Tom Griffin's guitar is part of the life of his class. He plays songs the children sing together as well as songs he sings to them. He makes up songs about favorite stories and poems. Tom and his music are an important part of the *way* his students learn every day.[12]

A word of encouragement for those of us who are *not* talented singers and musicians (especially yours truly). Children are *not* critics. They learn from you, their role model, that making music and singing are expressions of the human spirit, part of our uniqueness and universality. The joy, fun, and importance of making music with your kids takes precedence over your possible reluctance to be an active participant in this valuable process. A very self-conscious substitute kindergarten teacher was urged by the children to sing a song. With great hesitation and embarrassment she choked out the lyrics to "Twinkle, Twinkle, Little Star." When she thankfully finished the song, the children applauded. One of the kids patted her cheeks, reassuring her, "Don't worry. You did your best!" We have so much to learn from our children!

### Pass the Instruments Around

Once again, sit in a circle. Ask the children to shut their eyes and not to peek as you place rhythm instruments in their hands. Then they can open their eyes and explore their instruments. Ask a child to play a rhythm or melody on his or her instrument and have the others join in, one at a time, to accompany or play a variation until all the instruments are playing. Then signal each child to stop, one at a time, so that the music diminishes. Exchange instruments and begin again.

Part of the "Our Uniqueness" theme is the discovery that we have such a range of choices and abilities. "I played a hundred instruments today," a young musician puffed proudly. Add this idea to "Kids Count"!

### Gather Songs

I saw a poster that read: "Birds don't sing because they have answers, they sing because they have songs."

We have more songs than answers! The number of songs we remember is astonishing. Even very young children know numerous songs.

In appreciation of our human minds, talk with the children about all the songs they know and remember. Begin a class list of songs and keep adding to it. Include the children's original songs, which will soon become class songs *if you sing them*. Make large colorful song charts or song books. Make up dances to the songs. Use the children's suggestions. The more often you enjoy moving and singing together, the looser and freer the children will be in experimenting with movement ideas. Imagine all the language development in the learning and loving of lyrics!

### Back to the Basics!

Marlene Robbins helps children move and shake in imaginative and often startling ways.

One of Marlene's favorite challenges is to work with all of the children using three basic movement ideas such as *run*, *jump*, and *freeze*, or *timid*, *silly*, and *bold*, or *forward*, *backward*, and *sideways*. Even though everyone is centering on the common themes, "these same moves are different for each child. They stamp the movement with their own expressions, intensity, courage, sense of risk. They interpret it in their own ways—revealing their special qualities. Some kids are gentle, some humorous. Maybe Len feels rambunctious today. Pietro is thoughtful."

The movement will shape mood, feelings, and qualities of character.

"Remember," Marlene says with a grin, "even in a field of daisies, every petal is different! As a teacher, that's the joy—to see the look on the children's faces when they realize the ownership of what they do. You see the thinking and doing—the live child in front of you!"

No matter what the idea or theme, creative teachers encourage the children to use their own interpretations, to assimilate suggestions in their own ways. They don't limit learning to worksheets. They don't do formulas. As the students and teachers develop ideas together, comprehension deepens and imaginative ways of expressing those ideas evolve. Be open to the many possibilities inherent in any suggestion. Take a risk![13]

## The Wonder of Growing

Nothing celebrates our uniqueness as delightfully and effectively as discovering how we grow and what we can accomplish now that we could not accomplish before. This rich experience can be launched in so many ways. As you read just the two general approaches described here, think about how *you* would most enjoy sharing these ideas with your students. With the virtually thousands of children I've "grown" with, I usually started out with a talk session. We try to remember being infants (in multiage infant/toddler programs, these talks are very relevant to our toddlers' direct daily experiences!). This is a very popular topic with young children! Out of these talks emerge movement, drama, sounds, expressions, rhythms—completely blended in the "story" of our growing journey. Here's an example. The children love demonstrating every step of the way!

> When we were very new babies, we were very tiny and small. How tiny and small can we make our bodies?
>
> We could hardly do anything except sleep (soft snore), make funny noises (googly goo sounds), and cry (Waaaaaa!).
>
> We couldn't even turn over from our tummies to our backs or our backs to our tummies. We were stuck.
>
> We tried and tried to turn over. Lots of times. Finally, we did it! Turned over by ourselves. Yaaaaay.
>
> But, we couldn't turn back over and we kept trying and trying, until we did it! Yaaay.
>
> When we were babies, we didn't know that our hands and feet belonged to us, belonged to our bodies. We thought they were toys or mobiles. (Show it!)
>
> We couldn't even sit up by ourselves. Every time we sat up, we flopped right back over. (Do it!)
>
> But, we kept trying and trying to sit up, and finally, one day, we did it! We sat up all by ourselves without falling over.

The story continues with crawling, reaching, standing, and walking. Each accomplishment is the result of great effort, patience, and determination. The development of the story is exciting and dramatic. After reenacting all the steps along the way, children burst into enthusiastic celebration!

Now we can walk, lots of ways—quietly, noisily, tiptoe, sideways, backward, bouncy, stiff, high, low.

We can hop, skip, jump, turn, leap, slide.

We can march, run, dance, race, prance, gallop.

We can . . . (What else?)

There is no end to what we can do now that we are growing more every day. (Show us!)

This activity may take one twenty-minute session or it may be continued for days. Add illustrations and creative writing. Turn it into songs!

Another approach to this activity takes one item at a time rather than developing the whole idea:

When we were babies, we couldn't even turn over.

Now we can turn over.

When we were babies, we could only crawl.

Now we can walk. (Explore.)

When we were babies, we couldn't stand up without falling down.

Now we walk, run, hop, skip, and jump.

This is a great moment to remind the children that we all grow in our own special ways, in our own special times. The children have many ideas about the wonderful things they can do now. Remember, show the idea!

While the children are resting after their "growing," it's an excellent opportunity to share *Leo the Late Bloomer*, the classic story of Leo, who took his good old time to "bloom"! (We need to pass that reassurance on to often-anxious families!)[14]

### Try It Another Way

Children are the true explorers. Through free-spirited experimentation, they make great discoveries and learn in satisfying ways. To avoid getting into ruts ("This is the way I do this, and don't show me any other way!"), enjoy this fun challenge as often as possible. If you're walking, try to walk a different way. How many ways can we sit? Let's experiment with thirty-six varieties of jumps! We can change heights, stretch and bend, show angles, show curves, express qualities such as bouncy, heavy, straight, crooked . . . we keep amazing ourselves.

### DYOT and/or Playing Favorites

Even the youngest children understand something of their own uniqueness. We give information, directions, and suggestions to children. We demonstrate patterns and ideas. We offer them components of con-

FIGURE 3–13  *When we were babies, we couldn't walk by ourselves. We had to be held.*

cepts. It's spread before them. The next step is to invite the children to Do Your Own Thing. For example, we practice clapping and jumping and turning around. This gives us three ideas. After the children are familiar with the three ideas, suggest that they DYOT. Encourage them to arrange the material as they want to. Play with it! Or, I like to say, "Do your favorite part!" After a minute, I'll challenge them, "Change—show another favorite part!"

When children are invited to move, sing, improvise, be playful with ideas, they learn that their own arrangements and combinations are respected. They learn that their handling of common materials is very individual and special. Many of the children's original patterns are much more challenging and creative than a book full of preset finger plays! (Not that there's anything wrong with instructions for finger plays!)

Patricia Hubbell's lively book *Bouncing Time* is a great example of our excellent resources that inspire playfulness and exploration. Oh, my! We have so many ways of bouncing! Try bouncing like a clown or a pouncy cat, or a tumbling tiger or a somersaulting monkey! The book and the kids will bounce ideas around the room![15]

### Musical Moves

Welcome into your minds and hearts the rhythms and melodies of diverse musical offerings and instruments. Shake out all preset choreography! Let the music fill you. Let the music decide how you want to move! It is astonishing how close to traditional movement patterns children dance in response to totally unfamiliar music. Our bodies will move differently to Scottish bagpipes, to Mexican mariachi bands, to Appalachian dulcimers, to Russian balalaikas, to Arabic ouds, to percussive/brassy circus music, and to Peruvian flutes. Add creative writing and illustrations. Create designs for the music and movement.

Because we are unique individuals, our responses to these musical offerings are very original. Tamal may find the powerful beat of West African drums totally freeing and exciting while Isabelle's feet move in tiny, exact steps to an English country dance. Your public library is a great source for music representing the world's cultures. Use it!

### Jokes and Laughs

Remember the importance of humor as a basic ingredient of creativity. Humor usually reflects playfulness, comprehension, imagination, and language proficiency. Encouraging and celebrating humor with your children is a precious gift very needed in this too often humorless educational arena. As we mentioned before, take the first syllable of *fundamentals* away and you get a word something like "demental." We and our children *need* that first syllable. Often our sense of humor helps define our uniqueness. Be sure to begin with yourself. Be flexible! Hang loose! As the kids say, "Chill!"

A teacher who needed this advice was visibly upset with a kindergartner who, when asked what he brought in for the letter N, said, "Nothing!"

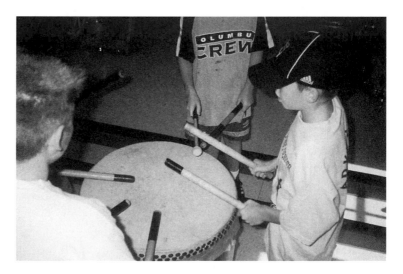

FIGURE 3–14  *Drums call to the kids.*

FIGURE 3–15    *Children remind us of the value of fun and laughter.*

The child was scolded for not doing the assignment!

Most children have marvelous wild and wacky senses of humor. They seem to be tickled by certain things at particular ages. Often what sends three-year-olds into explosions of laughter triggers cool and sophisticated (over the hill) four-and-half-year-olds to shake their heads and say, "Mim, you're *so* silly!" with hardly a smile. Play around. Find the kinds of situations that your students really enjoy.

Discover how many ways you can share times of laughter. Gestures, body movement, voice changes, songs, stories, facial expressions, dances . . . all help contribute to creative, joyful, mirthful shared moments (which of course will only happen in loving, safe environments where children know they are respected and affirmed).

A group of preschoolers and I were playing/dancing/chanting/improvising our variation of "The Tortoise and the Hare." (We played all the parts. We were all rabbits, all tortoises!) Everyone knows that Hare, aka Rabbit, was overconfident. We danced so far ahead of slowpoke Turtle, aka Tortoise, that we decided to stretch out and rest a while. That turtle would never catch up!

Munching our invisible carrots, lying relaxed on the floor, I kiddingly narrated, "The carrots sat under a tree eating their rabbits!" The kids collapsed, laughing, and continued laughing almost to the end of the session. For weeks after, children from that class kept repeating the line and dissolving into laughter.

To strengthen our uniqueness and originality, keep it light! Enjoy the playfulness of the process![16]

## Two Metaphors

We could fill these pages with metaphors that *didn't* work! But, the following two examples of really effective metaphors are offered to encourage children to use all their powers, all their strength and skills.

### Ten-Speed Bike

I usually ask the children to "show me" their responses:

"Friends, if you have ever heard of a ten-speed bike, stamp your feet!"

"Friends, if you haven't heard of a ten-speed bike, shrug your shoulders." (Always include all ranges of responses so no one is ever left out or feels devalued.)

"If you've ever seen anyone ride a ten-speed bike, tap your head." And so on.

After a series of movement responses to establish that most kids have heard of ten-speed bikes, the story begins.

Sometimes I ask the children to clap, stamp, tap ten times (just as an introduction to the story, which, of course, is accompanied by movement).

Once there were kids who had ten-speed bikes (show me ten fingers). But, they used only one speed (show me one finger). When they went up hills, they could hardly pedal (pantomime effort and strain). When they went down hills, they practically fell off (wobble). We met these kids and said, "You have ten speeds; why are you using only one?" Those kids looked surprised. "We forgot about our other speeds; thanks for reminding us!" Now they use all ten speeds—*all* their powers!

Then we talk about how we have even more than ten speeds. We have so many powers, but sometimes we use only one.

For the rest of the year, the children use the metaphor to remind themselves and each other to do more, not less; to expand, not shrink.

### Car

Friends, before we get started, we'd better check out our energy. (Bend down to your feet.) Put some air in your tires. (Tap your waist.) Put some gas in your gas tank. (I've had kids say, "Leaded or unleaded?") (Lift your head and open your mouth.) Check your oil. Oooooh—we need a quart of oil. We don't want to be rusty, do we? (Lift your arm.) Antennas up! (Wave your arm back and forth.) Get those windshield wipers on—we need clear vision! (Move your fingers as if moving a dial.) Check that radio station. Get a clear signal. Don't be static. We need clear thinking! (Burst into a shiny movement.) Turn on those *bright* lights! We can see so much more when we turn on our brights! That battery light is flashing. Turn the key and check that battery! (Good time to shake and wiggle.) That's better. Hold onto that steering wheel. Stay the course! (Hold-onto-steering-wheel movement.) Fasten that seat belt. We want everyone safe! Let's get into gear! Oh, some of us are in reverse. (Move backward in a non-participatory way.) Some of us are in park. (Don't move.) What do we need to do to get going? (The kids will tell you, put the car in *drive*!) OK! We're ready to go! Keep those *bright* lights on!

Once the children own these stories, it's so easy to remind them that they can turn on their bright lights, use all their powers, get into drive! The very valuable lesson inherent in these offerings is that, even at our very youngest ages, we are responsible for our own learning, our own developing of our potential gifts! For the too many children who have little support at home, this consistent strengthening is deeply nurturing.

I like to add on to the United Negro College Fund's excellent saying, "A mind is a terrible thing to waste." We extend it to "Our minds, our time, and our talents are terrible things to waste."

## ALL WAYS ART

### *A Room Rich with Materials and Offerings*

We are all hunters and gatherers. Children are always hunting for unusual discoveries—pebbles, shells, twigs, leaves, Styrofoam packing chips, glittered greeting cards. Gather materials. Sort them and make them available for many uses. Rebecca Kantor described her open-shelved, open-ended materials as being "everywhere." "If children want to write, pencils, pens, and markers are present and waiting all around the room. It's always the write time! Sometimes a particular material is the center for the children's attention. Perhaps they are fascinated by the possibilities of turning themselves into puppet characters. Today may be a day to decorate a forest scene with feathers, pebbles, and small pieces of colored cellophane. Today a child may feel blue or want to paint the town red! Our uniqueness is expressed even in the choice of materials, even as we arrange commonly used materials. We are *not* carbon copies of each other." Flowers are *not* always red, nor is grass always green.[17]

FIGURE 3–16    *Our uniqueness is expressed in the materials we choose.*

### Make Something Out of Nothing

From your ample (always accessible) collection of stuff and scrounged materials, invite the children to choose any items they want to and create something. Of course, there will be times these challenges are connected with themes, specific ideas ("Let's all make an animal."), but there is a joy in just being playful, free-spirited, and open to serendipity. The children and you will be delighted when you see the amazing works created out of such odds and ends as cloth scraps, shells, boxes of all sizes, toss-away plastic and Styrofoam containers, and so on. Michelangelo believed that the shape and idea for a sculpture was already hidden in the marble. He could see it there already and his main responsibility was to release it, chisel it out! Invite the children to see ideas in the materials and use their creativity and ingenuity to shape and release those ideas! (A more *process* way of looking at art rather than a product way.) Seven-year-old Dylan spent hours constructing a circus for squirrels out of a variety of boxes, paper towel tubes, fast-food packaging, and so on. When children feel secure, safe, and unafraid (no room for put-downs, ridicule, criticism), they will "go" with an idea, play with it, and see it grow. These are precious moments in the discovering of our uniqueness and in the exercise of imagination and problem solving.

### Stars

Every child is a star! Cut out stars of different shapes and colors and have each child choose one. In the center of the stars, the children write their names, paste their photographs, and paint or color original designs. On each point of their star, help them write a word that tells about their uniqueness. Spread the stars around the room so they brighten the walls and boards and give the children lots of places to look for words and pictures celebrating themselves and each other. Attach string and hang the stars from the ceiling!

## Mind Pictures

An always delightful experience begins with having the children close their eyes. Sometimes simply inviting them to turn their minds into paintings or scenes is enough of a suggestion to launch satisfying visual arts activities, transferring their mind pictures to paper! Or you might want to begin with a specific image: "Picture the sky. Is your sky clear or cloudy? Sunny or rainy? Under the sky is a field. What colors are your field? What textures? What season? Is there an animal in your field? A house? A fence?" As the children develop their ideas, their fingers will want to take brushes and crayons and depict their scenes.

One of my favorite series of suggestions is centered on trees, nests, and birds. First we stretch our bodies into strong tree shapes. Our arms, our limbs, our branches reach out and up. We imagine our colors, our leaves. Where would birds build a nest in our trees? And what if there were eggs in the nest, or hatched babies? Moving and imagining are magical ways to develop concepts, to express ideas, to demonstrate originality. The children's pictures or three-dimensional scenes of their trees, nests, birds, skies, and wind are souvenirs of an experience they will long remember.

## More in a Name?

Remember, children love their names; anything that has to do with their names is a popular activity. Give each child a large piece of construction or drawing paper. Write or have the children write their names on the papers. Be sure the names stand out clearly. The children decorate their name posters by drawing pictures or designs and by cutting out and pasting pictures or words to the paper. Encourage them to draw or cut out pictures of things that mean something special to them, so the poster is a kind of personal collage. The children can also add photos of themselves to the poster. Join the activity and celebrate your name.

## Only Me

When Michael Joel Rosen talks with students of all ages, his conversation focuses on their special ways of seeing, of noticing, of remembering. As they talk of common experiences, Michael asks them to think about and share more surprising observations, more exceptional discoveries. "What did *you* see that we may have missed?" He encourages

FIGURE 3–17    *Children love turning their names into art.*

the students to think beyond their familiar experiences, to look more closely at their surroundings, to fill "their sensory banks."

Magically transform these shared images into arts challenges. "Pierre, want to make a picture of the puffy cloud that looks to you like a cat? What kind of materials do you think you'd like to use?"

"What can you stuff into your cloud shape to make it three-dimensional?"

"LaToya, what an interesting idea—birds flying in the sky forming the letter V! How about finding a way to show it? Which way do you like the most?"

### Self-Portraits

Bring in an assortment of mirrors to be placed *carefully* on the ledge against the board or on shelves, or bring in a large dressing-room mirror. Invite the children to study themselves carefully and notice their own features.

Give out large pieces of paper and crayons or paint, and ask the children to color or paint pictures of themselves, self-portraits. Add names. Display all the self-portraits. Add titles!

Children enjoy creating their own self-portraits as well as drawing or painting the portraits of their classmates. Give them many opportunities to celebrate themselves!

When Dawn Heyman realized that a few of her third graders were painting self-portraits that did not include their skin color, she sat down with the children, reminding them that "all of us are beautiful in

FIGURE 3–18 *When Michael J. Rosen visits classrooms, he invites the children to contribute ideas, always celebrating the creative process.*

our own shades, our own colors." Reassured, the children chose combinations of beiges, browns, and other flesh tones that enriched their portraits and added to their feelings of self-worth and confidence.[18]

I visited a school that caused everyone who walked into the building to stop and stare! The entire corridor walls were covered with a self-portrait proudly displayed from *every* child in the school, from kindergarten to sixth grade. This visible affirmation of the children's beauty and individuality said more for the climate of the school than all the test scores put together!

### Three-Dimensional Body Sculptures

Extend the self-portraits into life-size figures. After outlining the children's body shapes on butcher paper, cut them out, decorate and paint them, add words and images to them, and prominently display them. Add a dimension by cutting out their shapes on double paper, so their body shapes will be front and back. After taping or stapling most of the shape together, stuff the shape with any kind of scrounge materials (even crushed newspaper). Now you'll have life-sized three-dimensional figures created by the children of themselves or of each other!

FIGURE 3–19 *Kids love creating their own unique images.*

### *"Me" Mobiles*

Mobiles can be made many ways, but the easiest is the hanger mobile. The subject is "me" and the material is any picture, design, word, or image that reflects the uniqueness of that child. In one kindergarten class, a mischievous five-year-old, with great effort, tied a piece of chewed-up bubble gum to his mobile. When asked about it, he said, "I chew so much bubble gum, my mom says I'm gonna turn into bubble gum!"

### *"We" Mobiles*

When all of the Me mobiles hang together from the ceiling or from a clothesline, they become We mobiles!

### *"Me" Books*

Young children like to watch these books grow from a few blank pages to thick, colorful collections of feelings, ideas, favorite things, memories, and wishes. Many classes work on their books all year. These books run the gamut from randomly constructed, all-inclusive collections to well-organized presentations of selected topics, such as favorite foods and games, family, and plans. When we gather our Me books into a collection, they become We books!

### *I'm Special! (Collages and Constructions)*

Any serendipitous happening can launch a fertile series of creative experiences clustered around the idea that every person is very special and unique. Such events as a loose tooth, new glasses, a colorful T-shirt, or a story bursting to be told, can inspire delightful sharings and materials for artwork. The topic of how we are special stimulated the kindergartners to excitedly dictate their ideas to their teacher. Nick Wilbat proudly shared: "I can run really fast. I still can't stop very good. I can jump high. I can even jump over my brother, Matt. I can roll like a ball and get dressed very fast. I can build really good stuff with Legos, like my castle. I give money to poor people. I know a lot of stories. Know why July is my favorite? Cause of fireworks. Why is Matt special? Cause he's fun to be with. We're good dancers. We do tricks and we both pick up our toys. . . ."

Nick and his classmates are encouraged to express some of those ideas in visual images. Pipe cleaners, wires, paints, markers, clay—all kinds of materials help the children shape their experiences. A large chart-size paper divided into sections, with each section highlighting one of Nick's observations (for example, "We do tricks") vividly illustrated is one effective way of celebrating the theme. Pipe cleaner or wire figures, wrapped with colorful wool and thread, enlivened with scrounged materials, easily convey action like "I can run really fast." Be open to all ideas and encourage the children to use what feels best to them. Expand such information into movement, drama, song, and improvisation. Celebrate!

### *"Once . . ." (A Magical Jump-Start)*

Young children are always ready to freely and gladly share real and made-up memories, experiences, wishes beginning with "Once. . . ." You'll find that it's hard to stop the flow of excited conversations that reflect our unique personalities and histories. If you have time, try not to limit the session, but go around the room and give whoever wants to contribute the opportunity.

These little gems can naturally be expressed in artworks! And they flow from the children's own life stories.

Title the pictures, posters, sculptures, constructions.

One of my favorite samples of such times was the kindergartner's picture featuring a very beautiful lady with gleaming white teeth and a wand. The title was "Once the Tooth Fairy left me five dollars under my pillow." (What does the tooth fairy look like to you?)

### *Our Own Bulletin Boards*

One wall of your space can easily be dedicated to poster-sized individual "bulletin boards" devoted to each child's individual works. The children decide themselves what they want on their bulletin boards and are welcome to change them or rearrange them any time they choose. A memorable example of such a display was the sighting of some first graders' wall of treasures. One child's map of his neighborhood filled his space. Another space was highlighted by pictures of dogs. Another featured various writings of the artist's name. What opportunities to celebrate the uniqueness of every child!

### Treasure Boxes

Young children notice everything! They are our original scavengers! Where to keep those found pennies, lovely pebbles and stones, bits and pieces of found objects usually packed into pockets? Treasure boxes, of course! With your collection of boxes of all sizes, invite the children to choose one to make their very own. Spread an array of materials for them to decide and use to decorate their boxes. I have seen treasure boxes sparkling with glitter, pasted and glued and papered and painted and buttoned. Inside are the special treasures children are saving to savor and share. Many of our children have no material treasures at home. Their treasure boxes at school remind them that they have a special collection of their own selected objects reflecting their own unique interests, and those boxes are respected and safe.

### Always Art Books at Our Fingertips

We can't stop reminding you of the numerous excellent offerings of children's literature rich with ideas and inspiration to celebrate our uniqueness. One of my favorites is Douglas Florian's *A Painter*, featuring color-splashed illustrations demonstrating simple ideas that remind our young artists that painters paint pictures, use all varieties of materials, paint morning and night (whenever they want to), and paint to create collages about any subject in the world! Another favorite, Gail Gibbons' *Art Box*, features all the materials in an art box, from pencils, paper, erasers, brushes, and all kinds of paints to tape and glue. These materials are in the hands of the artist, who decides what to do with them. Great information! In Nicola Moon's book *Lucy's Picture*, we meet Lucy, who wants to make a picture for her grandfather. Page after page, we follow her process as she creates a fabulous collage using paints, cut paper, bits of velvet, twigs, feathers, and other found and scrounged materials. Her wonderful gift to her grandfather celebrates the things we love. Your students will have many ideas of how to create unique and original paintings and collages for someone they love. Eric Carle's magical *Draw Me a Star* is a poetic tribute to the creative process. The artist responds to life's request and begins drawing a star, which leads to the star's wish to have the artist draw a sun and the sun's desire to have the artist draw a tree . . . and so on. This is such a good way for the children to learn about the process (rather than the product!), to follow their own arts-rich journey.[19]

*Note:* Every time you invite the children to participate in open-ended challenges that encourage them to respond with their own ideas and interpretations, their own styles and choices of materials, you are helping them grow more confident in their own abilities, sense of self, and respect for others. Sometimes the simplest idea is the most effective! Be sure to encourage and welcome the children's ideas for activities and projects. They will surprise you with their commitment and involvement in experiences generated by themselves.

## KIDS COUNT

Honoring our uniqueness, we are grateful to Howard Gardner for his multiple intelligences theory, which reminds us of the diverse combinations of learning styles, interests, strengths, experiences, and attitudes of every person. When we extend those understandings to integrating math into all the components of our day, we really help children learn in meaningful ways. We help children succeed!

The National Council of Teachers of Mathematics (NCTM) published its updated *Principles and Standards for School Mathematics* in 2000. Keeping in mind the various ways we humans learn, through categories like linguistic, logical-mathematical, spatial, bodily-kinesthetic, musical, interpersonal, intrapersonal (and Gardner continues to add more), we *must* provide numerous experiences, seeing relationships and creating representations in the ongoing and ever-growing process of understanding math concepts. Our children need ample opportunities to learn in relevant, enjoyable, authentic ways.

As you read the following suggestions, strengthen your connections and think of all the ideas that can be enriched by math awareness. Kids count all the time and in countless ways. Train yourself to be someone they can count on to honor their unique qualities as they multiply their time with challenging, exciting adventures in learning.[20]

### *Hunters and Gatherers Are Collectors*

Be with young children for ten minutes and you'll find many of them picking up such items as shells, rocks, dead bugs, and pennies. Encourage the collection of any treasures they find fascinating. From pinecones to pebbles, children are excellent finders/searchers/gatherers/collectors. Invite them to create boxes, containers, trays to house their treasures. Count them. Sort them. Categorize them. When these skills are connected to the children's own Magic Vocabulary choices, meaningful connections are made. Turn all the collections and their information into a museum! Invite people to come look and ask questions. Change the song "These Are a Few of My Favorite Things" to "These Are a Lot of My Favorite Things!"

## Ten-Speed "I Can" Pictures

Extend the ten-speed metaphor ("Are you doing your *most*? Your *best*?") to blend with "Things I Can Do" and begin with ten ideas! The children's large sheets of paper are divided into ten sections. With help from you (if needed) the children number the sections from one to ten. In every space, the children draw, cut out, or write something they can do. Cover the wall with their pictures. Multiply them. As this activity is shared, emphasize to the children that they can do many more than ten wonderful things and when they finish one sheet of ten, they can go on with another. That makes—how many? Keep adding! This is easy information to chart and graph. Even though some of us write or illustrate the same accomplishment, we express it in our own unique style. How many kids highlighted "I Can Throw a Ball" in their charts of ten? Watch ideas grow.

## Creative Ways of Counting and Measuring

Landen holds up two fingers for his two years. Ryan Joe announces that it's his "half year" birthday. Two kindergartners agree that their telephone numbers are exactly the same except "mine is one number higher!" My address has a two and a seven in it. Maggie is excited because her address has a two and seven in it, too! Next to our names, which are so very meaningful to us, such categories of numbers as telephones, addresses, heights, weights, ages, birthdays, days, and months add a rich source of material for math understandings. We are more than the sum of all our parts! But, it's challenging and relevant to talk about mathematical concepts as you compare, contrast, gather information, use mathematical representations, understand mathematical language in the ongoing exchanges and extended activities inspired by the conversations. Be open to the many (and many is a math concept) possibilities!

Our uniqueness is expressed in very individual ways of thinking and doing. Morgan can't wait for her older sister's visit. She asks her mom, "How many naps till Emily comes?" Tiarra is waiting for her dad's return from an out-of-town trip. "He's coming in three lullabies." Three nights! We must encourage the often original ways children measure time and space. Helen Lester's *Tacky the Penguin* reminds us that everyone is to be valued, no matter how unusually or differently a person looks at the world. When small children think about large numbers like "squillions and squillions," their imaginations are stimulated and challenged. There are young children who won't even enjoy the wonder of those almost unimaginable numbers, but your young students who are fascinated with all things mathematical will love the ideas in David Schwartz's *How Much Is a Million?* Be sure to add the children's own ideas.[21]

When children add math awareness and concepts to those areas most beloved and fascinating to them, the learning is joyful and the connections meaningful. Ryan is a young scientist. He pours, mixes, spills, and blends. He's very specific about how many teaspoons of dishwater liquid or cups of shaving cream go into one of his experiments. Ask him to write (if he can), illustrate, or dictate his procedure. Marissa loves all fairy tales. Fairy tales are very specific about how many wishes are granted by the good fairy or how many stepsisters are in the story. Ask Marissa to write, dictate, illustrate, or demonstrate the components of the story that count! How many Pokemon, Dylan? How many animals in your barn, Joe? Truck-crazy Ben, can you line up your trucks and count them? Draw them? Sing about them? When you tune into the children's interests, you can be sure that everything will add up beautifully!

Reminder: Classroom families, community resources, school neighbors, and friends are marvelous visitors and field trip programs. Human beings demonstrate uniqueness in countless ways. Artists, artisans, craftspeople probably come immediately to mind. Inviting them to visit your class and share their work and the ways they work is an excellent experience for your students. A visit to a studio is very exciting. Next week, Callie's third grade will visit her dad, Jim's, glassblowing studio. Imagine the questions and conversations from that valuable trip. Storytellers, musicians, poets, magicians, decorators, designers are examples of resources at your fingertips of enriching field trips and classroom visitors. Check the alphabetical list in the appendix for ideas in case you (temporarily) run out!

## IT ALL COMES TOGETHER

By now you are probably tired of hearing how we are always making connections, seeing relationships, creating combinations of ideas! But, in case you still need a reminder, let's visit Tom Tenerovich's kindergarten class. Tom and his students have been enjoying their study of nursery rhymes. One of their very favorites is "Humpty Dumpty." They recited it, sang it, chanted it, read it, and wrote it in their kindergarten handwriting and spelling. They loved it so much, they played it! And then, of course (unless time or an overly programmed schedule limits enriched expansion of ideas), children will jump into the visual arts. Together, they created a wraparound mural that covered their room.

The bricks for Humpty's wall were created by pressing sponges dipped in red paint against the classroom wall. They all, each and every child, wanted to make their own Humpty Dumpty, so instead of inflexibly holding to the literal rhyme, Tom flew right along as each child created a very original Humpty character and decided where on the wall to place that doomed Dumpty. One child even designed a falling-off-the-wall Humpty. The children talked about what their Humpties might be saying and Tom whipped out dialogue bubbles, which the kids filled with words for Humpty to say, shout, cry, or sing and added them to the mural. How could the children have had a Humpty Dumpty mural without the King and Queen's beautiful horses? That was the next challenge and the children met it joyfully, each horse a unique representative of a unique artist! No precut, predetermined horses here! When I spoke to Tom about all the fun, the children were getting ready to have a big parade—after all, the King and Queen's men and women, of course, marched to the scene of Humpty Dumpty's fall!

We just can't help remembering that it all comes together! Our only limit is time![22]

## NOTES

1. Wesley Brantford was a fifth grader when he wrote this note in his poetry journal for the DepARTures Program (a poetry and art partnership with the Columbus Museum of Art and the Columbus Public Schools).

2. "See Me Beautiful" by Red and Kathy Grammer from the recording *Teaching Peace* distributed through Red Note Records. 800-824-2980.

3. Tomlinson, C. A. 1999. *The Differentiated Classroom: Responding to the Needs of All Learners.* Alexandria, VA: ASCD.

4. Here are just a few examples to help you think about the uniqueness of each of your students:

Benson, P. L. 1997. *All Kids Are Our Kids.* San Francisco, CA: Jossey-Bass.

Duckworth, E. 1987. *The Having of Wonderful Ideas and Other Essays on Teaching and Learning.* New York: Teachers College Press.

Fisher, B. 1995. *Thinking and Learning Together: Curriculum and Community in a Primary Classroom.* Portsmouth, NH: Heinemann.

Isenberg, J. and M. Jalango. 2000. *Creative Expression and Play in Early Childhood.* (3rd ed.). Upper Saddle River, NJ: Merrill/Prentice Hall.

5. Harry Chapin's powerful song "Flowers Are Red" can be found on a three-CD set: *Story of a Life*, a compilation of Harry's works, produced in 1999 by Electra Entertainment Group. For more information, check out The Harry Chapin Foundation, 83 Green Street, Huntington, NY 11743.

6. Chenfeld, M. B. 1991. "In Four Easy Nudges—Everything You Need to Know About Being a Creative Teacher." *Kappan*.

Reprinted in Chenfeld, M. B. 1993. *Teaching in the Key of Life*. Washington, D.C.: NAEYC, pp. 7–9.

7. Moorman, C. 1985. *Talk Sense to Yourself: The Language of Personal Power*. Portage, MI: Personal Power Press, pp. 104–113.

Moorman, C. 1998. *Parent Talk: Words That Empower, Words That Wound*. Merrill, MI: Personal Power Press.

Alfie Kohn's writings are numerous. He continues to be at the center of controversy with his strongly articulated views. The December 1994 issue of *Kappan*'s cover story was Alfie Kohn's "The Truth About Self-Esteem." That issue generated an ongoing important dialogue in the field of education.

One of his most influential books is:

Kohn, A. 1993. *Punished by Rewards: The Trouble with Gold Stars, Incentive Plans, A's, Praise, and Other Bribes*. Boston: Houghton Mifflin.

8. Lionni, L. 1973. *Frederick*. New York: Pinwheel.

Nikola-Lisa, W. illus. Bryant, M. 1994. *Bein' with You This Way*. New York: Lee and Low Books.

Rosen, M. J. illus. Rand, T. 2000. *With a Dog Like That, a Kid Like Me*. New York: Dial.

Lester, A. 2000. *Ernie Dances to the Didgeridoo*. Boston: Houghton Mifflin.

Steig, W. illus. Euvremer, T. 2001. *Toby, What Are You?* New York: HarperCollins.

Hubbard, W. M. 2000. *All That You Are*. New York: G. P. Putnam's Sons.

9. Kroll, S. illus. Appleby, E. 1987. *I'd Like to Be*. New York: Parents Magazine Press.

Sharmat, M. W. illus. Choroao. 1977. *I'm Terrific*. New York: Holiday House.

Debbie Charna teaches at the Columbus School for Girls, Columbus, Ohio.

10. Boynton, S. 2001. *Yay, You! Moving Out, Moving Up, Moving On*. New York: Simon and Schuster.

11. Children's Music Network. P.O. Box 1341, Evanston, IL 60204-1341.

12. Tom Griffin teaches at the Cassingham School, Bexley, Ohio.

13. Marlene Robbins dances with the children at Indianola Alternative School, Columbus Public Schools, Columbus, Ohio.

14. Kraus, R. illus. Aruego, J. 1971. *Leo the Late Bloomer*. New York: E. P. Dutton.

15. Hubbell, P. illus. Sweet, M. 2000. *Bouncing Time*. New York: HarperCollins.

16. Chenfeld, M. B. 11/1990. "My Loose Is Tooth! Kidding Around with the Kids." *Young Children.* Washington, D.C.: NAEYC.

Reprinted in Chenfeld, M. B. 1993. *Teaching in the Key of Life.* Washington, D.C.: NAEYC, pp. 31–35.

Judy Fujawa's delightful *(Almost) Everything You Need to Know About Early Childhood Education* (1998, Beltsville, MD: Gryphon House) will keep your spirits merry.

17. Rebecca Kantor is professor of early childhood in the School of Teaching and Learning, the Ohio State University.

18. Dawn Heyman, now retired from the Columbus, Ohio, Public Schools, spent many years enriching the lives of children who attended McGuffey School.

19. Florian, D. 1993. *A Painter: How We Work.* New York: Greenwillow.
Gibbons, G. 1998. *The Art Box.* New York: Holiday House.
Moon, N. illus. Ayliffe, A. 1995. *Lucy's Picture.* New York: Dial.
Carle, E. 1992. *Draw Me a Star.* New York: Philomel.

20. National Council of Teachers of Mathematics. 2000. *Principles and Standards for School Mathematics.* Reston, VA: NCTM.

Adams, T. L. Winter 2000, 2001. "Helping Children Learn Mathematics Through Multiple Intelligences and Standards for School Mathematics." *Childhood Education International* 77 (2) pp. 86–92.

21. Lester, H. illus. Munsinger, L. 1998. *Tacky the Penguin.* Boston: Houghton Mifflin.

Schwartz, D. illus. Kellogg, S. 1985. *How Much Is a Million?* New York: Lothrop, Lee and Shepard.

22. Tom Tenerovich celebrated Humpty Dumpty with his kindergartners at the Roxbury Elementary School in Solon, Ohio. He now teaches at the Royal Palm Beach Elementary School, Royal Palm Beach, Florida.

# THEME 4 | OUR FAMILIES/ OUR FRIENDS

## THINK ABOUT IT

My family story is similar (and of course special, as are all family stories) to those of millions of Americans. I am a child of Russian and Rumanian immigrants. When my families came to America generations ago, they found new lives of extreme struggle, poverty, and very hard work in (the slums of) New York City. In those not-so-long-ago times, schools were distant, formidable, authoritarian, often intimidating kinds of (sacred) institutions almost never to be approached by families in the surrounding neighborhoods. If a teacher sent a message or called home about a student, it was very bad news! The child would be cowering in a corner, ready for punishment for whatever transgression the teacher reported. Rarely was there a trial by jury! The teacher was always right. In most situations, teachers and administrators had no idea of the home lives of the children. I'm sure there are hundreds of variations of this theme, but these are the experiences I learned about and know were pretty typical of those non-English-speaking, desperately ragged and needy newcomers to our land.

Bob Dylan's song "The Times They Are a-Changin' " accurately describes today's educational scene, where family involvement in schools and in the education of the children is a central component of all programs. The media constantly passes on the news that children's success in life and learning is heavily dependent on the quality and quantity of family support and encouragement. Douglas Powell even compared the education of young children to a woven fabric with three different colored threads, representing parents, children, and teaching staff. He described the threads as constantly interwoven so there is connection throughout the design.[1]

Prestigious organizations such as the National Association for the Education of Young Children (NAEYC) strongly advocate programs that reflect collaboration and cooperation between school and families, respect the diversity of family relationships that represent the children's lives, and build relationships that emphasize trust, respect, confidentiality, and continuous communication to guarantee and improve the welfare of the children.[2] Schools and programs across the country have made it their business to be welcoming. Doors are open, volunteer calls are sent home, the presence of family and community members in the daily school lives of young children is visible. The schools deemed most effective and successful are those with the highest numbers of responsive and caring families.

The reality is that most Americans believe that families should play a greater role in their children's education. Many do but still too many don't or can't because of work schedules, family pressures, and so on. While most schools and programs have welcome mats prominently displayed, many still have to make that "welcome" a true happening.

Head Start programs have been role models in their multimethod approach to family involvement, which is central to the success of their efforts. This is an ongoing process, not a one-shot, one-event token gesture.

An example of a yearlong dynamic program is described by Mary Sterling,[3] who writes about the weekly School Meeting bringing all members of the Loker School[4] together with families and community members—a time for sharing, celebrating, planning, communicating, and problem solving.

When meaningful and authentic relationships between families and schools are developed, everyone benefits. Families are strengthened in their understanding of their children's abilities, skills, and needs. Families feel more confident of their important role in their children's education and feel valued by the schools as they contribute in various ways to the success of the program. Of course, the children benefit! But, not as much attention is given in this dialogue to the benefits for teachers when there is strong, positive parental involvement. In our ever-growing heterogeneous multicultural society, it's more imperative now than ever before to have enlightened, informed teachers who are respectful of their students' social, cultural, and economic situations. As partnerships are formed between families and teachers, greater appreciation and understanding results. Of course, this challenge goes beyond teacher-family relationships, extending to the climate of the school or program. *What's really happening?* Are the doors truly open and welcoming, or are there welcome mats outside of closed doors? Do we mean what we say when we invite families to become part of our school community? This topic is so important that many educational journals devote numerous articles and research studies to it. In the July 2001 issue of *Young Children*, an entire section of the journal was titled "Families and Teachers: Parents in Support of Young Children." Deborah Eldridge's essay "Parent Involvement: It's Worth the Effort" is an example of the excellent materials clearly supporting this goal and reviewing the research that substantiates the value of such vital relationships.[5]

The variations and possibilities are endless. Bottom line: How do *you* feel about your relationship with the families of your children and community friends? Is your view of families narrow or open-hearted and sensitive to the many definitions of family we understand nowadays?

Families and friends come in all sizes, shapes, ages, colors, and patterns! Your attitude, commitment, and acceptance of the family and community backgrounds of your children are of paramount importance. Are you a person uncomfortable being with people from different cultures, family patterns, and customs? Do you think you function best in situations in which you and the children share common traditions and family settings? These are deeply critical questions that only you can answer honestly to yourself. Your discomfort, disapproval, or insensitivity to the situations of various children in your class or program will affect every aspect of curriculum and learning.

*Who decides the composition of family, anyway?* Our more limited definitions of traditional families are out of synch with the realities of these changing times. Many of our children live in multiple households, have extended families, are being raised by grandparents or nonparental family members. Many of our children are growing up in foster homes, are children of adoption, single parents, community institutions. Only about half of America's children are living in "traditional" settings with both parents and siblings. Fathers are playing a more pivotal role in their children's upbringing than ever before, but we flip the coin and find more children growing up without a father or father figure than ever before.[6] These are challenging times for those of us whose lives are committed to being with children and helping them learn. Because of

FIGURE 4–2   *Who decides the composition of families, anyway?*

ever-developing awareness of our children's families and home lives, effective schools and staffs have redefined the goals of education to emphasize the building of community, the creating of a warm, safe feeling of family within the walls of their institutions. Especially for young children, the role of teacher has taken deeper meanings. For many children, their teachers *are* their families! (How many teachers are called "Mom" or "Dad" throughout the day?)

When I told Polly Greenberg[7] that the themes of "Families" and "Friends" were going to be combined in the last edition of this book, she was immediately articulate and supportive of that connection.

She said, "As most of us know, the world can be a harsh, unkind, and even cruel place. And harsher are the facts that the homes of so many of our children—no matter their economic levels or cultural or racial backgrounds—are often harsh, unkind, and cruel. Large numbers of our children come from homes saturated with severe problems such as drugs, alcohol or substance abuse, domestic violence, or destructive relationships. Even our children whose homes appear 'normal' may be very hurried children whose parent or parents are preoccupied with earning a living and the other innumerable duties involved in running a household. There may be no one at home who meets this child's emo-

FIGURE 4–3    *Fathers are playing more pivotal roles.*

tional needs for leisurely friendship and fun. The less time a child gets for family conversations, activities, and projects, the more time the child needs that in school.

"The less a child's life permits play with siblings, neighbors, relatives, or interested adults, the more urgently the child needs an abundance of such opportunities for spontaneous discussions, activities, and play in the classroom. In such classrooms, children are able to work and play with others in partnerships and small groups. Generally, children seek out others from whom they will learn as they play and work together. They need many opportunities to get emotional fulfillment from such friendships. Providing time for spontaneous play—language, games, math games, make-believe—helps children strengthen their sense of self and appreciation of others. We are always trying to pull in the left-out child!

"You and I know that each of us is better able to focus on learning and more open to learning when we feel secure, when we're not emotionally or socially desperate, and when our basic human needs for acceptance, appreciation, and friendship are met. Then our minds are freed for learning. This is such a difficult time for teachers. We may find what we know about some of our children's families to be appalling, but *it is not our job to judge.* We must accept and welcome every child," Polly said.

In every classroom, there is a lonely child, and in many classrooms, there are quite a few. Aren't all of us lonely sometimes?

FIGURE 4–4   *We learn best when we feel safe and loved.*

One thing we can offer to all of our children is a comforting, kind, and encouraging classroom rich with colorful and attractive materials and teachers who mix and mingle, assist, challenge.

Yes, I'm glad "Families" and "Friends" are now combined! Especially for children whose families are *not* their friends. Many children can count among their best friends members of their family, but, unfortunately, many can't. That's why committed and loving teachers must create family-style classroom communities for all of our children.

The importance of creating community in schools and childcare programs can't be emphasized enough. This book could be filled with nothing but stories of what teachers, care-givers, support staffers mean to our children. They are extended family members, often more present for the kids than blood relatives!

Bus drivers and cafeteria, custodial, and secretarial support staff were included in a citywide staff development program for Head Start. The bus drivers were wondering why they were invited to this workshop. After a few minutes of talking and sharing, they realized that they were the first people to greet and meet most of the children. One of the

FIGURE 4–5    *Our class is a family, a community.*

drivers told me, "There are some kids whom I know no one talked to that morning—no one said good-bye to them or would say hello to them when they got dropped off. I make it my business to give them a warm, friendly greeting!"

Lynda Barry shared a poignant memory of a lonely and neglected childhood. One morning, before the sun rose, she left a house tense with parental fighting and made her way to school. There was such anger in the house that "the only place where we could count on being noticed was at school. . . ." She waited outside the locked school building until the janitor arrived and let her in. He invited her to help him open the school. When the secretary arrived, she waved to the little girl. When her own teacher arrived, walking toward her and calling her name in a very happy and surprised way, she remembers, "Suddenly my throat got tight and my eyes stung and I ran toward her crying. . . . It's only thinking about it now, twenty-eight years later, that I realize I was crying from relief. I was with my teacher and in a while I was going to sit at my desk, with my crayons and pencils and books and classmates all around me, and for the next six hours I was going to enjoy a thoroughly secure, warm, and stable world. It was a world I absolutely relied on. . . . Without it, I don't know where I would have gone that morning. . . ."[8]

I believe that if you are not deeply moved by your role in creating, as Polly Greenberg described, "a family-style classroom community" where every child is hallowed and welcomed, where trust and friendships develop, where no matter the season outside, the weather inside your space is warm, then *you should consider entering a profession other than teaching.* For the children, you must be strong and fiercely dedicated. They need you so much!

The children are waiting for you.

Are you ready for them?

## DISCOVERY TIMES/WONDER TIMES: POINTS OF INTEREST

- Family is basic to all people. Just think: no matter where people live in the world, most belong to some kind of family.
- Families have many members, including mothers, fathers, stepmothers, stepfathers, sisters, brothers, grandmothers, grandfathers, aunts, uncles, nieces, nephews—so many interesting relationships!
- Sometimes we have such good friends and neighbors that we think of them as members of our own family.
- Friends come in all ages, shapes, colors, nationalities, and religions.
- It's fun and easy to make new friends.
- Friends and family members are usually people who care about us.
- People are very unique. They have many ways of showing feelings and approval. Aren't we lucky we're not all exactly the same? We're not robots!
- There are many kinds of family arrangements. Children are intelligent; they usually understand even the most complicated family relationships!
- It's sad when parents divorce or when a family member or friend is sick or dies. It's good that children have teachers and friendly classmates to talk to and share feelings with.
- Sometimes family members and friends may disagree or argue, but it's often possible to settle differences in healthy ways. When people respect the feelings and ideas of others, a climate of trust and safety grows. It's always amazing to know that we can learn to cooperate and be with others in friendly ways.
- When a baby is born in the family, it's fun to be a big sister or brother! But sometimes new babies can be a "pain in the neck." Remember, everyone was a new baby once! We have a lot of experiences to share with friends and family.
- Aren't we all members of different kinds of family? Our school family? Our church, mosque, or synagogue family of friends? Our Scouts or after-school program family of friends? *The human family?* (Many children who come from negative family situations find very great comfort in their membership in other kinds of family-type groups.)
- Whether at home or at school, life is more pleasant when people help each other and care about each other.

FIGURE 4–6    *It's fun to have brothers!*

## SUGGESTED VOCABULARY

| | | | |
|---|---|---|---|
| mother | friend | trucks | laundry |
| father | buddy | chores | clean |
| mommy | pal | helpers | take turns |
| daddy | neighbor | car | cooperate |
| mom | partner | van | agree |
| dad | classmate | give | disagree |
| parents | teacher | trips | argue |
| stepmother | meals | outings | make up |
| stepfather | breakfast | picnics | talk |
| sister | lunch | visits | shop |
| brother | supper | parties | hug |
| stepbrother | bed | birthdays | kiss |
| stepsister | bath | holidays | smooch |
| baby | clothes | care | listen |
| grandmother | medicine | praise | share |
| grandfather | games | invite | friendly |
| uncle | toys | celebrate | happy |
| aunt | books | company | sad |
| niece | bikes | come in | glad |
| nephew | pets | house | scared |
| cousin | dolls | apartment | lonely |

| disappointed | you're nice | cry | company |
| excited | you're funny | jokes | forgive |
| please | let's play | church | baby-sitter |
| you're welcome | let's plan | synagogue | school |
| thank you | together | mosque | help |
| may I? | stories | gifts | apologize |
| I'm sorry | songs | puzzles | divorce |
| excuse me | poems | blocks | adopted |
| I love you | riddles | greeting cards | foster home |
| | laugh | hold hands | |

Your vocabulary list will represent your particular group of children. *Buenos dias, amigo, jambo, shalom, salaam, aloha,* and *yo* may be words your children use to communicate friendliness, greetings, or welcome. They may have different terms for family members and friends—especially grandparents! Continue gathering all their words, remembering that the qualities of friendliness are manifested in many ways. No matter our particular collection of words, I hope that we are teaching our children the vocabulary of friendliness in everything we do!

*Note:* A very beloved book expressing the vocabulary of friendliness is Chris Raschka's *Yo! Yes?* which uses a minimum of words to movingly convey the building of a friendship. You and your young students will be delighted with the simple illustrations and very basic dialogue that is immediately touching and understandable.[9]

## TALK/LISTEN/READ/WRITE: THE GIFTS OF LANGUAGE

### *Teacher Talk*

When children talk, we must listen with all of our senses. When children don't talk, we must observe with the ear inside our hearts. (Isn't there an "ear" inside of the word *heart*?) Awareness implies sensitivity and caring. Because you know that seven children in your room do not live with their mothers, you adapt your celebration of Mother's Day. Many teachers have created expanded celebrations like "Favorite Lady Day" to be more inclusive. In many schools, children celebrate such special times as "Grandperson's Day," opening the doors even wider. You respect the variety of home situations. You no longer automatically say "Mommy or Daddy" as your major reference to family without watching the pain of sudden loss sadden the face of a young child. Aware, respecting, accepting teachers learn new ways to refer to the adults at home. They say things like, "Ask a grown-up at home to please sign this note," or "Maybe a baby-sitter or friend or someone bigger than you at home will help cut out pictures of flowers for our project."

My special person is Judy. She always wears a bandana. She wears glasses. She is nice. She meditates. Judy is a friend of my mom. She is special because she loves me and I love her! By Nate

FIGURE 4–7    *Judy is honored to be Nate's Special Person.*

Be alert at all times to what the children are telling you and how you respond to them! Your responses could make the difference between life and death of the spirit.

## Welcome Children!

We all, and especially young children, want and need rituals or ceremonies that help set a climate of warmth and friendship. Special songs, gestures, words of welcome, chants, and poems take just a few short moments but have long-lasting effects. You are saying, "Come in! I'm so glad you're here today! We all need each other to have a happy group!" A few well-spoken, warm words of greeting and welcome are more meaningful to children than a bulletin board spread with commercial posters.

Here is an immediate chance to honor different languages, different cultural ways of "welcome" and greetings. Even if all your children speak English, they easily and eagerly learn words in other languages. This also gives the message that people of all cultures have vocabularies of friendliness.

Traveling the country, I have enjoyed sharing many ways teachers have created environments of welcome through special greetings, songs, gestures, stories, and rituals. These few moments of beginning each day in a sacred way will not mess up your schedule (as a teacher who did *not* teach in the key of life warned me). Be playful. Tune into the children's interests and talents. Integrate their ideas into your welcoming "caremonies." If you need any more inspiration than the joyful expression of your students as they enter your room, enjoy books like Charney's *Teaching Children to Care: Management in the Responsive Classroom* or Kriete's *Morning Meeting Book*.[10]

## Help! Helpers Needed!

Even the youngest children love to help. When everyone is asked to participate in the upkeep and well-being of the group, cooperation is strengthened and a feeling of cohesion brings everyone together. Here's a challenge. Figure out enough real jobs for every child in your class or group to have a responsibility every day. Be creative. Expand your concept of classroom helpers to such responsibilities as plant waterer, calendar helper, song leader, and paintbrush cleaner; the children will have many good ideas. This is another way to strengthen that home-school relationship. Children want to talk about the ways their families help at home, what jobs they do around the house, how it's good if people work together and help each other.

Create colorful charts or helpers' boards that feature the children's names and the various jobs needed. Add onto the helpers' collection as you and the children think of more. After a while, even the children who are nonreaders or beginning readers will recognize the various items displayed and used every day.[11]

How do we create safe and happy no-risk environments? Ask the children. Invite them, encourage them to talk together with you about some simple but powerful rules that will help keep their group cooperative, friendly, and happy. That will help create a family feeling! This is not a one-shot session but a continuous process. The classroom lists of rules that are often given to children by teachers or ordered from a catalog and taped to the front door are not nearly as effective or successful in inspiring sharing, respecting, caring about one another as those the children suggest and agree upon themselves. Keep it simple. If we want the children to respect, accept, and consider each other, we must model that behavior every day in everything we do and say. Integrate drama, role playing, songs, puppets, visual aids, and mime to help enhance ideas.

Concepts need continuous reinforcing in a variety of ways. Meaningful repetition strengthens understandings. Take one of the classroom rules, for example, and demonstrate it. Perhaps the kids decided that one of their rules is "Be helpful." "Children, let's think of some ways we can show the idea of being helpful. Let's not only say it but do something that demonstrates it." When children feel their opinions and ideas are valued, they are eager to contribute. Marcel shows the idea of picking up a book his neighbor dropped. Roma helps tie Mario's shoelace. Sumaya mimes helping by distributing books. She asks the children to guess what she's doing. Rules also make great song lyrics!

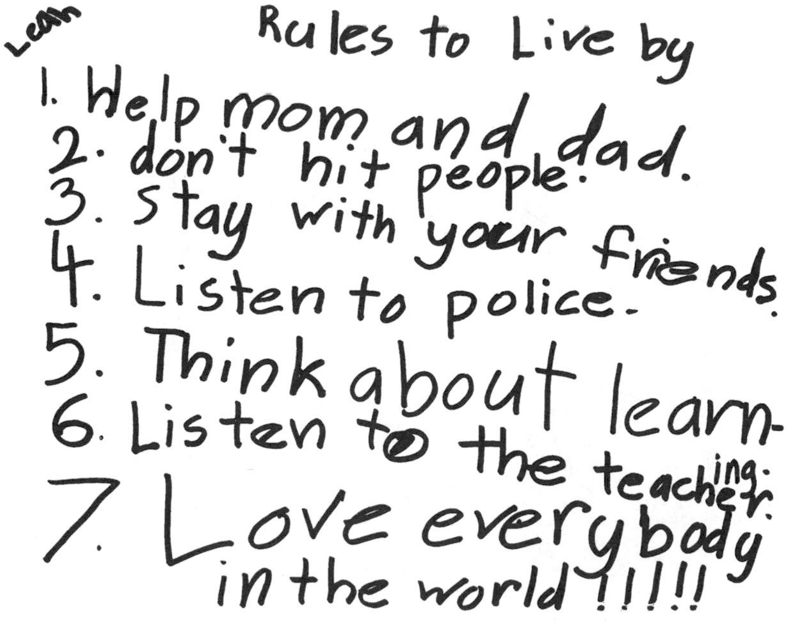

Rules to Live by

1. Help mom and dad.
2. don't hit people.
3. Stay with your friends.
4. Listen to police.
5. Think about learning.
6. Listen to the teacher.
7. Love everybody in the world!!!!!

FIGURE 4–8    *The first graders decided on their most important rules.*

·Read and talk about the agreed-upon rules. Ask the children to sign their names or letters or symbols to the rules chart! Add designs or photos.

Becky Bailey travels the country helping teachers find positive, loving ways to build respectful, cooperative, friendly groups. Her book *There's Gotta Be a Better Way: Discipline That Works!* is used extensively.[12]

### Buddy Up!

Talking about friendliness and friendship is an always relevant topic for young children. They will gladly give their opinions about friends in their lives (and don't be surprised if they include animals and toys). Add another F word, *families*, and you have the makings of *fabulous* talking/listening/reading/writing sessions.

But, even very young children often fall into cliques, and without loving "management" by a caring teacher, lonely children too many times remain outsiders. Encourage children to work and play with others in spontaneous relationships of their own choosing. But be ready, if needed, to offer the children opportunities to "buddy up" with others so that by the end of the school year, most of your children will have worked and played together, if only for one day. (More on buddies throughout the book.)

### Kids' Plans

Schedules, field trips, walks, arts activities, open house programs, holidays, and celebrations are all excellent subjects that need the input of

FIGURE 4–9   *Friends are important in school and everywhere.*

the children to truly succeed. Even the youngest children discover that their opinions and the opinions of others are valuable when they are full participants in planning their own learning activities. Exchanging ideas, listening to others, making choices, and cooperating to carry out class decisions are valuable experiences through which children learn cooperation, friendliness, respect, and responsibility. Use large chart paper to gather the names of children and their suggestions. Not only are such charts excellent souvenirs from stimulating talk times/listening times, but they are also excellent language resources.

### Family Circles/Magic Circles/Friendship Circles

Sometimes these kinds of gatherings are scheduled in daily or weekly programs. Sometimes they respond to the situation of the moment. Often, especially with young children, you'll find almost everyone has something important to say. This is the time to gather in your special place, sit quietly together, and give each child a chance to share feelings, questions, or concerns. This is a time for solving problems, for planning, or for simple human sharing and fellowship.

Remember, just because you are sitting on your special rug or in your magical friendship circle doesn't mean your time together will be special and magically friendly! I have seen children sit stiffly and quietly in these formations that occur at a prescribed time with a teacher-dominated preset agenda. It's very easy to squelch participation and trust when such exchanges as the following happen:

**Teacher:** Let's talk about some of your favorite ice cream flavors. Tell me your favorite ice cream flavor, Derrick.
**Derrick:** Chocolate.
**Teacher:** Wrong!

Teachers like Alice Aron Cohen embody the ideas of openness, trust, and friendliness in everything they do or say. Eavesdrop on Alice as she talks about talking.

"We talk all the time! We talk, sing, discuss, share, exchange. We sit together, help each other, ask questions, solve problems. There's always room for sharing. The more the children listen to each other, the more they learn about each other. Our kids have real conversations. I encourage them to help each other, to listen to each other. Cooperation develops. We have a close group feeling that just keeps growing!"[13]

An African proverb says, "Talking together is loving one another."

### Favorite Books Talk to Our Hearts

Nothing ignites more interesting and relevant conversations, shared feelings and experiences than rich literature. Aren't we lucky to have such a treasure of excellent resources at our fingertips? I like to hum the old chant, "Something old, something new, something borrowed, something true," as I think of the many outstanding books teachers have enjoyed with their children, strengthening their understanding of family and friends.

Barbara Topolosky holds a tiny, well-worn book, *A Special Trade*. It's about a little girl named Nelly and her dear friend and neighbor Old Bartholomew. When Nelly is a baby, Bartholomew wheels her in her stroller, taking her on lovely walks in the neighborhood. As Nelly gets older, her friend Bartholomew gets older, too, and one day he falls down and gets rushed to the hospital. When he comes home, he must stay in a wheelchair for a long time. Now it's Nelly's chance to take over and wheel her good friend around the neighborhood on delightful walks together.

*A Special Trade* tells a story that demonstrates the value of intergenerational relationships. Barbara and the children talk about how the story helps young children see the value of human friendship no matter the ages of the friends. The story never fails to inspire the kids to tell about their own older relatives, friends, and neighbors who are dear to them. Of course they love writing and seeing those names and descriptions on pictures, original books, charts, and song lyrics.[14]

In books like *Celebrating Families*, children learn that families come in a variety of patterns and usually find themselves somewhere in the array of possibilities. They will easily talk about their families in environments of trust and safety. See how easily the children's talks expand to creating their own "Celebrating Families" projects—constructions, poems, labeled illustrations, and so on. Stories like *Family, Familia* re-

FIGURE 4–10   *Young children are interested in all kinds of family stories.*

mind children that even though people speak different languages, like Spanish, and come from perhaps more unfamiliar backgrounds, like Latino, they share universal feelings about families. Adopted children, children born in other lands, *all* children will listen to and talk about books like *Allison*, about a little Chinese girl who comes to live with her new American parents. Stories like these evoke questions, wonder, empathy, important discussions, and understanding. Urban children are directly touched and rural and suburban children can learn that cities are full of more than buildings and bustling traffic. Stories such as *Abuela* (grandmother) and *Tar Beach* are examples of two books that help children find the warmth of family even in a metropolis like New York City.

Even a dog can be a best buddy, a best friend! *My Buddy* is a trained guide dog helping a child with disabilities. Mr. Rogers writes about the friendships of children with special needs and helps shatter stereotypes. In an Oklahoma intertribal community, a little girl learns about being a *Jingle Dancer* from her grandmother and other relatives.[15]

Linda Goldsmith and Jo Ann Bell consider *Sylvester and the Magic Pebble* a book that can never be read enough times. It's an enchanting story that entices children into imagining themselves turning into a rock totally devoid of family love. The happy ending reassures the kids and inspires important talks about how we all need each other![16]

### *Play Time Is Talk Time*

Family and friends are primary prominent topics for young children to talk about, think about, play about. With or without prompting, children become family members, neighbors, baby-sitters. Tune into their role playing, their dialogues, monologues. Who takes which parts? Is Kendra always the baby? Is Morgan always the mommy? Be a good listener and observer. Be ready to contribute a suggestion if needed. For example, children who want to join the game can be included with a simple idea like, "What if Jenna is the aunt who comes to visit?" The children naturally blend conversation, singing, improvisation, drama, reading (how many times have you seen a child reading to a stuffed animal, puppet, or doll?), movement (all skills and arts!) into one rich, multilevel experience. Through their play, they try on roles, comprehend relationships, learn major lessons in cooperation and language development. Nowadays, the time for young children to play has been too often drastically cut. I call it amputation of the spirit. This deprivation diminishes creativity and the joyful processes of imagination, problem solving, and learning to be with others as well as a multitude of valuable life lessons.

Besides the evidence always before you when you spend time with young children, excellent resources like Gretchen Owocki's *Literacy Through Play* will support your advocacy about the importance of play in our students' successful learning adventures.[17]

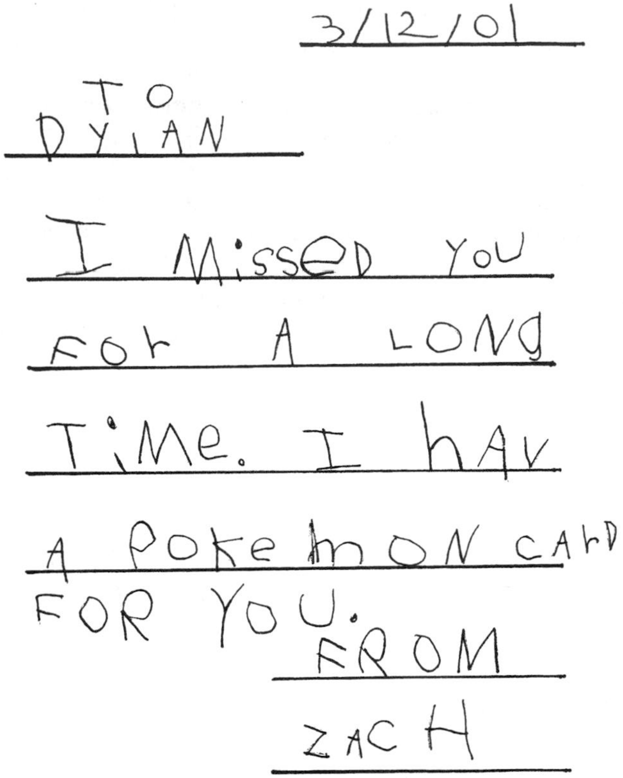

3/12/01

TO
DYIAN

I MissED YOU
FOR A LONG
TIME. I hAv
A PokemON CArD
FOR YOU. FROM
ZACH

FIGURE 4–11   *Kids love getting letters from their pen pals.*

### Pen Pals

Even in this age of emails, we love to receive hand-written letters and cards—we feel so special! All the children's names are written on pieces of paper and put in a hat, box, or whatever container you choose. Everyone picks a name. Your pen pal for the day! Write a letter or a card, draw a picture, send a greeting! The letters are either delivered or placed in the children's cubbies or folders or taped to their special bulletin boards or post office slots (if you organized that exciting project). Even toddler scribbles with pictures send messages of friendship. Do it again and again! Everyone receives a letter. Spread the cheer! See how such a simple idea contributes greatly to creating a friendly, family feeling.

## MUSIC MAKERS/MOVERS AND SHAKERS

Throughout this book, musical times are highlighted as times to celebrate ourselves, each other, and the creativity that stamps us as members of the human family. *Any* musical suggestion in this book fosters feelings of friendliness if it is shared with warmth, fun, reassurance, and flexibility. Music and dance bring people together through all seasons and events along the journey of life. Families, friendship groups, interest groups, communities of every kind have favorite kinds of music and dance. When we honor family songs and dances, we honor the cultural heritage of the families. We share in their rich traditions. In your own knapsack of memories and experiences, you have collected songs, games, and dances that you can trace back to family times, schools, camps, friendship groups.

In the classes you would want *your* children to attend, singing, music, dance, and play happen throughout the day, part of everything they do.

Don't limit yourself to packaged songs for children. Be eclectic in your selections. Choose music, songs, and dances that *you* love! Enthusiasm is contagious!

### More About Welcoming Ceremonies

Every day is sacred, never to come again, a new beginning, a little world of its own. The smallest gesture of welcome, little song or chant, rhyme or special rhythm or dance can make the difference between the life and death of the spirits of children as they begin a new day with you. Begin the day with life-affirming welcoming rituals. The children will learn them quickly and love them always. They will eagerly help you choreograph or compose improvised material for your very important welcome ceremony that starts every child on a day's journey of warmth, safety, acceptance, and fellowship. What a way to launch a day!

Young children throughout the country have started their days with special hand-clap rhythms, movement patterns, playful variations of such old favorites as "Old MacDonald."

> Mrs. Selinger had some kids, ee-I-ee-I-o.
> In her class she had a Joshua . . .

> Where is Thumbkin? (Where is Lauren? Where is Destiny?
> Here we are! Here we are! . . .)

Keep adding ideas!

### Lullabies

Peaceful, soothing, and loving songs that lull babies to sleep, lullabies are probably the most basic kinds of loving musical messages. Lullabies come in every language, representing every culture on the planet. During quiet times or after snacks or strenuous activities, share lullabies from around the world with your children. Make room for their own lullabies, original or learned. Listen as they sing to the "babies," to each other, to themselves.

## Songs and Dances as Gifts

The ancient tradition of giving one's own songs, dances, poems, artworks to others is easily understood by young children.

> I have a song that I love.
> I want to share it with you.
> I want to give it to you as my gift to you.

My Shinnecock princess friend, Bess Chee Chee Haile, told me long ago about a Native American custom of giving songs as gifts. When I visited schools in Canada, native people told me of their custom of finding and making one's own dance and chant that belonged to that person. Sharing that precious dance and chant with others was a deep mark of friendship.

Encourage the children to make their own songs, dances, poems, and chants. In safe and loving environments, children will teach and share them with others.

"We learned Jasmine's dance today!"

Remember that your children represent some of the rich diversity of our country. Your learning community will be enriched with gifts from homes including songs, music, instruments, rhythms, chants, and dances reflecting the cultural backgrounds of your students and their families. Because yours is a safe and accepting environment, children will want to share. *We begin with the world in our room!*

## Classmate Riddles

Children love guessing games! The popularity of the I Spy books demonstrates that fact. Ask the kids to turn on their power lights, lift their antennae, charge up their batteries, and get into gear for this fun, active way of honoring their classmates. Here are a few examples:

> "I'm thinking about (or I spy) a helpful boy who's wearing a blue T-shirt with the number three on it. If you know who he is, say his name and jump ten times."

> "I'm thinking about (or I spy) a girl with lots of extensions, beautiful beads in her hair, and a big smile. If you know who it is, say her name, skip over to her, and give her a thumbs up!"

Here is an easy, lovely way to emphasize positive attributes and feelings toward others and to ensure success for all who participate.

## Special Instruments Bring People Together

Throughout history, musical instruments and rhythms have communicated important messages to groups. Families sometimes ring dinner bells. Drums call people to gather for a special event. Bagpipes begin the

FIGURE 4–12    *I spy a girl wearing a red hat.*

excitement. Blowing a whistle for order or for instructions and directions is probably a relative of this old tradition. I use my tambourine for numerous signals and messages. Marlene Robbins' conga drum, Lester, is listened to attentively by her students. Tom Griffin's guitar strums have ideas to share with his students.

If possible, bring your instrument into class. Give it a language. Let it become an important part of your day.

Let it truly gather your children together.

### Rounds, Call-and-Response Chants

When children sing rounds, such as "Row, Row, Row Your Boat," they must listen attentively, sing closely with their group, and learn their place in the whole scheme. They also hear how much richer a song sounds when different parts are sung at the same time. *Harmony* is a musical term, but it is also a fitting word for a chapter on families and friends!

Call-and-response chants are rooted in tradition. They are almost extensions of conversations.

Come out and play.
OK.
Come out and play.
OK.

This is an example of a simple call-and-response song improvised by two children as they climbed a jungle gym.

A group of five-year-olds sang a call-and-response song as they hiked along. They made up the words as they walked.

> If you come with us
> You'll have fun.
> If you walk with us
> You'll have fun.
> If you swim with us
> You'll have fun.

Dante told his classmates about his baby sister, Jewel. The class made up a song about her.

> Jewel keeps crying.
> Waah waah.
> Jewel keeps crying.
> Waah waah.
> Jewel stopped crying.
> Yaaay. Yaaay.

Ella Jenkins, one of the most popular and earliest of the nation's singers to introduce children to the fun of call-and-response songs, sings call-and-response songs and chants from such cultures as Hebrew, Arabic, Spanish, French, African, and American. Before the term *multicultural* came to town, Ella sang and lived multicultural with children around the world. Ella sings to and with the world's children. She has taught us to honor their play songs, chants, and jump rhymes. Her "Miss Mary Mack," sung in the streets of her childhood and carried to towns, villages, and cities around the country, around the world, is an example of songs children never tire of and love forever.[18]

When children sing together, friendliness and goodwill prevail. Because music is the most universal language, we feel close to those with whom we share musical experiences.

Accompany singing and musical moments with visual arts, movement, drama, poetry, and stories . . . keep connecting!

### Choruses, Bands, Orchestras—Harmony at Work!

Whether we get voices together or instruments together, the underlying value is the same—we must work together to create the musical piece, whether a rap song or a symphony. Sing and play familiar songs together. Go beyond those experiences to improvise music. Play with rhythms. Begin with a heartbeat rhythm. Ask each instrument to pick up the rhythm and join in. Invite the children to experiment with sounds, words, and melodies to accompany the instruments. As often as possible, ask the children to pass their instruments along so they experience different sounds. Experiment with melody, tone, pitch, and tempo so children appreciate the range of possibilities for their voices. Together, create some new music, new harmony!

## Transitions and Cooperation

Imaginative and free-spirited teachers help children create cohesive, friendly places to learn with enjoyable ways to encourage helpfulness and cooperation. They sing and dance "cleanup songs"! They sing and dance "lineup songs"! Here are two examples:

- (To the tune of "This Old Man"): "I'll help you. You help me. Clean up everything we see. Jump down, turn around—clean up the room. We're doing great and don't need a broom!"
- (To the tune of "Twinkle, Twinkle, Little Star"): "Line up, line up everyone—we'll go out and have some fun. . . ."

Be playful! It's fun and important to help contribute to the happiness and well-being of the group.

## Playful Movement Songs That Feature Friends and Families

Popular songs such as "The Wheels on the Bus" that already name family members ("The mommies on the bus go sshh sshh sshh . . .") can be easily expanded to cousins, uncles, sisters, and brothers. Change the basic song into an active game by giving every friend in the class a chance to be on the bus doing something that is demonstrated by movement.

"Pierre on the bus does jumping jacks . . ."
"Crystal on the bus can touch her toes . . ."

"Farmer in the Dell" turned into a family affair when all kinds of relatives were "taken."

"The baby takes a brother . . ."
"The brother takes a sister . . ."

Or a friendly gathering when the teacher turns into the farmer and takes each child in the class.

"Mrs. Reedy takes a Yael . . ."
"Mrs. Reedy takes a Mohammed . . ."

Until everyone is "in."

### Exercise Families

This is a variation of the game Mother, may I? or giant steps, in which children differentiate between giant steps and baby steps. Children enjoy doing "baby jumps" then increasing the height of their jumps to "big sister (brother) jumps" to "baby-sitter jumps" and finally to "mother (father, stepmother, stepfather, grandmother, grandfather) jumps."

Choose any exercise that the children enjoy. Give them a steady beat on a tambourine or drum or play music with a steady, lively rhythm. Increase the volume as you increase in exercise. Always begin with the "baby" category because even the most reluctant movers will show they can do baby jumping jacks or baby hops.

### Animal Families Exercises

Children love animals and animal movement. Adapt the previous activity to the theme of animals. Kanga, a mom kangaroo, is a big jumper. Baby Roo takes little jumps. Grandfather horses have high prances and strong gallops. Baby horses have little prancing feet. The children enjoy the fun of demonstrating animal families in action, with specific movements for different family members. This is a great way to learn differentiation. Make up stories to go with the exercises. Illustrate them.

### Twenty Ways to Love a Circle

A circle is a perfect shape for encouraging friendship. It has no beginning and no end, no front and no back of the line. Everyone faces one another and no one is left out. A circle provides a feeling of belonging and safety. (*I am not an advocate of games played in circles where people are tagged out or cast out!*)

Of the thousands of circle activities, twenty are offered to start you thinking about your own family circle of friends.

1. Sit in a circle and shake hands with one another.
2. Wave to everyone in the circle.
3. Sing songs, clap hands, slap thighs, and stamp feet while keeping the circle.
4. Blink your eyes, wiggle your nose, and make a funny face for everyone around you in the circle.
5. Tell round-robin stories while sitting in a circle. Everyone has a turn to continue the story.
6. Roll the ball to each child in the circle and ask a question like, "What's your favorite color?" or "What's your favorite food?" The child responds and rolls the ball back to you.
7. Sit in a circle and pass around an imaginary shape that changes as each person receives it.

8. Sit in a circle and listen to a story, poem, or song. Improvise hand and body movements to accompany the action.

9. Pass an expression like "hello" around the circle. Everyone gets a chance to say it in a different language or different way. The children discover that even a wonderful phrase such as "I love you" can be said with anger or meanness. They are astonished that a playful phrase like "You cucumber!" can be hurtful when spoken in a negative way.

10. In your circle, talk about sign language and the language of gesture. Learn signs for phrases like "I like you" or "friends." Make up gestures for familiar ideas.

11. Sit in an unfriendly/friendly circle. Take turns making mean, unfriendly faces and body shapes. How does that feel? Change the circle into a friendly circle with friendly expressions, words, and body shapes. How does *that* feel?

12. Hold hands. How many ways can the circle move? Experiment. Walk into the center. Walk back. Hop, jump, kick, slide. Move the circle.

13. Play follow the leader. Choose your favorite music and give everyone a turn to lead some kind of movement in the center of the circle. (Don't force a shy child to be leader. Skip to the next person. Minimize tension!)

14. Turn your circle into a balloon. Stand very close together, bunched up and holding hands. Take deep, exaggerated breaths and expand into a large circle. Then breathe out and walk into a small circle again. Children enjoy pretending that the air went out of the balloon and pulled everyone into the middle.

15. Form a noisy circle, quiet circle, musical circle, clapping circle, tiptoeing circle, marching circle.

16. Turn your circle into a circle of giants, trees, robots, animals, elves, or characters from stories.

17. Turn your circle into a tribal dance circle. Play African, Native American, or Caribbean music, for example. Let the children dance freely to the music inside the sacred dance circle.

18. Make a circle of slow-moving, fast-moving, sideways-moving people.

19. Make a ten-speed circle. Everyone holds hands and walks very slowly. Begin walking a little faster, then faster and faster. Speed it up ten times until the children are moving in the fastest gear. Accompany with drums or tambourine or hand claps.

20. Brainstorm circle ideas with your children and turn your circle into a wheel, a pizza, a merry-go-round, a melting ice cream cone, the moon, or a puddle.

I know you can easily think of twenty more ways to love a circle!

## Literature Is a Moving, Musical, Playful Experience

Chances are that many of the children in your room will experience being a big sibling, cousin, or neighbor to a newborn baby. Across the country, newborns are "students" in infant-toddler classes. Babies are a relevant topic to most young children and are important to deal with! Books like the delightful *Everywhere Babies*[19] reassure young children in demonstrating that babies are not confined just to their households but are everywhere, and no matter where they are or what their backgrounds, they have a lot in common: for example, they all play games like peekaboo, patty cake, and roll the ball (and these are enjoyable games for your students to remember and play to music or to the text). Stories such as these help young children find camaraderie in family situations as well as confidence in all the things they can do now that they are bigger and older! Of course, infants and toddlers love nothing more than seeing infants and toddlers on the pages of books!

Bill Martin Jr.'s beloved book *Brown Bear, Brown Bear, What Do You See?* is another example of a book that inspires play, movement, chant, and improvisation as it contributes to the growing of friendship in your group. Play with the text. Use everyone's name—"Jillian, Jillian, who do you see?" "I see Marco skipping to me!"[20]

The immense popularity of the Berenstain Bears books, Winnie the Pooh, and Frog and Toad materials reminds us of how young children love stories about families and friends.

Invite children to celebrate the choreography and musical possibilities in their favorite books! You don't have to move or sing to every word in a text! Be selective.

### Walking Together

"Let us walk together" is a phrase, a wish, and a blessing from the traditions of many cultures. Walking together (unless you're lined up in a strict, rigid line with no chance to talk or sing or play as you walk) inspires warm, friendly feelings of sharing. An ordinary walk can be transformed into an extraordinary experience that strengthens camaraderie and cohesion while encouraging authentic learning.

A simple walk around the school or around the block when mixed with imagination and fun can become a peak event.

Here are a few suggestions. Add your own!

*Buddy walk:* Buddies walk holding hands.

*Singing walk:* Hold hands, swing hands, sing, and "bouncy walk."

*Animal walk:* The children walk like animals. Monkeys walk differently than giraffes.

*Noah's ark walk:* A variation of the previous idea is a procession of animals walking two by two. Buddies choose which pair of animals they want to be.

*Hello walk:* Greet everyone and everything you pass with a friendly word or movement.

*Stop-look-listen walk:* Walk with your senses in high gear. Stop and look behind you, around you, above you. What do you see? Listen; what do you hear? Share observations.

*Walk tall:* Heads high, shoulders straight, muscles strong—make big footsteps.

*Discover-the-world walk:* Wear your imaginary magical glasses, which help us see more clearly. Close in on a specific spot. One group of kindergartners spent almost a half hour on a patch of grass, noticing ants, ladybugs, caterpillars, birds, seeds, worms, roots, weeds, blades of grass, and holes in the dirt.

*Storybook characters walk:* Walk softly like Hiawatha. Walk rigidly like the Tin Woodsman, loosely like the Scarecrow. Walk *big* like a giant, *big* like Paul Bunyan. Walk like a monster from *Where the Wild Things Are.* Skippety-walk like Dorothy on the Yellow Brick Road. Walk like best friends Frog and Toad.

When you return from your walk, invite the children to talk, sing, draw, paint, construct, or dance about the experience of walking together.

## ALL WAYS ART

Our families/our friends are not ideas you have to introduce to children. They are already drawing (at whatever level) family members and people closest to them without any instructions. With all visual arts experiences the possibilities of encouraging friendships, sharing, respect, cooperation, and acceptance are enriched. Once again, key phrases to remember are "open-ended" and "safe at any speed." Rigid rights and wrongs have no place in the encouraging and safe environment you want to create for children. When children are chastised for "going out of the lines" or using the "wrong" color in their painting, no child feels safe. These ideas are for you to play with. Mix and match. Combine and change. Connect and add.

### Family and Friendship Trees

Following a talk about families—who do *you* live with?—the children enjoy cutting out different tree shapes from cardboard, construction paper, or any scrounged material. Of course, our trees need leaves, and cutting leaf shapes is so much fun. On each leaf, the children draw, color, paint, or paste a picture or name of someone in their family or someone special to them. The leaves are pasted to the branches of their trees. Find a wall big enough to display your forest of family and friendship

FIGURE 4–13  *Love Outstanding!*

trees. A variation of this popular idea is to bring a small bare-branched tree into the classroom and paste or tape the leaves to the wooden branches.

### Collage of Shared Family/Friends Activities

After talking about such happy times together, gather the ideas and suggestions on a chart or a section of the chalkboard to keep as reminders. The children cut pictures, draw, or paint any of the activities suggested that they enjoy with friends and family. They paste their drawings or cutouts on large sheets of paper arranged and designed as they choose. These collages are not only interesting and lively but also tell a lot about the children's lives. In five-year-old Lynette's collage, I noted a cutout picture of a car, a TV set, an outdoor grill, a garden, and cat food. Included was an original drawing of two happy faces: "That's me and Mom at the Ice Capades."

I always make room for even the one child who may feel left out because of home situations. Add to your suggestions, "If there are some activities you haven't enjoyed yet but think you would love to experience someday, draw about them or cut them out," or "Kids, do include some of your favorite times with friends in school." (If your classroom is a loving community, *every single child* should be able to create a collage, picture, book, sculpture, or other artwork.)

### Family/Friendship Scrolls

The children are fascinated by stories of long ago. Talk with them about how long ago, before people learned how to make books, they used scrolls to tell stories. Cut butcher paper into long sheets that roll easily. Give all the children a sheet. Encourage them to write names of family members or special friends and to put next to each name drawings as well as descriptive words to highlight their characteristics. Stories about the family and/or the friendships can be added with words and colorful illustrations. When the scrolls are finished, the children choose a strand of colored wool to tie them. Be sure to share and celebrate all of the scrolls before they are given to families and friends as gifts.

### Family Symbols/Classroom Symbols

Scottish clans have tartans, Cub Scouts have animal names for their dens, Native American nations have totems honoring animals or natural forces. Talk with the children about choosing a symbol for their family—perhaps it's a star or a fish. Tyrone said that his family went to church "almost all the time," so he chose a church steeple for his family's symbol. After the children chose all their symbols, they used them as often as they wanted. One first-grade teacher wrote all the children's names on a large sheet of paper. The children signed their names after the printed list; next to their own signatures, they drew their family symbols. Soon the children knew the symbols for everyone in the class! How many ways can you think of for these designs to be used?

### Family and Friends Place Mats

I personally have learned more from some place mats than I have from lectures! On plain sheets of paper, the children design place mats for their family members or the people they live with. Encourage them to create a special place mat for each person, including the person's name and any designs or pictures that person would enjoy. Somewhere on the place mats, include the family symbol. Louie's place mat for his baby brother, Harry, featured a collage of pictures of baby food jars. "That's his main thing," Louie explained. "Eating!" Laminate them if possible. Clear contact paper can be stretched over them if no laminating machine is available. They make wonderful gifts.

### Friendship/Cooperation Posters

Expand a talk about what makes a good friend, what is cooperation, and invite the children to illustrate their ideas in words and images to demonstrate those important ideas. One first-grade class loved their cooperation posters so much that the posters were prominently displayed for the entire year! A continuous source of conversation and learning.

## Gifts for Friends, Classroom Buddies, and Families

Doesn't "gifted education" mean giving gifts to others? Children enjoy making special gifts for special people. With scrounged materials, bits and pieces, hunks and chunks, chips and scraps, children create charm bracelets, earrings, pins, treasure boxes, posters, picture albums, and T-shirts with original designs using tie-dyeing, markers, or paint (to name just a few popular ideas from around the country). Of course, an original greeting card should accompany each gift!

## Group Projects

(Every page of this book encourages you to create, with your children, a family feeling, a friendship community.) Respect and affirmation build when all the children contribute to projects such as these:

*Wallpaper:* As a group, the children decide the pattern for their wallpaper. Cover a portion of a wall with paper and ask the children to contribute their portion to the whole. I have seen walls of footprints, handprints, circles, stars, and animal designs (very ancient patterns).

*Quilts:* In the last few years, quilts, using many materials, from paper to cloth, have become very popular. Family quilts or "Our Class Friends"

FIGURE 4–14  *We're happy when we make gifts for others!*

quilts are excellent projects for cooperative learning and group enjoyment. A quilt can't be complete unless it has a section from everyone!

*Turn your whole room into . . .* Nothing brings children together
more quickly and effectively than deciding on a story or theme that is
especially exciting to the group and turning your whole room into the
idea. For example, one kindergarten class so enjoyed *Charlotte's Web*
that they decided to turn their room into a web. They connected string
from corner to corner and place to place by taping it. The project emphasized cooperation because the process of deciding where and how to
connect the string was complicated. The children wrote their favorite
words on colored construction paper, then cut them out and taped
them to the string of the web. They made marvelous mobiles of baby
spiders, shiny and twinkling.

I have seen whole classrooms turned into rain forests, oceans, Iro-
quois longhouses, and gardens. These ideas go on, sometimes for
weeks. Stories, poems, songs, games, play activities, and art projects related to the theme continue throughout the duration. The only limitation is time! The basic lesson is friendship!

*A.Y.O.* Add your own!

### Friends Make Connections

One portrait, sketch, sculpture, or body sketch is a powerful image.
Save a wall or a board to connect all the bodies, sculptures, sketches and
the effect is, as one first grader observed, watching the wall fill with
friends' images, "awesome!" Add names, words, dialogue bubbles!

### Buddy Works

Add to your buddy activities, creating a piece of art together. Choosing
their own materials and themes, children learn cooperation and friendliness and enjoy the exciting process. Be sure to celebrate all the artworks! (No competition!)

### Friend Ship

Out of scrounged objects, working together, build a boat. Into the boat,
put images of all the classmates created out of chosen materials. (I always like the children to have many opportunities to choose their own
materials. Break the molds!) Tell and write stories, songs, poems, and
games for all the friends in the Friend Ship. Illustrate them!

## KIDS COUNT

Once you become aware of how many times during the day you and
your students are demonstrating and constructing math concepts and
vocabulary, you'll remember how natural and easy it is to integrate
math into every area of curriculum and class management.

## Add a Friend

Begin with one child. Add another and another until all the kids are in. (In a circle, in front of the room, in a cluster.) I like to use Greg and Steve's popular song, "We're All Together Again,"[21] as we begin with one and celebrate the sum of our classmates. Celebrate with a parade!

## Who's Missing?

We need *all* the children to have the most fun together! As we take attendance and count heads, note the names of absent students.

"Friends, we have fifteen children in our class, but today, Kenyata is absent so now we only have . . . let's count!"

Not only do the children learn the concept of subtraction but they're learning an equally important lesson—every child counts!

## Friends and Families Share

When we work and play together, we learn to share. The art teacher distributes a clump of clay to each pair of partners. "Divide your clay in half," he instructs. Children learn that a whole of anything can be divided into halves, thirds, and quarters. How many children are working and playing together in this group? Are we in twos? Threes? Fours? We need to divide these pipe cleaners so that everyone gets the same number. The opportunities for such hands-on, relevant learning abound.

## Party Time!

Friends and family enjoy parties! For any and all reasons, parties are high on the list of popular events. Planning a party involves so much math! How many people are coming? How many invitations do we need? How many party favors shall we make? How will we divide the refreshments? Shall we have an animal party? (Young children are party animals!) Shall we teach everyone one or two songs? How about dancing and exercising? Colorful, fun-filled books like Arthur Dorros' *Ten Go Tango* give the kids many ideas. Toucans two step! Three bears do three cha cha chas! Six crickets jiggle and jitterbug across the floor! You can count all the ideas for a party of fun for all! Did we forget balloons? How many? What colors? What if the doorbell rings and everyone comes in at once? Hutchins' *The Doorbell Rang* inspires playful adding of guests. Rylant's *The Relatives Came* adds numbers and people! After the party, the children create their own party books with illustrations, words, and numbers.[22]

## Friends Play Together

Children need many opportunities to work and play together in non-threatening, noncompetitive situations: bouncing and throwing balls (keep the count); jump roping (how many jumps?); hand rhythms (expand on old time *patty cake* variations); cheers (how many jumps, how many turns and claps?). Taking turns, sharing, counting rhythms, choreographing movement, and making patterns are examples of the numerous ways children use math concepts.

A wild and wacky book packed with different ways friends can play together is Bruce Goldstone's *Ten Friends*. What kinds of creative ideas can ten friends enjoy together? Will they all do the same thing? Read the book and enjoy all the ways ten friends can divide their time and multiply their fun. A delightful book to adapt and improvise with the children's own numbered ideas.[23] They can play the book!

### Birthday Dancing Graphs

Children love their birth-dates! The months of the year are important vocabulary words as well as understandings of time and seasons. We talk and sing about the months of the year. (Children who speak languages other than English can contribute their words for the months.)

One of my favorite ways to share this activity is to divide the room into the months of the year. Be sure to print large labels for each month. As the children say the months, count them out, place their location around the room, invite the children born in January to skip over to the January section. The February birthdays can jump to their month. And so on. Now you have a living graph around the room. How many children have birthdays in June? Oh my, we have six friends with June birthdays. Create a chart/graph using stick figures for each number. The children understand that each of the stick shapes represents a child. They are the living, dancing graph you write for them. Now you can ask, "How many children have birthdays in January?" Count them. "How many friends have birthdays in February?" Count them. Which month has the most birthdays? Everyone celebrates! This is a great way to guarantee the summer birthday kids have a chance to celebrate.

### Wave Hello!

Nothing is friendlier than a warm wave. (Handshakes are friendly. High fives are friendly.) Peter Sis' *Waving: A Counting Book*, creates a warm, cheerful environment that begins with one taxi waved down by Mary's mother and progresses through such events as nine Girl Scouts who wave at school children, and fourteen firemen waving from their fire truck, until the culmination of fifteen taxi drivers waving friendly greetings.[24]

The children improvise their own ideas beginning with one and building to whatever number you decide. Illustrations, movement, and drama naturally blend into the action, multiplying the fun!

### Folk Dance

Remember the warmth of our circles? Most folk dances around the world are in the form of circles. Children create their own movement for their circle of dancers. How many counts to go around? How many stamps and claps? How many counts for us to march into the center? Use any rhythmic music with steady beats from any culture. Your choreography will work! Keep it natural, rhythmic, and fun.

### Grand March

Many cultures and communities have variations of the Grand March. This is a joyful way to reinforce important math concepts such as counting, sequential development, addition, multiplication, and so on.

The children begin marching in a single file, one behind the other. Help them divide into two branches as they move across the floor, winding back to their starting point. Now they march two by two. Branch off the twos and help them arc around to come across the floor in fours. Branch off the fours as they curve around and now combine to cross the floor marching in eights! Any marching music will work. It's very exciting for the children to see the progression from their singular beginning to the large group patterns. By ones, twos, fours, and eights are exciting concepts for our young students.

### Gifts for Friends

When children learn and live in safe, warm communities they freely express love for classmates and teachers. This is their family away from home. Sometimes, their only loving family. Eve Merriam's beautiful book that counts down from ten to one, *Ten Rosy Roses*, is a story about children picking roses, one at a time. The numbers and subtraction illustrations are delightfully presented. The surprise ending is that the children gather all ten roses together and give them to their teacher. Children want to hear the story over and over again. Invite them to make up their own countdown variations—share them, draw them, sing them, and illustrate them.[25]

"Our Families/Our Friends" is a theme so rich in possibilities for field trips and classroom visitors that this entire text could be devoted to that relevant idea. Look through the extensive list of suggestions in the back of the book. Don't limit these events to a single celebration. These are ongoing possibilities and can connect to every other theme!

## IT ALL COMES TOGETHER

Janis Pechenik, a highly honored teacher,[26] is a shining example of a loving, enlightened, dedicated educator whose kindergartners grow into a warm, family-style community. Every Monday, Janis' children,

FIGURE 4–15    *A visit from Grandpa is a special time!*

some with special needs who receive services in speech, language, and physical and occupational therapy, join the classmates in a hugging reunion so emotional that it's as if the kids were away from each other for six weeks!

Now in her fifteenth year teaching kindergarten "my way," Janis is strong in her beliefs about the importance of children learning to live cooperatively and joyfully with each other, whatever their individual abilities and needs. When she first started her "inclusionary" settings, parents of children who were not considered "physically challenged" were reluctant to have their kids attend Janis' class, as they thought the "other" children would demand too much attention and their children would miss out academically.

Janis asked them to give it a few weeks and then decide. She and the school would understand if a change was requested. In all the years, not one child was ever removed by parent request.

How does she do it? She demonstrates in everything she says or does with the children: "*This is your family in school. Here our ways are fun, acceptance, awareness, love.* We work and play together. We always have playmates to watch over and watch out for each other. Especially on the playground. There are always lots of choices about where they're playing and with whom. With more introverted children who choose not to have play partners, I take out something exciting, like puppets or snap blocks, and play with that child. Invariably, the others join in.

"I love to play songs for the children like Thomas Moore's 'I Am Special' or 'At the Easel' or 'I Like You.' We sing together, then tell each other what we like about each other. We draw each other and draw pictures for each other. Oh, we make up lots of circle games. We sing and dance to Thomas Moore's 'Hokey Pokey Dokey.' Then we make up our own verses and take turns being leader. There's always singing and moving going on in our room. Through movement, singing, and playing, the children are always developing higher-level skills. Talking goes on all the time. Lots of cooperative learning. Children more skilled in one area may not be skilled in other areas. We help each other and learn to respect each other. One of my kindergartners reads on an eighth-grade level but can't skip. The other kids try very hard teaching him how to skip. His best friend in the classroom is a child with Down syndrome.

"Throughout the day we work and play together as a whole group. The first hour of every day we are all together. It takes us an hour to go through the calendar, days of the week, counting. We sing and dance the days of the week and our numbers. Unless they're listening to a story, five-year-olds won't sit still more than a few minutes! As long as I keep the kids moving, they're happy.

"We learn a new poem every single week. We write them in our classroom poetry book. Most of our children are doing inventive spelling with lots of pictures. *My children who scribble think they're writing in cursive!* My child reading on an eighth-grade level prints in all

FIGURE 4–16   *Our friends in school are like family!*

capital letters. In our room there's room for everybody in every stage of development. We respect and acknowledge each other's specific gifts and talents. Learning is an ongoing process in our class, among all members of our classroom family!"

## NOTES

1. Powell, R. D. 9/1998. "Reweaving Parents into the Fabric of Early Childhood Programs." *Young Children* 53 (5). pp. 60–67.

2. Bredekamp, S. and C. Copple. (editors). 1997. *Developmentally Appropriate Practice in Early Childhood Programs.* (rev. ed.). Washington, D.C.: NAEYC.

3. Sterling, M. 9/1998. "Building a Community Week by Week." *Educational Leadership* 56 (1). pp. 65–68.

4. The Loker School is in Wayland, Massachusetts.

5. Eldridge, M. 7/2001. "Parent Involvement: It's Worth the Effort." *Young Children* 56 (4). pp. 65–69.

6. Articles like "Fathers' Involvement in Programs for Young Children" by A. C. Guthrie, published in *Young Children*, 7/2000, pp. 77–79, reflect a new interest in the vitally important role fathers play in the lives of their children. Note: The National Fatherhood Initiatives <*www.fatherhood.org*>.

7. Polly Greenberg was editor of *Young Children* (NAEYC) for fourteen years and the author of numerous articles and essays. She is now writing full time. One of her highly acclaimed books is *The Devil Has Slippery Shoes: A Biased Biography of the Child Development Group of Mississippi.* It was originally published in 1969 by Macmillan and reissued in 1990 by the Youth Policy Institute in Washington, D.C. Another is *Character Development: Encouraging Self-Esteem in Infants, Toddlers and Two Year Olds*, which was published by NAEYC in 1991.

8. Lynda Barry's essay "The Sanctuary of School" appeared in *The New York Times*, Jan. 5, 1992, p. 58.

9. Raschka, C. 1993. *Yo! Yes?* New York: Scholastic.

10. Charney, R. 1991. *Teaching Children to Care: Management in the Responsive Classroom.* Greenfield, MA: Northeast Foundation for Children.

Kriete, R. 1999. *The Morning Meeting Book.* Greenfield, MA: Northeast Foundation for Children.

11. See "Your Assistant Is Getting Her Diaper Changed" by M. B. Chenfeld in *Teaching by Heart*, 2001. Redleaf Press. Reprinted from original article in *Young Children*.

12. Bailey, B. 1997. *There's Gotta Be a Better Way: Discipline That Works!* Oveido, FL: Loving Guidance, Inc.

13. Alice Aron Cohen taught kindergarten in P.S. 153, Bronx, New York. She is now a speech-language pathologist with the pre-K program, in Mamaronek, New York.

14. Wittman, S. C. illus. Gundersheimer, K. 1978. *A Special Trade.* New York: Harper and Row.

Barbara Topolosky directs the Early Childhood Program at the Leo Yassenoff Jewish Center, Columbus, Ohio.

15. Hausherr, R. 1997. *Celebrating Families.* New York: Scholastic.

Bertrand, G. D. illus. Howard, R. P. 1999. *Family, Familia.* Houston, TX: Pinata Books.

Say, A. 1997. *Allison.* Boston: Houghton Mifflin.

Dorrow, A. illus. Kleven, E. 1991. *Abuela.* New York: Dutton.

Ringgold, F. 1991. *Tar Beach.* New York: Crown.

Osofka, A. 1992. *My Buddy.* New York: Henry Holt.

Smith, C. 2000. *Jingle Dancer.* New York: William Morrow.

An example of an excellent book to help in understanding the more complicated challenges of meeting the needs of children from multi-ethnic, biracial families is

Wardle, F. 1999. *Tomorrow's Children: Meeting the Needs of Multiracial and Multiethnic Children at Home, in Early Childhood Programs and at School.* Denver: Center for the Study of Biracial Children.

This theme of reaffirming children from diverse multiethnic and multicultural backgrounds is so urgent that numerous articles and essays have been dedicated to it. An example of an outstanding resource is the themed issue, "Considering and Reconsidering Culture, Diversity and Early Childhood Education." 2001. *Young Children.* 56 (6). pp. 18–39.

2000. *My Two Grandmothers.* San Diego, CA: Harcourt.

An excellent children's book that reflects relations in a two-religion family is

Effin, O. illus. Hayashi, N. 2000. *My Two Grandmothers.* San Diego, CA: Harcourt

16. Steig, W. 1969. *Sylvester and the Magic Pebble.* New York: Simon and Schuster.

Linda Goldsmith and Jo Ann Bell taught together at the Leo Yassenoff Jewish Center, Columbus, Ohio.

17. Owocki, G. 1999. *Literacy Through Play.* Portsmouth, NH: Heinemann.

I hope the pendulum may be swinging back and our society may be rediscovering the importance of play. Even *Time* magazine, April 30, 2001, pp. 56–58, featured a major article, "Whatever Happened to Play?" by W. Kirn and W. Cole. In May 2001, a global conference on Children's Right to Play drew hundreds of participants from more than forty countries to Hofstra University. Don't downplay play!

18. Ella Jenkins' most recent honor was the 2002 Early Childhood

News Directors Choice Award for her recording *Songs, Rhythms and Chants for the Dance*. Information on Ella's numerous musical works can be found by contacting Smithsonian Folkways Recordings, 800-410-9815, or folkways@aol.com.

19. Myers, S. illus. Frazee, M. 2001. *Everywhere Babies*. San Diego, CA: Harcourt Brace.

20. Martin, B. Jr. 1983. *Brown Bear, Brown Bear, What Do You See?* New York: Holt, Rinehart and Winston.

21. Information about Greg and Steve's musical resources can be found at 800-548-4063 or <*www.gregandsteve.com*>.

22. Dorros, A. illus. McCully, E. A. 2000. *Ten Go Tango*. New York: HarperCollins.

    Hutchins, P. 1986. *The Doorbell Rang*. New York: Greenwillow.

    Rylant, C. 1993. *The Relatives Came*. New York: Aladdin.

23. Goldstone, B. illus. Cahoon, H. 2001. *Ten Friends*. New York: Henry Holt.

24. Sis, P. 1998. *Waving: A Counting Book*. New York: Greenwillow.

25. Merriam, E. illus. Gorton, J. 1999. *Ten Rosy Roses*. New York: HarperCollins.

26. Janis Pechenik teaches kindergarten at the Green Meadow School, East Greenbush, New York. She has received many honors, including Teacher of the Year. In April 2001, she was honored with the prestigious Thelma P. Lally award for Elementary Teacher of the Year from the College of Saint Rose, Albany, New York.

# THEME 5 | OTHERS WE MEET/ OUR WORLDS WIDEN

*If I am not for myself, who am I?*

*If I am only for myself, what am I?*

*Separate yourself not from the community.*
—Rabbi Hillel

\*

*It takes a whole village to educate a child.*
—African proverb

\*

*Every neighbor is a teacher.*
—Arab proverb

\*

*Mitakuye oyasin. (We are all related.)*
—Lakota nation

## THINK ABOUT IT

Please consider this theme a natural continuum linked to "Our Families/Our Friends." Just as the divisions in this book have blurry boundaries, overlapping and continuously interconnecting, so the many worlds of human beings flow one into another. As we journey from wombs to rooms, to, as John Holt describes in his concept of "world three," "the world on the other side of the door,"[1] our awareness and experiences expand. Beyond our closest, most immediate circles of family and friends, other people and ideas wait for our recognition. Beyond that door (or doors) are greater communities. My colleague, Liz Harzoff, inspired by the theme "Others We Meet/Our Worlds Widen," began a collection of notes elucidating specific ideas. Here are some excerpts from her list:

- All kinds of "otherness": language, age, gender, ethnic, rural-suburban-urban, racial, religious, cultural, family grouping, diverse abilities . . .
- What about the world of work? Who are the people around us who help us? Around school? Around the neighborhood?
- How can we approach people of different ages? Older adults? Teenagers? Babies? What about people from other ethnic groups who live in our community? Who speak other languages? What can we learn from people who participate in service projects?
- How do we approach people who may have physical challenges? People from environments different from ours?
- Start close to the students and yourself. Move outward to the rest of your school or center, the neighborhood, the area, the nearest population center, other parts of the United States, and finally to other countries.[2]

Add your own ideas about "others" in our ever-widening circles.

Sylvia Ashton-Warner's wise words advising us to remember that before we teach others, we must teach ourselves points directly to this theme. Because we are such significant influences on the lives of young children, our own attitudes and beliefs about reaching out to "others" we meet, our feelings about the worlds outside the door, will be as much *caught* as taught! The children recognize integrity and honesty in adults. They know inconsistency when they see it. I like to say they "sniff" it! They know immediately if you *really mean it* when you tack up a multicultural display on your bulletin board. Do you *really* reach out to people different from yourself? Are you open to welcoming those from diverse and unfamiliar backgrounds, ages, abilities into your heart? Into your room? Is your behavior consistent with the edifying charts encouraging *respect* and *cooperation*? Recently, I was invited to a school to celebrate the theme of peace. Symbols, words, and pictures illustrating that excellent theme wallpapered the rooms and halls. Peace was the talk of the school. With one group of third graders, I decided to share a lovely circle dance to a song about peace and being together in a happy way. We formed our circle. When I asked the kids to reach out and hold hands, a few children pulled their hands away from their neighbors. This is a visually hurtful image and a very hurtful image socially and emotionally. How could I go on with a dance about peace in a school that prided itself on honoring peace when children felt it was OK to reject their classmates? *Where does peace begin?* To add to this disappointing scenario, the teacher, who had already reprimanded a few children for not being good listeners, had no reaction to the incident. Had I not stopped the entire celebration to discuss the negative actions, I'm sure the teacher would never have mentioned it.

After talking together about how we feel when we're left out, humiliated; after asking the children next to me to demonstrate exactly

FIGURE 5–1    *Where does peace begin?*

how pulling hands away from each other looked; after we showed the opposite—naturally and easily holding hands together, I asked the group to please form a circle. All joined hands without hesitation. The children loved the peace dance and made some beginning discoveries about its meaning.

What is your role in intervening, taking a stand, protecting and securing a true feeling of safety and respect in your own group, clarifying values? How can we reach out to others when we feel frightened, rejected, humiliated in our very own room? How do we build a classroom community, a family feeling in our *wider* world and ideally in the world the children will one day govern when we permit acts of betrayal to the principles we say we believe? It all comes back to you, to me, to we, as teachers and role models.

*Childhood Education*, the journal of the Association for Childhood Education International, devoted its annual theme issue of 2001 to "The Global Village: Migration and Education."[3] This most moving series of vitally important essays touched on many aspects of finding ways to welcome and effectively teach children from different cultures, children who often bring painful and traumatic experiences with them. As I read each piece, I found myself saying, "These ideas and implications apply to *all* of our children and families. Understanding, respect, support, communication, helping newcomers become valued members of the school community, creating family, safe learning environments for every child are 'strategies' we need all the time!" But, we don't role model strategies! We teach by demonstrating ways of looking at others, relating to that world outside of ourselves. In light of the dark events of September 11, 2001, our challenges are immense. How do we travel with our children on this journey of widening worlds? Begin with this moment, taking small/large steps.

D'Angelo and Dixey wrote a very helpful and provocative article, "Using Multicultural Resources for Teachers to Combat Racial Prejudice in the Classroom," for *Early Childhood Education Journal*.[4] Discussing the immediate reality that each day our society is growing more diverse, the authors closed in on racial and ethnic prejudice and the responsibility of teachers to honestly examine our beliefs and attitudes. They remind us to be acutely aware of how our behavior influences our students. Three questions were posed to help teachers assess viewpoints and feelings.

1. Do I believe some races are more capable of learning and/or have greater intelligence than other races?
2. Do I model respectful and positive attitudes in the classroom for all races and ethnic groups?
3. Do I integrate race and ethnic issues in the curriculum exclusively through thematic units, holidays, and celebrations?

The effectiveness of multicultural education is limited when it's confined *only* to calendar dates, holidays, and special events. As with the concept of whole language, multicultural education can't be isolated from the daily lives of the children, from all the strands in the curriculum. It has to be part of the air we breathe in our daily lives.

We can learn from our young children. They are fascinated with their world, curious about everything and everyone. They have dozens of questions for the bus driver, the trash collector, the auto mechanic, the group of Andean musicians playing in their school lobby. They are still open, nonjudgmental. Most young children perceive people and occupations in horizontal ways. Most young children are color-full. They see people in colors beyond black and white. They see wrinkles on the faces of older folks and accept them without hesitation. They are reassured to see people working together, contributing to the success of the whole. They are strengthened by the interdependence of people and institutions. As they daily make meaning out of their lives, they learn about their place in the pattern. They find connections. Too soon they will learn some of the prejudices and stereotypes that still infect our society biases. As the *South Pacific* song reminds us, "We've got to be taught. . . ." The children look to us, their caring adults, for direction, for information. We communicate our beliefs and attitudes verbally and nonverbally every minute of the day!

This is a time for self-examination. Our excellent first-grade materials on community helpers (a standard course of study!) lose impact when our first-grade teacher speaks to the school custodian and cafeteria workers in a condescending manner, which the children pick up immediately. Do we hold stereotyped, biased opinions? Are we suspicious of new and strange languages, customs, occupations, and family relationships? We must listen to ourselves and each other, be willing to communicate honestly, to learn to understand that *different* does not mean *bad*, that labels are hurtful, that our words have power—the power of life and death of the spirit. Our body language has its own vocabulary.

When I began teaching in the fifties, resources were sparse in the field of what we now call "multicultural education" or "educating for diversity." Let's say such materials were practically nonexistent! In most instances, we had to "wing it." For a few years in the sixties, I worked with teachers around New York state under newly developed guidelines from the State Department of Education to develop curricula and activities that would strengthen intercultural understanding and relationships.

It was a great idea but many teachers and school systems were not ready for it. As I traveled New York with my ideals and ideas, activities and lesson plans on how to develop positive relationships with others, I met many very resistant educated people! We're comfortable with our prejudices! Why rock the boat? This is another example of self-discovery. *What are your beliefs and commitments?*

Now, in this new millennium, we are not out there "winging it"! Influential educators like Louise Derman-Sparks and her widely acclaimed and very used *Anti-Bias Curriculum: Tools for Empowering Young Children* have strengthened schools and teachers around the country with practical, accessible, inspirational resources and activities that help children understand diversity and resist the harmful impact of bias. Powerful organizations like the Southern Poverty Law Center, which publishes *Teaching Tolerance*, and the Anti-Defamation League share ideas that work in this important and noble goal and are helping spread ways and means of achieving a more understanding, accepting, respectful society—a true democratic, diverse country. Resources abound in this crucially important area. They help steer the way![5]

Take the wide road when you think about "others we meet." Any suggestion from Liz Harzoff's notes or any idea can be the grain of sand through which you and your children discover the world! Be inclusive in your definition of "others." In the expanding worlds of young children, TV characters, cartoons, storybook characters, dolls, animals, and puppets are often as real and believable as next-door neighbors.

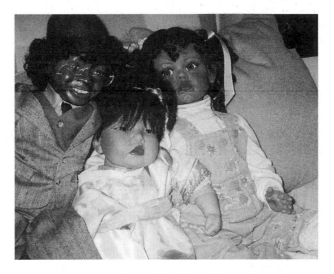

FIGURE 5–2    *Multicultural dolls help kids learn about others.*

This theme continues and extends the life lessons of openness, respect, mutuality, friendship, and welcome to others we meet along the journey. Don't we want our children to live in a society that recognizes individuality, differences, and similarities and builds positive interactions and relationships? Such qualities of mind and heart are sorely needed in this very complex, often frightening world. Maybe, just maybe, if we help children reach out and hold hands together in a circle dance, help children learn that rejecting and humiliating others is painful and unacceptable, the hands of those children will not be the ones that write headlines of violence in years to come.

## DISCOVERY TIMES/WONDER TIMES: POINTS OF INTEREST

- The success of a community depends on everyone doing a good job, taking responsibility, and caring about and cooperating with others.
- Everyone's work is important and should be appreciated. Isn't it astonishing to think about all the kinds of work possible for people to do? Explore the Yellow Pages!
- People, in their work and in their lives, contribute to the well-being of others.
- People depend on one another and have responsibilities toward one another. (I bet you can think of a hundred ways people help one another!)

- If people work hard, learn special skills, practice a lot, and achieve certain levels of accomplishment, they should be able to do any job to which they aspire.
- Sometimes the work people do is easily recognized and understood, but there are many kinds of jobs that are not as immediately obvious (doesn't someone shape the holes in doughnuts?). Obvious or subtle, all contribute to the working of the whole community.
- So many kinds of people, languages, customs, and cultures appear different from our own; we can find ways to learn about, get to know, and understand them. People always have ways of connecting with one another. It's fascinating to realize that with all the diversity, we are still members of the human family and have so many things in common. (Can you think of ten?)
- We have so many strengths, talents, skills, questions, and ideas about how our world works and the many wonders of our world. We have important contributions to make to others.

## SUGGESTED VOCABULARY

| | | | |
|---|---|---|---|
| neighbor | job | mail carrier | computer |
| school | chore | police officer | word |
| teacher | assignment | mechanic | processor |
| classmate | responsible | doctor | equipment |
| partner | cook | dentist | tools |
| principal | clean | social worker | ladders |
| nurse | store | clinic | art supplies |
| bus | gas station | volunteer | artist |
| bus driver | post office | Scout leader | studio |
| custodian | firehouse | ambulance | theater |
| helper | laundry | subway | sculptor |
| community | factory | taxi | symphony |
| neighborhood | office | airplane | instruments |
| street people | hospital | fire engine | TV |
| different | market | library | movies |
| same | supermarket | museum | videos |
| share | shopping | zoo | cassettes |
| repair | center | farm | magazines |
| fix | beauty parlor | city | books |
| collect | barber | country | cameras |
| sort | shoe repair | machinery | languages |
| clean | garage | skills | understand |
| customs | uniform | mayor | African |
| accent | food pantry | librarian | American |
| worker | truck | telephone | Asian |
| work | delivery | typewriter | American |

| Hispanic/ | Muslim | college | president |
| Latino | church | university | governor |
| Native | synagogue | welfare | United |
| American | mosque | worker | Nations |
| Christian | world | radio | Homeless |
| Jewish | senior citizen | news | shelter |
| Hindu | nursing home | newspaper | |

*Note:* Continuously add to these vocabulary suggestions with your students. Each word is a universe of possibilities!

## TALK/LISTEN/READ/WRITE: THE GIFTS OF LANGUAGE

### *More Talk About Play*

Remember, play's the thing in the lives and the learning of young children! Even in environments minimally equipped with articles of clothing, toys, scrounged stuff, children will play firefighter, police officer, doctor, nurse (all the occupations they know about!). Be aware of the importance of adding to play areas multicultural tools, utensils, clothing, books, blocks, and pictures as well as dolls representing diverse peoples and cultures. When children are surrounded with such props, their language expands along with greater familiarity with heretofore unfamiliar objects and the ideas they represent.[6]

Keep in mind that when children are at play in safe and loving environments, they are talking and listening to each other all the time.

FIGURE 5–3    *It's fun to play construction worker!*

You may have to enter their play occasionally to problem solve (or help them problem solve), but talking and listening are basic components of the play process. Blend in reading and writing! Even the youngest children learn very early how to hold pencils and crayons. Their scribble is their first written language, which soon evolves into recognizable letters and words.

I visited a kindergarten class that had been playing airport ever since their field trip to the airport more than a week before. They couldn't get enough of the game and kept adding ideas: posters of different places and people; books about other cultures; notepads; dolls representing diversity; berets and kimonos; a table turned into a ticket counter; chairs arranged like an airplane with a row down the middle; flight attendants serving beverages; mechanics fixing planes . . . no one was left out! Every child had a part in the ongoing drama.

Playing restaurant is another very popular game in the lives of young children. So many skills and concepts are mixed into their recipes, menus, signs, posters, place mats, decorations, dialogues, and decision making. Restaurant workers must be courteous and welcome all diners. It grieves me deeply to see so many play areas where genuine,

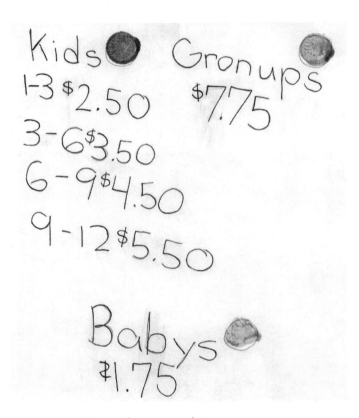

FIGURE 5–4   *C'mon! The price is right!*

meaningful learning happens removed from the rooms of early child-hood programs. If you doubt the value of such multifaceted experi-ences for our young students, sit down at one of their tables, read over their menu (you may have to translate it from the hieroglyphics of early writing), listen to their "specials" as your server greets you, and enjoy the meal, which will probably reflect an understanding of nutritious foods! The price is right!

### Talk About Spontaneity and Serendipity

Be open to the wonderful, unexpected gifts offered to you every day—the new child, a visiting relative, a telephone repair truck, or something shared by one of your students that ignites imagination and explo-ration. When the three exchange teachers from Kenya walk down the halls of your school, do you say, "We're not ready for Kenya yet!" or do you say, "Come on in!"[7]

### Talk Times: Shared Experiences and Observations

Every day, we need to make time for children to share observations and new experiences. Teachers need to share, too! When I was a child, I was amazed that whatever needed to be done, someone did it! Recently, talking with kindergartners about the ingenuity and industriousness of human beings, I wondered aloud, "Isn't it amazing, friends, that some-one is always able to do a job that needs to be done?"

That little comment triggered an avalanche of ideas about the kinds of work people do to help make things succeed. Brainstorming opened new opportunities for play, talk, drama, music, visual arts, and other as-pects of the curriculum. The children played veterinarians, post office workers, checkout clerks at supermarkets, and electricians.

When we teach in the key of life, we help children learn how to meet new situations, people, and ideas with courtesy and respect. Sometimes that's a challenge! Our own attitudes toward others spread easily. We need to be sensitive talkers and compassionate listeners so our own fears, suspicions, and prejudices are continually reduced. These talk times are excellent opportunities to model and encourage nonsex-ist language, open, respectful comments about people in their work, in their diversity. Be alert to how our language often reflects stereotyped thinking. Help the children learn to think and communicate in non-sexist ways. Doctors are women. Men are nurses. Men and women drive buses, deliver mail, put out fires, and work at construction. Change traditional titles like mailman, policeman, and fireman to letter carrier, police officer, and firefighter.

If the children are speaking about a person or people from a culture, race, or religion unfamiliar to them, be sure their language doesn't reflect prejudice. Model respectful words. Don't ignore labeling and name call-ing. Your sensitive but clear responses help children clarify values.

## Sometimes the World Comes to Us!

How do we handle unexpected situations? The parent who becomes unemployed; newly arrived immigrant families with very different customs and no English; the children from a homeless shelter or transient migrant worker family; the visually impaired new classmate? These are common events in classrooms and programs of countless teachers and children. Here are opportunities for the gifts of language to have deeper significance. As we talk *with* our children, freely sharing feelings and thoughts about such very difficult but relevant topics, we must match our words with action, with behavior. Do we see the rich possibilities for meaningful experiences within these situations?

When a timid, weary, raggedy newcomer stood at the doorway with the principal, her soon-to-be teacher, Dawn, did *not* greet the child with a frustrated, annoyed expression, as did her teacher in the last school she went to. Despite an already overcrowded class, Dawn smiled warmly at the frightened child, greeted her with a hug, turned to her curious students, and asked who would like to be the helpers of their new classmate and make room for her to share a desk until another desk was delivered. Dawn's genuinely caring welcome, words, and actions in harmony, inviting the children to reach out, made *all* the difference. It marked the way! The newcomer quickly became a member of the class family, all the children wanted to be her helpers, and Dawn added another valuable member to her already too many students!

The gifts of language mean we talk to each other. We listen. We write or dictate our ideas, feelings, thoughts. We read the many words surrounding us—in books, boards, doors, desks, charts, windows, and so on.

Don't we want our students to learn that all people have basic needs such as food, shelter, clothing, a sense of self, acceptance, and respect?

In talking together about Cindy's father, who is unemployed, we need to remind Cindy that he is a good dad, a good neighbor, a good citizen. Our homeless children are people of value whose contributions are important. Our frightened new child who just arrived from Cambodia, with memories and experiences unfamiliar to most of us, learns reassurance and encouragement from her classmates and you. The hearing impaired boy accompanied by his signer finds you, his teacher, and his classmates a supportive, sharing group. Look within yourself for ways to understand and accept situations and relationships that may be unfamiliar to you. Look to your children for examples of compassion and helpfulness. Your commitment is to help strengthen your young students with feelings of confidence, courage, and self-worth, however diverse and difficult their situations. Talking and listening helps a lot. Writing together and reading about it helps. Notes and letters, welcome mats, posters, chants, welcome cheers, and poems enrich the experiences. In the many ways our children have opportunities to work and play together, hopeful outcomes are possible.

## Kids Care!

Throughout the book, the importance of strengthening feelings of caring and kindness is reiterated! Many young children instinctively respond to troubled people or emotionally disturbing situations. Toddlers give sad or crying adults their binkies or blankets for comfort! Young children often cry along with another child in distress. We know that young children will perform many bumper sticker reminders of "random acts of kindness." *Phi Delta Kappan* devoted a special section of the journal to the theme "Youth and Caring." Numerous books and articles focus on this important topic.[8]

Because our youngest children are bombarded with media images of daily and hourly events, they learn about "others" very quickly. They need to talk about these often disturbing stimuli that bring the world to their immediate attention. Talking leads to action! News reports from around the country described how young children, including kindergartners and first graders, wrote letters and cards and illustrated gifts to cheer the firefighters, police officers, and rescue workers following the tragedies of September 11. Because they read that the rescue workers needed gloves to do their unbearable work, young children collected gloves and with their letters of love, sent the *care* packages to New York City.

Talk times lead to writing, reading, dramatizing, singing. I heard of one group of kindergartners that sang a medley of songs and sent their tape, letters, and pictures to the rescue workers to cheer them up. When given the opportunities, when you set an example by your words and actions, children respond positively with caring and compassion.

At holiday time, bins were packed in schools around the country with toys, cards, and letters contributed by all the students who wanted to send gifts to children whose holiday season looked grim. Be sure to gather the children's ideas and find ways of extending them into action. Young children are action figures!

## Pen Pals Across the Street and Across the Miles

All around the country young children and their teachers are enthusiastically involved in building close relationships with people of different age groups, areas, and, often, institutions like senior citizens groups; nursing home residents; children in hospitals or shelters; and children in schools representing diverse cultures. Pictures, letters, postcards, posters, stories, messages, collages are some of the gifts flowing back and forth between the new friends. I visited a nursing home where the residents were eagerly awaiting the arrival of their kindergarten "kids." Colorful paper plates, ice cream and cookies, songs and the exchange of cards were some of the activities featured for the special visit. Helping children reach out, practice kindness and thoughtfulness, and share with others is really very simple. But *you* must decide if that commitment is one you want to make. The children are already there, ready and willing!

### Cards, Notes, and Snail Mail

Sometimes in this speed-driven, high-tech millennium, we forget the satisfaction, feeling of goodwill, and connectedness derived from writing notes and letters to friends and others we meet. Many of our young children don't have grandparents living nearby. Many of our young children have little interaction with older people. This intergenerational connection is so important! Our older citizens and our children learn from each other, form bonds and friendships. Here are opportunities to invite community seniors to visit your children on a regular basis—reading with them, being with them. Notes and pictures flow back and forth. Greeting cards for all seasons and reasons are so appreciated. The gifts of language really involve *gifts of language*! Nothing is more exciting to young children than to receive mail. I've been enjoying my poet-in-residence role in a collaborative creative writing/visual arts program called DepARTures between the Columbus Public Schools and the Columbus Museum of Art. After I visit each of the ten fifth-grade classes, spending a half day with each of them writing poetry, I always send them a note or a postcard. I was so delighted to hear from the chil-

FIGURE 5–5   *I love getting letters from children.*

dren how much those little messages meant to them! Of course, many of them write back to me. We have to support our postal system!

### Books Open Doors to Others and Other Ways

Nowadays we have literature and resources that cover every topic needed to enrich our children's learning. Stack your shelves and tables with rich samplings of books celebrating the kids' traditional favorite occupations—firefighters, police officers, and so on. But, go beyond the familiar and offer stories about trash collectors, school custodians, sign painters, artists, even a zamboni driver! All contribute to the betterment of the community! All are exciting themes and plots for children to enjoy, talk about, write, illustrate, and dramatize. Say's *Sign Painter* expands awareness of how the visuals in our everyday environment are created. *The Feet in the Gym* helps children gain new respect for the school custodian who shines the gym floor so kids can leave their marks! *Stop That Garbage Truck* extends children's fascination with that everyday taken-for-granted necessary helper. *The Painter* gives young readers an insight into the life of an artist. Even in places where there is little ice, our young students delight in the idea of a zamboni; *Sam the Zamboni Man*, tells of a man who drives that special truck that spreads and evens coats of ice on an ice rink.

If you run out of ideas to read, talk about, play, sing, or illustrate examples of community helpers, enjoy *Community Helpers from A–Z* by Bobbie Kalman. If you're feeling poetic, share Gary Paulsen's *Work Song* and discover the poetry in work and workers.[9]

To help children learn about people very different from themselves, excellent materials are always ready to be welcomed into your room to read and inspire ideas of extending the stories into meaningful activities.

Shy kids, new kids, first-day-of-school jitters when the world is filled with the great "unknown" are themes all children relate to. Our first "others" are those we don't know, people new to us. Katie Couric's *Brand New Kid* is a touching story that triggers very relevant conversations. How do we welcome a new person who seems very different from ourselves into our midst? How do we learn to reach out to others? How would we feel if people made fun of us? Julie Danneberg's *First Day Jitters* captures the almost universal anxiety of wondering what a new school situation holds in store. Ivy Green finally welcomes school in *First Day, Hooray!* after a night of worrying and wondering about her new school scene. *Wemberly Worried* tells about a child who worries about everything! Especially about the new kids she would meet on that first scary day of school; about the teacher being mean; about the kids making fun of her name; about getting lost. Illustrated with very unusual photographs, *Russ and the Almost Perfect Day* will be talked about by the children for a long time. In it, Russ discovers a lot about friendship and reaching out to a child he doesn't know.

FIGURE 5–6   *It's hard being a new kid.*

In this era of inclusion, children must learn to relate positively to others with physical challenges. Brian is blind but he and his beautiful parakeet have excellent lessons for all to learn. *Brian's Bird* teaches about acceptance and love. *Moses Goes to a Concert* and *Moses Goes to School* tell of a boy who, with his hearing impaired classmates, communicates clearly in sign language while enjoying the everyday activities typically developed children know so well. The universality of understanding and empathy, acceptance and respect is built into the text and pictures on every page. Make time for your young readers to learn some simple sign language words!

So many alphabet books are in print that the list is dizzying! An example of a beautiful alphabet book that introduces a culture unfamiliar to most children is *Navajo ABC: A Dine Alphabet Book*. Children who know little or nothing about people of Asian heritage find reading, talking, and enjoying extended activities inspired by *Henry's First Moon Birthday* all valuable experiences. Even though people look different, speak in other languages, eat different foods, and have different customs, they share many common bonds.

Such books and resources are available under the multicultural umbrella that the National Council of Teachers of English, NCTE, released—a third edition of *Kaleidoscope: A Multicultural Booklist for Grades K–8*. Remember, books are not only ends in themselves but excellent means to wider and richer ends—understanding and learning about our ever-expanding worlds, making connections, finding meanings. Read, tell, talk, discuss, write about, illustrate, sing about . . . extend your experiences.[10]

*Others We Meet/* **161**
*Our Worlds*
*Widen*

## MUSIC MAKERS/MOVERS AND SHAKERS

Tell the truth—isn't it difficult to sustain suspicion of a people or a culture different from your own when you enjoy their music and dance? The arts have been so often referred to as the "universal language," one that criss-crosses time and maps and links us together. I like to think of the arts as the connective tissue that keeps the structure of the human spirit intact. Celebrating concepts through music, dance, and play are truly joyful ways of learning. When I visit early childhood programs and hear no music (singing, instruments, rhythms, chanting), when there are no signs of movement (dance, play), I despair for those kids. *What are they learning* and *how?* You don't need to master an instrument, be an agile, graceful dancer, or have a trained voice to share memorable musical times with your students.

A poignant reminder of the power of music and the love for music by all peoples lies in the headline news stories following the freeing of Afghanistan cities in the aftermath of the terrorist attacks of September 11. After years of total repression and the forbidding of music, poetry, and the arts by the extremist Taliban rulers, the people of Afghanistan immediately turned on their radios, played and sang music, danced in the streets to rejoice in their very fragile shreds of freedom. The metaphor of the canary in the coal mine takes on greater meaning when we think about the canary who can smell the odorless poisonous gas sometimes emitted in coal mines and warns the miners of the danger by its silence. By its death. As long as the canary is singing, the air isn't poisoned. When the singing stops, everyone is in grave danger. The arts have been compared to the singing of the canary.

We must keep our singing alive and strong! Our music, our arts full of courage, spirit, joy, and hope!

### *Music and Rhythms from Around the World*

Every culture that has ever lived on earth created its music. Many instruments are common, beloved and used the world over, like drums, flutes, maracas, bells, stringed instruments. The astonishing variety of instruments is, as the kids say, "cool"!

In an interview with Bob Blue, the acclaimed songwriter, teacher, and performer talked about children's love of music and song. "It's really important for music to be fun. . . . One way to deal with cultural differences is to bring in music from around the world. Just the tunes from around the world give children a sense of other cultures. Learning to sing songs in other languages and what those songs mean expands their awareness of the world. . . ."[11]

Remember, our youngest children are the fastest learners of languages. We miss the boat when we don't introduce children to languages other than English until they're in middle school or high school! (Who are the slow learners?) Leslie Zak sings in sixteen languages! When she shares her music with children of all ages, they quickly learn songs in Japanese, Swahili, Russian, Hebrew, Arabic, and more. All the songs are simple, repetitive, delightful. They sing of nature, friends, seasons, weather, playfulness. Children easily recognize the stories, the lessons in the songs from around the world.[12]

National treasures like Ella Jenkins and Pete Seeger were pioneers in introducing the world of music to the world of early childhood. Now, almost every musician, composer, and singer creating music for children understands the importance of offering a smorgasbord of works representing the diverse cultures and peoples of the world.

If you're focusing on a specific culture, play music or teach a song, dance, or game from that culture. Be sure families and community resources are invited to share such gifts. Libraries are waiting for you to check out their unusually ample sources of multicultural music. The materials are there. The children are ready and eager! And they are waiting for you to share joyful times with them, not instruct them in the tight structure of a folk dance or game with absolute rights and wrongs and correcting of children who don't "get it." You don't need to know any folk dances to invite the children to listen to the rhythms of the music and let the music move them. All people clap, jump, bounce, sway, tap, skip, turn, and kick. The children's own freely interpreted movement to rhythms come very close to the actual folk dance patterns from those specific traditions. If you want your students to enjoy the delight of moving to exciting music, *you must enjoy it with them*! Teaching is a moving experience!

The great American poet Langston Hughes wrote eloquently about the universality of music and rhythm. He wrote: "Rhythm is something we share in common, you and I, with all the plants and animals and people in the world, and with the stars and moon and sun, and all the whole vast wonderful universe beyond this wonderful earth which is our home."[13]

### Work Songs

Throughout history people sang as they worked—on canals, railroads, ships, ranches, and farms. Work songs popular with children of all ages include "Sixteen Tons," "Pick a Bale of Cotton," "Erie Canal," "Banana Boat Song," "Rock Island Line," and "John Henry." When you enjoy work songs with your children, be sure to include songs from other cultures.

Fill your room with the sound of singing and music! Add movement and drama!

Compose and improvise original songs honoring community helpers, classroom helpers. Present them as gifts to those special people. Invite puppets to sing along, choreograph movement patterns (the children have great ideas); in safe and loving environments, they freely share. Don't wait for Secretaries' Day to honor the school secretary. Turn the celebration into a parade! When the pre-Ks invited their bus driver into the room for a surprise, he glowed as the children sang their original song to him expressing their appreciation for his work!

### Movement Games of the World's People

Even when they meet a person who initially appears to be different, the children soon learn that people of unfamiliar backgrounds and situations offer much to share and enjoy and have many things in common.

Every culture features circle games/dances in which people take turns going into the center, performing some movement that the others follow, and choosing another person to be the leader in the center of the circle. These variations of follow the leader are universal. Find chants that you know and love, use music easy to circle to, and dance to any and every culture. Discover the ways your children enjoy this kind of game. Books like Mary Lankford's *Hopscotch Around the World* or Jane Yolen's *Street Rhymes Around the World* are examples of excellent resources that inspire you to play with your children in old and simple ways.[14]

All peoples have variations of hand-clapping games like patty cake. Nowadays, our city kids have lifted those patterns to new heights of complexity and creativity. Watch children sit together on stoops or playground benches and perform dazzling feats of eye-hand coordination, small and gross motor skills, high-level language development, counting, sequential learning, listening skills, comprehension, rhythm, and timing as they show you their hand-clapping routines.

When children learn to love the songs, dances, games, and stories of cultures and people unfamiliar or strange to them, they break down barriers and turn keys in locks that open new doors.

### A Note About Children with Diverse Abilities

No game, dance, or song was chiseled in stone on some sacred mountain! Be flexible, playful, and inclusive! No child should ever be left out! *Change the rules to make it possible for everyone to participate.* With a group of first graders I was celebrating a Chippewa story about the sun hiding and darkening the earth because the people were so mean to each other. Only when the children flew up to the sky to the house of the sun did the sun slowly come out from the stormy clouds and begin to brighten the darkness. One of the children was in a wheelchair. As the dancing children circled with their rhythmic movement to Native American powwow music, she rolled her wheelchair around with the others. It took hardly an instant of communication to give her the idea of steering into the center of the circle and hiding her eyes. She was a terrific sun and the whole gym beamed as she slowly revealed her face and began shining on her classmates!

There's no rule that says you have to do "head, shoulders, knees, and toes" if some children can't move their heads or their shoulders. Change it to "eyes, eyebrows, noses, and chins" so everyone succeeds!

Know what your children *can* do and integrate those skills into any song, game, or dance.[15]

### Dances of the World's People

As the group of kindergartners filed barefoot into the dance studio, Amy Polovick talked about bringing the world to the children.[16]

"I always show places on maps, introduce the music, movement games to the music. . . . But let's back up—we spend most of our time showing the human element right in our classroom. . . . We go beyond verbal . . . moving together, building connections every day so no one is ever an outsider. . . . These lessons have to be taught within the classroom community—then we are strong enough within ourselves to expand. . . . It really starts with *us right here together*. . . . Now we can look 'out there. . . .' "

Very often dances from different cultures express various kinds of work—numerous dances from around the world show aspects of farming, transportation, building, and mining. Not only can we honor the work people do in dances, but we can also honor their cultures. People the world over celebrate seasons, friendships, important events, rites of passage, natural wonders. All people have processions for special occasions. You can't go wrong if you honor a visitor from another culture by finding music from that culture and presenting a welcome parade or procession. If you can learn simple dances from other cultures, that's wonderful. If not, use music from the different cultures. People the world over dance in circles. Listen to the music. Let the rhythms move you. Circles can walk, march, stamp, and skip. They can change directions: clockwise and counterclockwise. They can face the center and clap and jump. Your children will have excellent movement ideas that will fit perfectly to the music no matter how unfamiliar.

### So Many Choices! What Will We Be When We Grow Up?

Books like *Career Day* by Anne Rockwell and *Jobs People Do* by Christopher Maynard inspire a myriad of activities from dramatic play to games

FIGURE 5–7    *What fun to be bakers and bake real treats!*

to riddles to movement patterns to songs to your own Career Day or Days![17] The Rockwells introduce special visitors to the class who share their work. The children love to turn themselves into orchestras playing beautiful music, paleontologists digging for dinosaur bones, and crossing guards directing traffic. Each career suggestion can be played and dramatized separately as you read along or invite the children to show their favorites and add on (always) any of their ideas not included in the book. Celebrate the careers with a parade of workers! Choose lively music from diverse cultures. Improvise movement that describes different kinds of work. Add words, drama, creative writing, or songs.

### Stories, Rhymes, Songs Travel the World

Where is it written that Jack Be Nimble jumps over a candlestick only in America? Can't Jack and his nimble friends run and jump over a candlestick in Japan or Spain or West Africa? Wee Willie Winkie and the other Town Criers have run/danced/hopped/skipped/leaped around towns the world over. Easily following the choreography chanted in the rhyme, the children demonstrate upstairs/downstairs/knocking/shouting/rocking/time ticking in global rhythms.

This is the era of folktales and stories from around the world.

Just as our singers and songwriters are committed to expanding and enriching their repertories to represent music from the world's countries and cultures, so our libraries, bookstores, and storytellers are bringing the rich diversity of global literature to our children, pulling the world closer every day. We have a plethora of possibilities.[18] Choose any culture. Collections of tales from that particular people wait for your consideration and are ready to engage your children. If you want a more eclectic offering, a representation of a variety of cultural treasures, you'll have many resources to enjoy. I always look for stories with movement, music, and play possibilities. Stories that naturally and immediately inspire musical, rhythmic, drama, and dance interpretations. Stories, poems, and songs that are easily illustrated and inspire creative writing. Stories to sing and dance to! The Asian Monkey King, West African Ananci, Native American Turtle, Winnie the Pooh and his many friends and neighbors are examples of beloved stories easy to move to and sing about. Remember, throughout history, storytellers sang/danced/mimed/chanted/enacted their stories. Costumes, makeup, musical instruments, props, banners, masks, and puppets traditionally accompanied the celebration of stories! Our young children naturally integrate ideas. Encourage them to recognize common threads in many stories of the world. Think of how many variations of Cinderella have been documented! Tricksters play their mischief in every culture! Familiar characters with different names and living in different times and places are recognized by the children. After weeks of enjoying stories in the most multidimensional ways possible, a first grader asked, "Mimi, did the Wicked Witch know the Giant (from *Jack in the Beanstalk*)?" A greater underlying lesson is built into these valuable, enriching experiences. Children begin to appreciate that people throughout the world and through all time have had very similar feelings and needs: fears, courage, disappointment, dreams, wondering, problem solving, searching, friendship, love . . . the substance of folk literature, of song and dance, interrelated and inseparable.

If you are teaching a more homogeneous group of children with minimal experiences with people different from themselves, *it's urgent that you surround them and immerse them in rich multicultural materials and activities.*

## ALL WAYS ART

### Create a Multicultural Arts Environment

I hope that by now you can't help but think of your room as a dynamic space/environment that is always in process—full of action, exploration, and participation. Your space is more than a room, more than, say, "Kindergarten Room 4." It's a gallery. It's a museum. It's an archeological dig. It's a convention center. It's an exhibit hall. Walls are for pictures, painting, murals, collages, posters, and portraits. Hooks are for hanging mobiles, balloons, and sculptures. Windows are for painted colors. Your room tells a story. Is it product-centered or process-centered? Does it reflect the excitement, the energy of what's happening with your children, or is it perfectly framed in static, packaged images mail-ordered from commercial catalogs? Be eclectic in your gathering of

FIGURE 5–8    *You'll know a process-centered room when you walk in the door.*

visual materials, especially if, as we noted, your group of children reflects more uniformity. The need for them to be surrounded by faces and images that show diversity is vital. In many classrooms around the country, the only faces different from theirs seen by the children are pictures on their walls. Always make room for the faces and stories of people, for people at work, for the rich complexity and fascinating heterogeneity of the human family. Keep the images flowing throughout the year.

Because your scrounge materials will always be plentiful, you will never be short of magazines, cards, scraps, snips, ribbons, buttons, glitter, sparkles, or treasures that most people toss, like Styrofoam packing chips and fast-food containers. You and your children will be able to enjoy hands-on visual arts experiences daily.

Bonnie Neugebauer offers extensive suggestions for creating a consistently multicultural classroom. She reminds us that when we "bring bits and pieces of the world into the daily life of our programs, the unfamiliar becomes familiar; what was outside our experience becomes part of our frame of reference. From that point on we have real objects and experiences that serve as a basis for asking questions and initiating conversations." And let me add, inspiring works of art, play, drama, music, and movement.[19]

### *Decorate Ordinary Objects*

Creative teachers who are dedicated to bringing "the world into their classrooms" are scavengers. Their rooms are rich with such stimulating items as photos, posters, materials, designs, instruments, paintings,

FIGURE 5–9   *Kids are always ready to create.*

sculptures, artifacts from diverse cultures. UNICEF offers extraordinary materials, as do travel agencies—vivid images of the world's people and places. In such colorful and dynamic rooms, children discover that people throughout history and from places around the globe honor objects by decorating them: plates, flower pots, and bowls are painted; instruments are enlivened with feathers, beads, ribbons; useful items like rugs, pillows, tablecloths, and chairs boast imaginative and traditional patterns. These realities inspire children to follow that idea and paint and decorate their own everyday useful objects. Talk about and explore patterns, colors, designs, and symbols that are meaningful to the children. Encourage them to add those visual images to their own homemade instruments, kitchen utensils, housekeeping centers, dramatic play areas, walls, spaces.

### Symbols, Colors, and Patterns

A good example of the universality of many symbols is a study of the flags of the world. Note how many have stars, circles, lines, and stripes of colors. Note the variation of common designs: animal shapes, nature patterns like clouds, flowers, rainbows, mountains, trees—beloved images shared by people the world over, carved in totems, chiseled on jewelry, tie-dyed on shirts, painted on stone and wood, waved in flags and banners.

After the events of September 11, 2001, American flags and flag patterns of all sizes appeared everywhere in the country.

What do flags and symbols mean to us? To the people whose culture they represent? Why does Mahila's Hawaiian grandmother wear

FIGURE 5–10  *Children proudly wear the flag symbol!*

clothing of tapa print design? Patrick's uncle Daniel always wear a green shamrock, not just on St. Patrick's Day?

Encourage your children to design their own flags, banners, totems, posters, signs. Add words! This is an excellent way to highlight shapes and colors.

### Illustrate Song Books

As you write down the words to the songs children sing (their own original songs included), invite them to illustrate the songs. Imagination will mix with awareness as they create images for songs from cultures different from their own. I like to talk, sing, play, and dance *before* visual arts and writing! The children's heads are filled with lively and vivid ideas easily translated with greater clarity into visual art works.

Songs like Raffi's "One Light, One Sun" are excellent examples of deeply meaningful concepts we want our children to learn and live. One sun over all the earth. Jack Grunsky sings the idea that one sun shines over all of us, rain falls on all of us. Red Grammer's haunting song "We Are All Brothers, We Are All Sisters" is a curriculum in itself of helping children learn about others in our world.[20] No matter our differences, we are all members of the human family and must learn to live together in peace. Children sing, dance to, and interpret those ideas into very moving and powerful pictures and posters.

### The Colors of the World

My mother came to America from Rumania when she was fourteen years old. She lived in New York City till her mid-eighties, when she moved to Ohio to be near us. Just before she left New York, she sat with my father on a city bus in downtown Manhattan as it neared Rockefeller Center. She looked at all the proudly waving flags of the world, searching for the Rumanian flag. Alas, she forgot the colors of that flag. Miraculously, she remembered a little song that all the very young children in Rumania learned that taught them the colors of the flag. She sang it to herself in Rumanian. Instantly, she found the Rumanian flag! Eighty-three years after she learned the song, she remembered!

Cultures have their favored colors. Chinese people wrap gifts in red. Purple was a royal color. Halloween's colors are orange and black. Color patterns mark traditional textiles of many cultures. Polynesian people favor tapa prints and splashes of brightly colored nature designs. Kente cloth has great meaning in African cultures. Let the colors of the world's peoples inspire our children to paint their own interpretations, to enrich their own works. Children are especially excited about materials shared by classroom visitors or field trips. These are such potentially peak experiences that *not* to give children the opportunities for follow-up activities is truly a sad disservice.

FIGURE 5–11  *Dylan shares his great-grandmother's story of coming from Romania to America.*

FIGURE 5-12    *The clothing, patterns, colors of the world's people are beautiful.*

## A People Procession

When the children talk about, read about, visit with, and observe people coming into your room and your lives, honor those experiences with symbols, cards, pictures, posters, collages, sculptures, and mobiles—works of every style and dimension.

Now more than ever before, our children are learning about people unfamiliar to them. Whether from firsthand experiences or through books, posters, pictures, TV, and movies, we demonstrate our new awareness, our new knowledge, in colors, shapes, forms, and textures.

Inspired by the diversity of the human family, our children choose their favorite ways to express exciting ideas—masks, sculptures, clay, paintings, drawings, collages, constructions. Encourage them to look carefully at the beauty of features, skin colors, hairstyles, clothing of the fascinating people of the world. Remember, our youngest children's artwork looks very much like the walls of ancient cave ancestors with dots, lines, designs, strokes, symbol-like images. As they are introduced to the rich variety of faces, bodies, cultural patterns, their works are enriched, as are their minds and hearts.

## Images of Peace

We all want it, pray for it, long for it. But, how do we express the idea of peace, then translate that into a shape, a design, a contraction, a mobile, a poster, a mosaic, jewelry, a T-shirt, a place mat, a banner, a sculpture, a poster, a card, a quilt?

Talk first. Sharing feelings about a peaceful world, community, classroom, family . . . (in that order?) is an essential component of comprehending such a concept. For most young children, the world is their immediate surroundings and familiar faces. The idea of a greater world expands through their own experiences, through the media, through means under our "control" and ways often out of our control.

Write all the ideas shared. I jotted notes from a first-grade gathering as I stopped by the room on the way to the gym. Peace was the topic. Some of the ideas reflecting peace offered by the children were:

Peace is:  people shaking hands      nobody yelling
people helping            kids playing together
each other             no mean people
everyone happy            people taking walks
nobody picked on            together
people nice to animals      everybody friends

When I visited the class at the end of the day, the children were totally involved in creating images for their ideas about peace. Some were working on a large mural, some were making constructions out of wires and tongue depressors, some were shaping clay figures, many were painting pictures and adding words.

Throughout the country, young children have painted, sewn, sculpted, and constructed such symbols of peace as flowers, rainbows, sunshine, smiling faces, and hands holding each other. Be open to the

FIGURE 5–13   *Let there be peace!*

children's original ideas. Turn their ideas into Peace Cards to be sent to others, posters, murals, quilts, and so on. Always add words.

### People, Places, and Things

When, through direct experiences or through books, videos, movies, songs, and stories, children learn about other people, places, and customs, they are eager to extend their knowledge and understanding into visual arts experiences. Even our very young children hold crayons and markers in their small fingers and create their earliest hieroglyphics! Make room in your room for the children's works! Paintings, carvings, mosaics, puppets, jewelry, cards . . . always celebrate the creative works of your students. I have seen too many instances where the children's paintings or three-dimensional creations were stacked in a corner of a shelf, throwaways! Engaged children are eager to continue exploring ways to express their interest and fascination. When the new child from Turkey arrived, the children loved learning that he had an uncle who was a shepherd. The children created shoe-box scenes of clay hills, cotton puff sheep, construction paper trees and wire shepherds. These were city children whose only prior familiarity with sheep was "Mary Had a Little Lamb"!

*Go with the children's often enthusiastic interest and response.* Their own opportunities to initiate ideas and projects are the best motivations!

Another example of discovering the wonders of others happened after a group of first graders listened to the story *When Africa Was Home*.[21] Peter and his family live in Africa. They are a white family working in their beloved African village with friends all around. Peter's family is transferred to America but Peter misses his best friend, Yekha, their barefoot, sun-bright African days running with goats and children, listening to monkeys in the trees, eating sugarcane under a jacaranda tree. After a contrasting time in America, the family returns to Africa, their home. The first graders wanted to make a mural with one-half images of America, one-half, Africa. That's just what they did when they returned to their classroom!

### Images of Helpers

"Community Helpers" is such a familiar theme in early childhood. A plethora of materials is constantly available for enriching experiences. Sadly, I've noticed too many handouts, dittos, worksheets about common helpers like firefighters, police officers, and letter carriers. Let's not limit our children's experiences to such minimal activities.

When good talks and good books are constant stimuli, children have their own imaginative pathways. Leah is fascinated with veterinarians. Shai is in love with firefighters. D'Angelo wants to be "the guy who builds the highway." Give the children time and encouragement to follow their interests and celebrate their own ideas in the media of their

FIGURE 5–14 *Give kids boxes and they'll construct the world.*

choice. Shai draws a series of pictures of firefighters in different actions. He can't stop looking at his favorite book, *Firefighters from A to Z.*[22] His firefighter paper-bag puppet helps put out the make-believe fire that started in his classmate Salvatore's building of blocks and boxes. After the trip to the firehouse, almost all of Shai's classmates were eager to paint pictures of firehouses and firefighters, to play fire engines and make up songs about those heroes. They made colorful thank-you cards to send to their firefighting friends.

*Note:* Creating a multicultural environment is not an idea limited to a week's study or around a special holiday. It's an ongoing, consistent reality. A daily awareness. Part of every day. When music, visual images, stories, games, and dance reflect the amazing diversity of the human family, the children's artwork will express those important influences.

## KIDS COUNT

### *Numbers in Every Language*

Names and numbers are our very first vocabulary words. It's exciting to see the faces of young children when they discover that all people have words that count numbers!

Singing and chanting numbers is even more fun than just saying numbers! I have so many favorite songs, like Miss Jackie's "Uno Uno, Dos Dos," sung in cha-cha-cha, and Sweet Honey in the Rock's "African Numbers."[23] Most of our fantastic music makers feature songs highlighting counting and number words in other languages.

You don't need a child from a Latino or Hispanic background to be a member of your class to introduce the children to counting in another language! It's fun and easy to learn and helps widen our worlds.

And when children see the numerical sign for the number, the English word, and a word or words in different languages, their learning is multiplied.

### Basic Shapes in Multicultural Images

Children love making dream catchers from Native American cultures. The shapes are circles. Chinese children share their love of kites. Many kites are in triangular shapes or diamond shapes. After a visit from a friend from the Chinese community, the children enjoyed Stuart Murphy's *Let's Fly a Kite*.[24] The children discovered the concepts of symmetry, fractions, and shapes. Good preparation for geometry! Mix in colors! American-style baseball diamonds are spreading around the globe! Hopscotch played by children of many cultures in a variety of forms usually uses squares or rectangles. Jade amulets in circle shapes are worn by many Asian people for good luck. As children learn to count and see mathematics concepts in their everyday lives, information becomes meaningful. Blend in that awareness throughout your days. Name, color, count, and compare those basic shapes.

### Everything in the Whole Wide World and Other Stuff

Observing, comparing, categorizing, and counting are basic ingredients of math comprehension. One of my favorite books to enjoy with children is *Grover and the Everything in the Whole Wide World Museum*,[25] a wacky story that tries to categorize everything in the whole wide world with labels like "tall things," "very light things"—well, you get the point and can imagine the many categories for things in the whole wide world that you and your students can organize, count, chart, and measure. The children's own original interpretations of the book inspire classroom museum collections and exhibits! Be sure they are labeled, counted, compared, and categorized. Even our youngest students are often excellent docents!

### Stars and Stripes and Other Symbolic Images That Count

Remember, flags fascinate children. Our American flags flew proudly all around the country following September 11, 2001. Even our very young children recognized the red, white, and blue, the stars and stripes. But how many stars? How many stripes? How many of the world's flags have stars? Have stripes? Have moons? Or half moons? Have suns? A wonderful way to sharpen observation and clarify comprehension. How many flags have red, white, and blue in them? What other colors? This is easy information to measure, chart, and graph.

### Count Your Money

As children's awareness of community expands, they have many more experiences with money. Community helpers like bell-ringing ice cream truck drivers, supermarket clerks, and postal workers demonstrate the idea of money for goods and services to our youngest children, who almost always have treasures of pennies tucked safely into their precious pockets! For our kindergarten and primary children who may be familiar with people from other countries, comparing coins, noting differences in sizes and colors, and talking about their worths are fascinating activities.

### Counting Beads and Other Universally Loved Materials

Beads are very old materials used by humans from hundreds of cultures. Colors, sizes, and shapes are qualities to consider. Making patterns in beaded bracelets, necklaces, and decorations is an important aspect of beading. Counting, sequential learning, decision making are a few built-in skills. When I brought a large assortment of beads of all sizes and colors to Callie and Ryan, I thought we would spend about an hour making bead bracelets for a huge family reunion. I found out that stringing beads is the equivalent of eating popcorn. It's hard to stop. Callie, Ryan, and I strung bead bracelets *all* day! The next day, five-year-old Ryan woke me with the request, "Grandma Mimi, can we do more bracelets?" We arrived at the reunion loaded with one hundred bead bracelets.

When a bag of colorful feathers was brought to the kindergarten room by a garage-sale-addicted teacher's assistant, the children were immediately excited. Time had to be carved out for the kids to create feather designs on construction paper. Regular and glitter glue helped keep the feathers intact. Feathers were counted, divided, distributed. Every child received ten feathers. How they decided on their original configurations and patterns was an example of creativity, math, problem solving, and comprehension of shapes, colors, and numbers.

Mosaic designs created from small colored shapes, fabric fragments, tiles, buttons, beads, and a wide assortment of found and scrounged materials are known and loved throughout the world. While children work with their materials, encourage language and math thinking with your always relevant questions and conversations. For example, "How many squares do you think you want to use?" "Will all your colors be the same? Which colors do you think you want to have in your design?" "I like the way you created this pattern of red and yellow squares. It

FIGURE 5–15    *It's fun to count beads and use colors to make patterns.*

looks so bright. Are these your favorite colors?" "How did you decide how many squares in your pattern?" Just as young children very early on begin constructing knowledge about the world around them before formalized teaching begins, so that natural gathering of observations, thinking, problem solving in the domain of math awareness is happening all the time.[26]

### Community Helpers Count a Lot

Multiply enjoyable lessons gleaned from discovering and appreciating the many ways people contribute to the success and well-being of the community. Our postal workers are the keepers of stamps that have different prices on them. How many stamps to mail a letter? Our parking attendants stamp parking tickets that tell time and money owed. Transportation is a fascinating area of study for young children who never tire of learning about and playing bus driver, train conductor, airline pilot, or toll booth operator. How many miles? How far? How fast? How many people on this bus? Take advantage of every opportunity to engage the children in meaningful conversations about these areas of interest. Talk leads to action. The children will write their own bus tickets, make their own stamps, and track their own journeys.

### Far and Near, Others We Meet

When the Somalian children arrived in Columbus, creative teachers pulled down maps, pictures, information to share with new classmates. How far away? How many miles? How long was the trip? Manuel's family arrived from Guatemala. Which was the longer journey? Somalia to Ohio or Guatemala to Ohio?

How many streets away from the school is the house Arkady and his newly arrived Russian family moved into? When Randy and his family moved from New York City to a suburban area of Michigan, his classmates listened in wonder as he told them of his apartment on the fifteenth floor of a tall apartment house on a bustling city street. Books like Stuart Murphy's *Elevator Magic*, combining counting and subtracting as elevator buttons are pushed with playful fantasy, helped Randy's classmates imagine the everyday ups and downs of elevator travel in a very unfamiliar high-rise building.[27]

---

**Classroom Visitors and Field Trips**

We can't emphasize enough the importance of these experiences. (If they are conducted with rich preparation and enjoyable follow-up activities in a spirit of respect, curiosity, appreciation, and openness.)

---

The extensive list at the end of the book will trigger ideas if you hit a dry spell! You don't have to go very far to help children welcome other people from their ever-widening worlds. Look around you for opportunities. Often our American communities offer great resources and stories our young children need to experience. After a year of learning trust and safety in a loving environment, two high school sisters from Ethiopia overcame their shyness and visited young children in a nearby elementary school. They shared their music, dance, and memories of their country. A high point in everyone's year!

## IT ALL COMES TOGETHER

In our city, the Greek Festival and the Native American Powwow are celebrated on the same weekend. With the Greek community, I dance till the music stops. The next day, I dance every intertribal dance the powwow master of ceremonies announces. After one of the intertribal dances, I was leaving the dance circle when a woman waved me over.

Glaring at me, she said, "Didn't I see you dancing at the Greek Festival last night?"

I told her yes, she had.

"And now you're dancing at the powwow?"

I smiled, thinking a joke was coming.

She was clearly upset as she asked, "Just what are you, **anyway?**"

I was flabbergasted! This was my instant response: "I guess I'm just a festival girl!"

This festival girl has participated in thousands of festivals in schools, cities, and neighborhoods. I love them all! Think generically. What do most festivals, whatever their reason or season, have in common? Themes, colors, foods, clothing, symbols, games, music, crafts, dancing, parades or processions, rituals, information, history, every curriculum area, every skill, all the multiple intelligences at work, cooperation, celebration. With your children, choose a theme. It doesn't have to be connected to a calendar holiday. Some of the themes I remember clearly are Nursery Rhyme Festivals, Friends Around the World Festivals, Peace Festivals, Favorite Books Festivals, 100 Days of School Festivals, and we can go on and on. Do we need tickets? What

FIGURE 5–16    *Festivals mean great stuff to do!*

shall we name it? What special activities, songs, games, pictures, posters, invitations, tickets, announcements, directions, information, signs, symbols do we need? Will we wear special clothing? A delightful book that celebrates clothing, colors, geography, and friendship is Nicki Weiss' *World Turns Round and Round.*[28] High-level thinking, problem solving, listening skills, and cooperative learning are essential to the success of such a delightful event. If it's possible to cook in your room, invite the children to make some of the refreshments. Be sure to keep count so you have enough for everyone. I remember some years ago, a kindergarten class was planning a storybook festival. They wanted to dress up as storybook characters, eat storybook refreshments like Winnie the Pooh's honey, the Moose's cookie, gingerbread cookies, and raspberry tarts. They wanted to sing storybook songs like "Mary Had a Little Lamb" and "Three Blind Mice." They made up a song for *Goodnight, Moon.* They wanted to invite their families and maybe one other class. By the time I arrived, their original festival idea had spread like confetti. The whole school was now invited and the building was absolutely packed with families, neighbors, the mayor, the city council members, police officers, firefighters, and other community helpers and guests. Every class turned its room into a mini-festival featuring the storybooks theme. One room had created three houses: one of straw, one of sticks, and one of bricks. They used a variety of scrounged and commercial materials. All the classes joined a huge procession moving through the entire building. Banners, flags, signs, posters were waving as the costumed storybook characters marched to lively music played by the instrumental music kids. I'll stop the description now only because of time and space, but talking about this one festival alone could fill a text! Do you think this event will be remembered by the children in years to come? I think its many lessons were learned by heart!

## NOTES

1. Holt, J. 1970. *What Do I Do Monday?* New York: Dutton. (See Chapters 3 and 4.)

2. Liz Harzoff teaches early childhood special ed at Nisonger Center's University Affiliate Program, Columbus, Ohio.

3. Theme Issue. 2001. "The Global Village." *Childhood Education.* 77 (5). pp. 256–322.

4. D'Angelo, A., and B. P. Dixey. Winter 2001. "Using Multicultural Resources for Teachers to Combat Racial Prejudice in the Classroom." *Early Childhood Education Journal.* 29 (2). pp. 83–87.

5. Derman-Sparks, L. and the ABC Task Force. 1989. *Anti-Bias Curriculum: Tools for Empowering Young Children.* Washington, D.C.: NAEYC.

The Southern Poverty Law Center publishes *Teaching Tolerance* (a journal) and *Starting Small* (1997), a book for young children.

The Center can be reached at 400 Washington Avenue, Montgomery, AL 36104.

The Anti-Defamation League (ADL) is at 823 United Nations Plaza, New York, NY 10017.

Examples of some of the excellent resources addressing these life-and-death issues of learning to live with others in our widening/narrowing world are:

McIntyre, E., A. Rosebery, and N. Gonzalez. 2001. *Classroom Diversity: Connecting Curriculum to Students' Lives*. Portsmouth, NH: Heinemann.

King, E. W., M. Chapman, and M. Cruz-Janzen. 1994. *Educating Young Children in a Diverse Society*. Boston: Allyn and Bacon.

Ramsey, P. 1998. *Teaching and Learning in a Diverse World: Multicultural Education for Young Children*. (2nd ed.). New York: Teachers College Press.

6. So many wonderful materials abound. Check out such readings as:

Huber, L. K. Summer 2000. "Promoting Multicultural Awareness Through Dramatic Play Centers." *Early Childhood Education Journal* 27 (4). pp. 235–238.

Boutte, G. S., I. Van Scoy, and S. Hendley. 1996. "Multicultural and Nonsexist Prop Boxes." *Young Children*. 52 (1). pp. 34–39.

Gann, C. November 2001. "A Spot of Our Own: The Cultural Relevance, Anti-Bias Resource Room." *Young Children*. 56 (6). pp. 34–36.

7. I wrote about the gifts of serendipity in:

Chenfeld, M. B. 2001. "Get the Elephant Out of the Room! We're Finished with the E's!" *Teaching by Heart*. St. Paul, MN: Redleaf. pp. 110–119. Originally published in *Young Children*, November 2000.

8. Chaskin, R. J. and D. M. Rauner. (guest editors). May 1995. Special Section on Youth and Caring. *Phi Delta Kappan*. 76 (9).

Examples of fine books and articles on the vitally important topic are:

Fisher, B. 1998. *Joyful Learning in Kindergarten*. (Rev. ed.). Portsmouth, NH: Heinemann.

Levin, D. E. 1994. *Teaching Young Children in Violent Times: Building a Peaceable Classroom*. Philadelphia, PA: New Society.

Whitin, P. September 2001. "Kindness in a Jar." *Young Children* 56 (5). pp. 18–22.

Swick, K. J. Winter 2001. "Nurturing Decency Through Caring and Serving During the Early Childhood Years." *Early Childhood Education Journal*. 19 (2). pp. 131–137.

9. Say, A. 2000. *The Sign Painter*. Boston: Houghton Mifflin.

Daniels, T. illus. Foster, T. 1999. *The Feet in the Gym*. Del Ray Beach, FL: Winslow Press.

Glaser, L. illus. Schmidt, K. L. 1993. *Stop That Garbage Truck*. Morton Grove, IL: Albert Whitman.

Catalnotto, P. 1995. *The Painter*. New York: Orchard Books.

Stevenson, J. illus. Stevenson, H. 1998. *Sam the Zamboni Man*. New York: Greenwillow Books.

Kalman, B. 1998. *Community Helpers from A–Z*. New York: Crabtree Publishing.

Paulsen, G. illus. Paulsen, R. W. 1997. *Work Song*. San Diego, CA: Harcourt Brace.

10. Couric, K. illus. Priceman, M. 2001. *The Brand New Kid*. New York: Doubleday.

Danneberg, J. illus. Love, J. 2000. *First Day Jitters*. Watertown, MA: Whispering Coyote.

Poydar, N. 1999. *First Day, Hooray!* New York: Holiday House.

Henkes, K. 2000. *Wemberly Worried*. New York: Greenwillow Books.

Rickert, J. E. photos McGahan, P. 2000. *Russ and the Almost Perfect Day*. Bethesda, MD: Woodbine House.

Rickert, J. E. photos McGahan, P. 2000. *Brian's Bird*. Morton Grove, IL: Albert Whitman.

Millman, I. 1998. *Moses Goes to a Concert*. New York: Farrar, Straus and Giroux.

Millman, I. 2000. *Moses Goes to School*. New York: Frances Foster Books (Farrar, Straus and Giroux).

Tapahonso, L. and E. Schick. illus. Schick, E. 1995. *Navajo ABC: A Dine Alphabet Book*. New York: Simon and Schuster.

Look, L. illus Heo, Y. 2001. *Henry's First Moon Birthday*. New York: Anne Schwartz Books (Atheneum).

Yakota, J. (editor). 2001. *Kaleidoscope: A Multicultural Booklist for Grades K–8*. (3rd ed.). Urbana, IL: NCTE.

Other excellent sources are:

Beaty, J. J. 1997. *Building Bridges with Multicultural Picture Books for Children 3–5*. Upper Saddle River, NJ: Prentice Hall.

Kiefer, B. Z. 1995. *The Potential of Picture Books: From Visual Literacy to Aesthetic Understanding*. Upper Saddle River, NJ: Merrill/Prentice Hall.

11. From an interview with Bob Blue in:

Neugebauer, B. (editor). 1992. *Alike and Different: Exploring Our Humanity with Young Children*. (Rev. ed.). Washington, D.C.: NAEYC. pp. 64–66.

12. Leslie Zak directed Days of Creation Arts for Kids until her retirement in 1999 to devote her full time to making music.

13. Hughes, L. 1995. *The Book of Rhythms*. New York: Oxford University Press.

14. Lankford, M. illus. Milone, K. 1992. *Hopscotch Around the World*. New York: Morrow.

Yolen, J. 1992. *Street Rhymes Around the World*. Honesdale, PA: Wordsong.

15. A few suggestions of very helpful materials are:

Allred, K. W., R. Brien, and S. J. Black, 9/1998. "Collaboratively Addressing Needs of Young Children with Disabilities." *Young Children* 53 (5). pp. 32–36.

Soriano-Nagurski, L. 1998. "And the Walls Came Tumbling Down: Including Children Who Are Differently Abled in Typical Early Childhood Educational Settings." *Young Children* 53 (2). pp. 40–41.

Wolery, M. and J. W. Wilbers. (editors). 1994. *Including Children with Special Needs in Early Childhood Programs*. Washington, D.C.: NAEYC.

16. Amy Polovick is the dance teacher at Duxberry Park Arts Alternative Elementary School, Columbus, Ohio.

17. Rockwell, A. illus Rockwell, L. 2000. *Career Day*. New York: HarperCollins.

Maynard, C. 1997. *Jobs People Do*. New York: Dorling Kindersley.

18. Information on excellent sources for multicultural literature is plentiful. A few examples are:

Banks, J. A. 1994. *An Introduction to Multicultural Education*. Boston: Allyn and Bacon.

Forest, H. (compiler). 1995. *Wonder Tales from Around the World*. Little Rock, AR: August House.

Lenox, M. F. 2000. "Storytelling for Young Children in a Multicultural World." *Early Childhood Education Journal* 28 (2). pp. 97–103.

Saldana, J. 2000. *Drama of Color: Improvisation with Multiethnic Folklore*. Portsmouth, NH: Heinemann.

19. Neugebauer, B. 1992. "Where Do We Begin? Bring the World into Your Classroom." From *Alike and Different: Exploring Our Humanity with Young Children*. Washington, D.C.: NAEYC. pp. 16–19.

20. For information on Raffi's works, contact Rounder Kids at <www .Rounder.com> or 800-ROUNDER.

For information on Jack Grunsky's works, contact Kimbo Educational at <www.kimboed.com> or KimboEd@aol.com, or call 800-631-2980.

For information on Red Grammer's works, contact Rednote at 800-824-2980.

Be sure to check the music makers noted in the appendix for more outstanding resources.

21. Williams, K. L. illus. Cooper, F. 1991. *When Africa Was Home*. New York: Orchard Books.

22. Demarest, C. L. 2000. *Firefighters from A to Z*. New York: Margaret McEldery Books (Simon and Schuster).

23. Information on Miss Jackie's (Jackie Silberg) works can be found at

800-432-6307 or <*www.jackiesilberg.com*>. Miss Jackie's album *Joining Hands with Other Hands: Multicultural Songs and Games* is outstanding!

Information on Sweet Honey in the Rock can be found through Rounder Kids at 800-ROUNDER.

24. Murphy, S. illus. Floca, B. 2000. *Let's Fly a Kite*. New York: Harper-Collins.

25. Sesame Street. 1974. *Grover and the Everything in the Whole Wide World Museum*. New York: Random House.

26. Considering mathematics as an emergent curriculum, energized by children's natural interests, observations, experiences, and problem solving, is helping teachers create more meaningful, integrated learning opportunities. In July 2001, *Young Children* devoted a special section of the journal, titled "Making Math Natural and Fun." Eugene Geist's article, "Children Are Born Mathematicians: Promoting the Construction of Early Mathematical Concepts in Children Under Five," inspires readers to think of emergent math just as they accept emergent language development as an important way to consider that vital interconnected strand of learning.

A few examples of excellent resources full of stimulating ideas and concepts are:

Copley, J. V. 2000. *The Young Child and Mathematics*. Washington, D.C.: NAEYC.

Zaslavsky, C. 1985. *The Multicultural Math Classroom: Bringing in the World*. Portsmouth, NH: Heinemann.

Katz, L. G. and S. Chard 1989. *Engaging Children's Minds: The Project Approach*. Stamford, CT: Ablex.

27. Murphy, S. J. illus. Karos, G. B. 1997. *Elevator Magic*. New York: HarperCollins.

28. Weiss, N. 2000. *The World Turns Round and Round*. New York: Greenwillow.

# THEME 6 | OUR NATURAL WORLD/ OUR ENVIRONMENT

*May green be the grass you walk on.*
*May blue be the skies above you.*
*May pure be the joys that surround you.*
*May true be the hearts that love you.*

—old Irish blessing

## THINK ABOUT IT

My friend Paula was evaluating an early childhood playground for developmentally appropriate equipment needs when a little boy ran over to her, eagerly asking, "Are *you* Mother Nature?"[1]

Smiling, Paula had to answer no, but she, along with numerous educators and community and national leaders, is passionate in her concern for Mother Nature, for the condition of our natural world and environment and for our children's relationships with those vital areas of our lives.

The headlines are grim. The reports of global warming, air and water pollution, deforestation, the expansion of new communities on old farmlands, the shrinking of our natural resources as modern life

185

with its demands and needs continues to threaten the gifts of nature. Add to the bad news the sorry fact that many of our children spend more time than ever before indoors, in very structured programs with limited experiences directly connected to nature.

Carl Pope, the executive director of the Sierra Club, in an article subtitled "Kids' Inalienable Right to Mess Around Outdoors,"[2] reminds us that when we lose our contact with the natural world, we lose something precious, lose part of what it means to be human. "We evolved in nature, dependent on its rhythms, inextricably connected to other living things." He believes that our experiences as children forge our relationships with nature. He sees our children bombarded by consumerism, electronic games, TV, and shopping malls. He fears that nature is losing out to the virtual world. We need to recommit ourselves to helping children develop a sense of our human community as part of the wider, natural world.

The hopeful news is that there is a growing concern that we must remember and strengthen our connections to the natural world. Julie Davis writes eloquently about the need for environmental education.[3] She believes that environmental education has three overlapping approaches: "education in, about, and for the environment." Young children, in order to develop positive feelings and attitudes toward the world of nature, must enjoy direct experiences. At the same time, we need to help children learn *about* nature and the often miraculous and mysterious ways nature "works." And lastly, because we are (or should be) the guardians, the stewards, the protectors of Earth, we must become stronger advocates for ways to care for this planet of ours.[4]

*Do you care?*

FIGURE 6–1   *Children are connected to the world of nature.*

Do you care that the places where children can enjoy outdoor play are slowly disappearing? Mary Rivkin, probably Mother Nature in disguise, is an articulate advocate, educator, and author whose work over the years has been relentless in reminding us of our children's need and desire to play freely, make discoveries, find fascinating treasures, and develop a love for the riches of the natural world. She is especially distressed at the reality of children from inner-city, low-income, minority communities, who are disproportionately deprived of safe and beautiful outdoor play areas. Her widely used book *The Great Outdoors: Restoring Children's Right to Play Outside*[5] has a wealth of suggestions and information to inspire creative ways of integrating this theme in the everyday curriculum and life of young children. Remember, our children will be the caretakers of the earth!

*Do you care?*

Ruth Wilson, another Mother Nature in disguise, devotes much of her writing and teaching to environmental education. She asks us to remember that the Environmental Protection Agency promised all Americans that they deserve clean air, pure water, land that is safe to live on, food that is safe to eat. *All* people, not just those who live in the cleanest and safest communities, but everyone deserves to be protected from pollution. The disparity between those who live in poverty and those who live more privileged lives is great. Even though we all live on the same planet, the air we breathe is not always the same, nor is the water we drink, nor the soil children play on.[6]

Let's look at our children. They don't read headlines or lobby in Washington as environmental advocates. They live their everyday lives—their lives in the land of childhood.

Whether they live in high-rise tenement houses in urban neighborhoods or on farms miles from their nearest neighbors, it seems that most of our young children have a built-in readiness to revere nature. One look around at the play of lights, shadows, colors, movement, shapes, and designs—the swirl of the natural world—and young children immediately understand Liese Millikin's delightful description, "The world is flipped and damzled about!"[7]

Our young children are like Ptolemy. Not only is the earth the center of it all, but they are also at the center of the earth! Most young children think that the world is a big, red, juicy apple waiting for them to sink in their new teeth and suck out its sweetness. Nothing is ordinary. Noticing everything, they catch the beginnings of breezes, dust particles shining in the noon window light, a stray ant carrying a crumb. A young child looks at the moon and the moon looks at the young child. The child doesn't say, "The moon!" The child says, "*My* moon!" Stars twinkle and shine so children can wish upon them. Those early years are rich with ownership!

And, those early years are rich with meaningful connections. Remember, our young children are already learning in an integrated way!

Too often, it's the adult world that chops up curriculum into little compartments, isolated and separate. Steven Levy, in his beautiful essay "To See the World in a Grain of Sand,"[8] concludes with his goals: He wants his students to "find the universal in the particular, to discover metaphors that connect personal experience to the struggles of humankind, to see worlds in grains of sand and heavens in wildflowers. . . . They will look at anything and discover the deep and broad connections that weave the threads of the story that unite the web of the world. . . ."

As we ponder the wonder of our natural world, our environment, let us remember how relevant, vibrant, and engaging a curriculum it is. It is a true treasure chest and treasure hunt! Long before our students come to us, they have already become fascinated with this theme. Even our youngest students, newborn infants, watch the light, shadows, shapes, and colors around them. Our children are children of the earth and already communicate with animals, plants, trees, sun, moon, and stars.

In her excellent article "Nature Education and Science," Ruth A. Wilson suggests some goals for nature education:

1. the development of a sense of wonder
2. an appreciation of the beauty and mystery of the natural world
3. opportunities to experience the joy of closeness to nature
4. respect for other creatures[9]

The simplicity of these goals reminds us that children learn through interaction; through hands-on experiences with accessible, concrete materials; and through ample time to explore, experiment, observe, and reflect. This is a curriculum, as are all our life-affirming themes, that goes beyond information, beyond the gathering of facts. Wilson writes, "Nature Education offers a way of knowing that includes, but is not limited to, rational knowledge. Its focus is on a way of knowing that moves the heart and soul and imagination of the one involved. . . . While it is, indeed, good to have factual information about the natural world, it is also important to have a sense of connectedness, love and caring for the world of nature."

Once again, I call on that other Mother Earth, Mary Rivkin, to share some of her philosophy:[10]

"Appreciate where you are. Develop a sense of place. Start anywhere, anytime! Thoreau said, 'The earth is more to be admired than used.' Learn to become attuned, not controlling. Notice and respond. Keep your sense of wonder and your curiosity. We're natural creatures and we need to be connected with the 'unbuilt environment.' Don't worry about memorizing the names of things. That's the least important part. What's important? Take the kids out. Sit together. Close your eyes. Listen. Tune in. Walk to a park. If you don't have a park, look at a puddle! See the reflections in it? Sit and watch. Let yourselves experience the fullness of things. I like to tell the kids, 'I don't want to take it home. I don't want it. I just want to look at it!' But the children *do* love to collect things like pebbles, stones, rocks, shells, leaves, and twigs. We have to guide, inspire, model. We have to help our children look for beauty, patterns, predictability, cycles, seasonality. This is not a passive study. We have to respond creatively, poetically, figuratively to nature's gifts. We help our children experience both interaction and transformation. What can we do? What can we make? How can these experiences, this knowledge be transformed into poems, maps, songs, exhibits, games, paintings?"

I asked Mary about her deepest concerns in regard to the teaching of nature. Children of poverty, children living broken lives in depressed neighborhoods are children who hold a special place in Mary's heart. She sees nature providing unique lessons for all of our children, for all people, but especially for children who feel hopeless.

"Nature can be an antidote to despair. It's important for a sense of hope for children to see the incredible abundance of nature. They need to see the spaciousness of sky and the beauty of clouds. That's available to everyone. Even weeds in sidewalk cracks and insects on asphalt remind us of the enduring and adaptable qualities of nature, that ongoing

FIGURE 6–2  *Children learn they are part of the natural order of life.*

intensity to *live*. And our children living in these confused and chaotic times are comforted by the reassurance of orderliness, night and day, cycles and seasons. It's tragic that so many of our children say, '*If* I grow up.' Nature says to them, 'I want you to grow up. Everything young is supposed to grow, to get older. You are a part of the natural order of life.' "

As Mary so passionately states, the study of nature, the love of nature in the lives of children is one of hopefulness, of *life*, and of continuation. We are part of nature, children of the natural world. We are caretakers as well as residents!

This is the curriculum beyond information. This is the curriculum of wonder and appreciation, of connectedness and caring, of ownership and empowerment.

There is enough material in the rich offerings of nature to select areas of study you love, are fascinated by, and feel comfortable with. If you're not an animal person, look at rocks and plants. If you are allergic to plants, keep your eyes on the sun, moon, and stars. Millions of animals, plants, and rocks are waiting to find their way into your classroom. All across America, children and teachers are going outside to discover nature's treasures, and all across America, children and teachers are inviting nature in.

Mary Rivkin advises, "Start anywhere, anytime." Whether you and your children are blowing the fuzz from dandelions, watching chicks hatch from eggs, sunning your plants, or filling an entire school with birds, fish, reptiles, mammals, plants, and recycling centers, you are participating in a life-rich curriculum, totally engaging the children, demanding interaction, inviting "hands on," connecting minds and hearts.

Within the world of nature are the human-made worlds we construct for ourselves. Our children live in amazingly diverse communities in our geographically heterogeneous land. The communities we live in and their natural settings and surroundings deeply affect us. After our son returned to visit in Ohio from months in Arizona, he couldn't stop appreciating the lush green colors of trees, bushes, and grass. Our Arizona grandchildren live in the shadows of gigantic, strangely shaped saguaro cactus plants growing miraculously from dry sandy soil. Most of the snow they know is in pictures or the pages of books. Our New York City grandchildren don't even blink at skyscrapers, the screech of traffic, the rush of thousands of pedestrians as they speed through crowded streets on their skateboards. They know every playground in Central Park, that fabulous oasis in the middle of Manhattan. Some of our American children live near oceans. The sea and the language of fish, sails, tides are daily components of their lives. Our suburban kids watch their communities grow, see malls multiply, listen to the often vitriolic dialogue among those who want more construction, more development and those who argue that the spread of suburban communities destroys wetlands, farmlands, forests, and animal sanctuaries. Our children know about pollution. Many of them worry about lakes and rivers dangerous to fish and humans. Nature and our environment are inextricably linked. Our children will be the guardians of the future, the caretakers of the earth and its communities.

There are many lessons in this theme. One is humility. Throughout history, humans have tried to fathom the mysterious workings of nature. Even today, with our incredible technoscientific instruments, many of nature's secrets have not been revealed. Coming to this study with a sense of wonder, an open mind, lively curiosity, and questions (even questions that may take centuries before answers are in sight!) is an antidote to smugness. Closed-in, right/wrong, short-answer questions and answers learned by rote and recited for grades are not the stuff of inquisitive, adventurous, and courageous minds. Plato told us that there is no other beginning of learning than wonder. Einstein believed that imagination is more powerful than knowledge! Wonder, imagination, curiosity, courage, patience, caring, responsibility, and enthusiasm are some of the qualities necessary for this journey.

Are *you* ready for this journey? Are you prepared to soar beyond information? Are you ready to turn Earth Day into a continuum of Earth Days rather than a single event determined by a calendar date?

The children are always ready and waiting.

## DISCOVER TIMES/WONDER TIMES: POINTS OF INTEREST

- Our planet is called Earth.
- Even though people speak different languages and live in different places, we all live on the planet Earth.
- Our planet has air for us to breathe, water and land, a sky above us, and countless plants and animals of every size, type, design, and color.
- Not even the smartest scientists know all the answers to how our planet works, how plants and animals grow and change. Questions and curiosity are the best ways to begin learning about things.
- There are many beautiful parts of Earth: oceans, rivers, mountains, fields, valleys, deserts, and forests. Each part has special features, such as special animals, birds, kinds of weather, and plants.
- Even though it seems impossible to count all the trees and fish and plants, they can be used up or wasted. It's very sad when people don't appreciate the gifts nature gives us and waste them or destroy them (like forests and rivers).
- We need to take care of our home, our Earth. There are many ways we can help keep it clean and clear.
- All living things are connected. We are all a part of life, of nature.

Callie

**Water**

I think we should be more carful about what we put in the water, like wrapers, cans, plastic bottles, and bags. So don't polut rivers, oceans, streams, seas, ponds, or lakes.

**Air**

The air can be poluted by motersikels, trucks, cars, moter boats, and trains. So car pull, walk, ride your bike or scooter. So Don't Polut The Air!

**Land**

Everyone needs land. You use land to grow fruits and vegtibles, and trees to give us air. All animals live in trees and on land so don't litter!

FIGURE 6–3    *Talking, thinking, writing go together.*

- Nature is very orderly: morning and night, dark and light, seasons, tides, birth and death, growing and changing.
- We have fantastic "instruments and machinery" for study and for caring for nature: our senses, our language, our memory, our curiosity, our understanding, our imagination, our talents, and our creativity.
- No matter where we live, we can help make our environment and communities safe, clean, beautiful, and peaceful.

## SUGGESTED VOCABULARY

Every word included in this starter vocabulary is a universe of possibilities for joyful learning experiences. The words themselves are motivating and inspiring! Start anywhere, anytime.

| | | |
|---|---|---|
| sun | clouds | rivers |
| moons | mist | lakes |
| stars | hills | trees |
| wind | valleys | grasses |

birds
animals
insects
mountains
oceans
sea
lakes
puddles
forests
sky
mud
earth
dirt
stone
air
fly
dark
light
twinkle
sky
rain
sprinkle
thunder
lightning
snow
ice
breeze
sand
water
waves
fish
branches
leaves
seeds
roots
hibernate
feathers
paws
shells
claws
wings

beaks
hop
crawl
fins
grass
crops
grow
harvest
preserve
fruit
vegetables
eggs
hatch
bugs
insects
reptiles
mammals
endangered
pollution
clean
clear
recycle
protect
swamp
fossils
shore
pebbles
webs
cocoons
gallop
scurry
morning
night
afternoon
winter
spring
summer
autumn
seasons
weather
colors

animal shelters
veterinarians
park rangers
greenhouses
naturalists
scientists
herbs
gourds
patterns
designs
rainbows
hurricanes
tornadoes
flowers
plants
gardens
swim
climb
environment
environmentalists
astronomers
city
country
highway
stores
malls
parks
farms
factories
houses
streets
trucks
cars
buses
trains
hospitals
traffic
traffic lights
buildings
movie theaters

Obviously, if we included all the possible words under "animals" or "plants," every page in this book would be covered with names. Words beget!

### *Wonderful Talks*

Young children help us rekindle wonder. High on their Magic Vocabulary lists are words of nature and the natural world. They are always ready to talk about animals, plants, weather, familiar terrain like mountains, hills, or rivers. Be sure to record their wonderings on charts or boards if the children cannot yet write. They still know the words they say have shape and form. Add their names. "Megan wonders about baby tadpoles. Does it hurt when they change into frogs?" Their ideas will steer the way to the library for books about their favorite topics. (Remember, this is open-ended. No absolute right or wrong answers have places in these talks!)

Talk with the children about their neighborhood and immediate environment. They will surprise you with their observations and knowledge.

### *Walk and Talk (Look, Listen, Smell, Taste, Touch—in Other Words: Come to Your Senses)*

The ancient Greeks followed their teachers around, walking and talking about the great themes of life! They called that *peripatetic* education. With your children, take a walk, even around the school. What do we see? Stop and talk about it. Stop and listen. What do we hear? What do we smell? Pine? Mint? When the beloved educator Herb Sandberg was visited by friends just a few days before his death, they wanted to share with him that the daffodils were now in bloom and waiting for him to recover and see them. Unable to talk because of a respirator, Herb wrote on his clipboard, "A child once said, 'Yesterday I heard a daffodil bloom!'" His friends knew that Herb was telling us to take the time, like that little child did, to listen to the daffodils bloom.[11] *Synesthesia* is not a disease! It's a gift young children remind us that we have and should cherish. With a group of children, we were playing with changing images into sense impressions. We were talking about the afternoon, say, about two o'clock. I asked the kids what color two o'clock reminded them of. One of the boys immediately responded, "Orange." His seatmate jumped to his feet, in some kind of bewilderment. "What's so orange about two o'clock?" he asked. In these walk-abouts and talk-abouts, be open for very creative ways of describing what we discover. Extend the ideas into stories, word walls, charts, posters, poems, and more.

Encourage the children to gather sense images for all aspects of our natural world, for our surroundings. For example, we collect winter sounds/sights/smells/tastes/touches/feelings. All ideas are welcomed.

The more we think about, the more we think about! How easily those images are enjoyed in vivid talks and sharing times. How naturally they flow into poems, pictures, and a myriad of extensive activities. Our only limit is time! (Boo time!)

### *Talk About Pets and Plants*

As children dig, plant, water, feed, and clean animals and plants, they talk. They observe, compare, and share. They learn to take turns, take responsibility, and respect others. This incidental talking and listening is so important, perhaps the most valuable kind of language enrichment. Caring for classroom pets and plants generates important conversations about responsibility and caretaking. Even very young children clearly discover that the actual lives of the pets depend on being cared for by people. "Before we eat our snacks," kindergartners decided, "we should be sure our rabbits and turtles are fed." We learn by doing. Caring for pets and plants means *doing*. It's important work, and talking together about such life-affirming work is essential.

Here's a great example of such a class in action: Carol Highfield and Linda Muzzo's pre-K kids don't walk, they run to school every day, to the world of nature living in their room. Plants, fish, birds, animals, and children share dynamic times in this room of feathers, fins, and fur. Animals and nature are high on Carol's Magic Vocabulary list and her students catch the love of living creatures from her. Visit and you'll be given a tour by any one of the children. They are filled with information, responsibility, excitement, and curiosity. Books, pictures, projects, mobiles, poems, and journals color the walls and tables. The children are busy and involved. Their enthusiastic interest is evident in every space. There's no end to the ways Carol, Linda, and their students celebrate their yearlong love affair with nature, which we hope becomes a lifelong love affair![12]

### *Please Ask!*

Our natural world is a popular subject for children's numerous questions. Many of their questions help us see life in fresh, new ways. I love this question that I heard about a young child asking: "Where does the white go when the snow melts?" In relaxed, safe-at-any-speed rooms, questions are always welcomed. Often special time is set aside for questions on the children's minds. Many teachers designate a space featuring the children's questions recorded on charts or boards. Value the questions in themselves even if you don't know the answers. Each question is a seed and questions beget questions. Before you know it, your kids may give you the direction and guidelines for an enriched curriculum on our natural world. Go with the energy and the curiosity! The children will learn from you that wonder, exploration, and discovery are exciting touchstones of this amazing journey of ours.

## Problem Stating/Problem Solving

A story, news report, direct experience, and class-sharing item are examples of ways problems can be introduced to your children. Perhaps the playground is littered. Maybe the gerbils' habitat is neglected. What about the smog-clogged sky? Why are fish dying in a nearby stream?

These are important opportunities for encouraging problem-solving discussions. Be sure that everyone understands the situation being discussed. Write on the board or a chart as the children talk. They must always see the connections between oral and written language. Listen with respect to all ideas and suggestions. Brainstorming means all contributions are welcomed; put judgment on hold. Once all the ideas are gathered, the group can begin selecting, arranging, and combining. Remember, a silly idea may trigger a really significant idea! That's the way the creative process works.

Very young children can understand the importance of, for example, helping to pick up litter or not wasting usable materials. Our youngest students have signed their names, symbols, scratches, and pictures on letters to local, state, and federal officials on behalf of problems they want to see solved. Sometimes those messages from children carry more weight than the statistical testimony of lobbyists!

FIGURE 6–4   *Children can be wonderful problem solvers.*

### Windows and Weather

Children the country over devote part of their "calendar" time to describing the weather. I've watched countless occasions when this item was a perfunctory number on the morning's agenda. "OK, put the sun symbol up and let's move on." Creative teachers and their loved students who know they are safe and free to express themselves often turn that ordinary weather item into extraordinary discussions—full of wonder, questions, memories, understanding, and comparisons.

If you have a window, be sure to look out it every day with your kids. You may be surprised at the valuable resources waiting for you to notice them. Outside the window of a third-grade class was the most beautiful, lush oak tree that was rarely noted. We spent about ten minutes at the window, admiring the tree, discovering a nest hidden in its branches. The children wrote, drew, talked, celebrated their wonderful discovery!

The weather is waiting outside your window, too! You don't need a clear day to see forever. Cloudy days can clear the air and inspire very poetic talk times.

These are opportunities for colorful observations. The sky isn't always blue. Leaves change hues. Sunlight brightens colors. Mix colors into all language celebrations. Extend your conversations, discussions, observations to art projects, poems, songs, charts, movement patterns, and stories. The children's ideas generate the best enriched activities.

These daily events are simple but fascinating ways to add the dimension of shapes to the children's observations. Are buildings outside our windows flat or pointed? Are trees straight or crooked, wide or narrow? One spring day, a group of first graders and I looked out their window together. We focused on the redbud tree outside the building. One of the boys jumped with delight at the discovery, "The leaves are in the shape of hearts!"

Everything goes into the mix!

### City Kids/Country Kids/All Around the World Kids

Imaginations are fed with that wonderful "What if?" question. "What if we lived in a big city in a tall apartment house?" asked of children living in a farm community evokes lively responses to record, illustrate, build, sing, and dramatize. Of course, the reverse is also true. City kids often have difficulty imagining life in the country. Keep enriching your discussions with topics that evoke imaginative responses. Keep the senses central.

"What sounds might kids who live in country communities hear?"

"What sights would city kids see every day?"

"Would city kids see crops growing? Fields and meadows and farmers working? What do you think?"

Books like Rylant's *When I Was Young in the Mountains* or McPhail's *Farm Morning* add vivid images that nourish creative possibilities. For children who can't imagine city life, try books like Soentpiet's *Around Town*, which invites readers into places where "some people live in the city, where houses are built close together and backyards are tiny and streets are always busy. . . ." Patricia Polacco's almost classic *Mrs. Katz and Tush* adds the elements of diversity and neighborliness to an urban setting. Our children need these important book talks to expand their own awareness and knowledge. Our world is a wondrous place! The more we learn about its different regions and people, the greater our appreciation and understanding.

Even in the midst of a very harsh, high-poverty urban area, Sharon Dennis Wyeth tells us that anything is possible in *Something Beautiful*. Our children need to know that they have the power to make things beautiful if they believe that with their effort and faith it can happen.

Children from every region of the country must be reminded that they are children of the earth! The powerful poetic sweep of the title *Did You Hear Wind Sing Your Name?* is a great reminder.

All of our children, no matter their geography, will gladly take a walk with you in the magical web of a tiny spider. Jonathon London's *Dream Weaver* closes in on a tiny story that catches the wonder.[13]

A rich offering of quality children's books are not just for practicing reading skills! They are for talking, thinking, sharing, and comprehending on many levels. We bring the world to the children through these connections that touch our spirits, that nourish our imaginations.

### Bird Words

A most delightful experience is suggesting to the kids that they take time to *really* listen to the sounds of birds. If they can write, ask them to write the sounds as they hear them. If they aren't yet able to write, ask them to remember the specific sounds and have a person at home write them down or just bring the information into class to share. We gather *all* the sounds, the songs and language of birds. One group of first graders dictated about forty different phonetically spelled sounds! Bird words such as *caw caw*, *cheep cheep*, *coo coo*, *chirrup chirrup* filled the chalkboard. Our board was chirping with bird songs! Of course, the children wanted to draw pictures of birds. As we gave out drawing paper and crayons, I encouraged them to decide what words the birds were singing, copy the ones they chose from the board, and use dialogue bubbles if they wanted to. As an added spice, I asked the kids to pretend they could translate the birds' words into English, so somewhere on their pictures, they included the translation! The children's pictures of bird words are among my most precious possessions! Try it. See for yourself.

## *Mother Nature Rhythm Band*

Many of our city children rarely have opportunities to enjoy "outdoor education" or frequent field trips to nature centers, ponds, or forests. Few of them see a real field on a field trip! Sylvia Wallach Motin[14] takes her inner-city Chicago children to the nearest park. They have already talked about nature and music.

Sylvia's lessons are imbued with energy and commitment. The children have heard her say, "All the instruments we ever knew came from nature—for example, drumming on tree trunks, shaking seeds in pods from trees, blowing into seashells. . . . In ancient days when we experienced storms, lightning, thunder, phenomena we didn't understand, we tried to make it more understandable by imitating the sounds and rhythms of natural events. We lessened our fears by saying to Nature, 'Listen. We're part of you and we're honoring your powers!' We became composers, performers, and listeners. . . ."

The children gather materials for their Mother Nature Rhythm Band, picking nothing but what they find on the ground. They bring their pebbles, sticks, seed pods, tree bark, and other natural items back to the classroom. They experiment with various sounds. It's exciting for them to decide where they will "go" to create their Mother Nature soundscape using imagination, voices, bodies, and rhythms from their gathered "instruments." One class decided to "go" to a pond before a rainstorm. What kinds of sounds would they hear? The children had many ideas, like crickets, birds, frogs, raindrops, wind, and leaves rustling.

They taped their soundscape. *Inspiration has no limits.* The children created a large mural, which everyone worked on. They wrote haiku-style poems about the pond and the rain and placed their poems in the middle of the mural.

"Of course, we include movement for each of our sound sections," Sylvia adds.

Once again, Mother Nature's daily gifts of weather are constant connections to the natural world. Children love making rainsticks. The easiest way I know is to use paper towel rolls. Close one end. Gather small pebbles, sand, bits and pieces of scrounged materials. (Six-year-old Dylan filled his rainstick with a variety of different-shaped shakable materials.) Teachers help the children add little sticks, cotton swab sticks without the cotton, or any hard, protruding object that will keep the shaking materials from falling evenly in the rainstick. The children, after both ends are covered, love to decorate their instruments. We had a glorious time playing our rainsticks and paper-plate tambourines and coffee-can and oatmeal-container drums, accompanying Jack Grunsky's dramatic and exciting song "Big Thunder, Dark Cloud."[15] You can imagine the thunderstorm poems and pictures created after our musical/movement celebration!

### Sing a Song About the World of Nature and Environment

This is a very old idea!

All tribal peoples sang poems, called their poems "songs," and honored every aspect of nature. Thumb through any anthology of, for example, Native American poetry. You'll find countless chants/songs/poems with titles like "Mouse Song," "Bear Song," "Beaver Song," "Rain Song," "Thunder Song," and so on. Think how many "songs" you and your children can compose, sing, chant, and accompany with rhythm instruments and movement! (Many young children already carry on this ancient tradition by humming and singing their own little songs about the sun shining or stars twinkling or rain pattering!) Expand sharing original songs about neighborhoods, playgrounds, the life of streets, and the buzz of traffic!

### Nature Is a Moving Experience!

Earth revolves around the Sun. Seeds grow into flowers, plants, and trees. Wind blows leaves. Tides roll in and out.

Every aspect of nature can be shown through movement and body designs. When children "show you" on a daily basis, movement becomes a stronger integral component of their vocabularies. Because they are moving purposefully all the time, they are able to develop more complicated movement ideas. Working individually, in small groups, or as one large group, we have demonstrated and celebrated the ocean (complete with water, tides, fish, and sea plants) and the solar system (including the revolution of Earth around the Sun as well as the rotation of Earth on its axis). Do it slowly, with dreamlike music, so no one gets dizzy (especially you). From the crawling of the smallest snail to the buzzing/blowing/swinging/climbing/hiding/blooming/pulsating life of a forest, children delight in expressing ideas through movement. You'll find that after they actively interpret themes and suggestions through movement and play, their visual arts creations as well as their original writings are extraordinarily enriched. Move and play first! Settle down to the visual arts and creative writing *after* movement/music/play sessions.

### Metamorphoses/Changes/Cycles

From seeds to trees, plants, and flowers; from caterpillars to butterflies; from tadpoles to frogs; from winter to spring; the possibilities for movement celebrations abound! Wrap the thematic material in a story and the experiences are enhanced. After the first graders' movement story about chicks hatching (we began curled up on the floor oh so tightly, feeling our shells around us as we grew, we felt closed in, crowded—we

FIGURE 6–5   *After we played and danced hatching, we illustrated the idea.*

had to get out—*crack*—we jabbed our shells but were too exhausted to get out—*crack* again—we kicked, we pecked—finally, we hatched—and our new lives began), a few children came back to the multipurpose room. "Tasha can't find her earring." We looked for it on the floor. One of the children asked, "Tasha, where were you when you hatched?" We found the earring!

Think about the children interpreting the melting of snow, the forming of ice, the frozen shapes, the melting again, the changing of frozen shapes, puddles, and evaporation—there are so many movement possibilities in the dance of nature! Music from *everywhere* that has changes (slow/fast, loud/soft, high/low) will inspire movement.

### What If? Turn Yourself Into . . .

(More words to get kids moving.) "What if you were a deer? How would you leap?" "What if you were a sunflower? How tall would you grow?" "What if you were a monkey? What tricks could you do?" "Turn yourself into a river. How would you flow?" "Turn yourself into a star. How would you shine?" "Turn yourself into a horse. How would you gallop?" These children are always ready. Within each challenge are many possibilities. Encourage the playfulness.

### Books That Help Kids Get Moving

These are so plentiful that no one text could contain them all! One of my favorites is Eric Carle's *From Head to Toe*. Animals show children one of their movements and ask the children if they can do it. Of course, the children can! Frogs (and kids) always enjoy Ellen Stoll Walsh's *Hop Jump!* Betsy the Frog wants to dance. Hopping and jumping and leaping and turning, frogs discover (as do their human choreographers) that there's room for dancing and hopping!

Taro Gomi's *My Friends* strengthens feelings of connectedness to animals and nature. Children love to move to the ways their friends teach them—lovely lessons like learning to sing from birds, learning to kick from their friend Gorilla and even learning to watch the sky at night from their friend Owl.[16]

(Give me a book about *any* aspect of nature and I'll show you a resource for movement, drama, play, and music activities intrinsically woven into every illustration and word!)

Remember, animals are creatures of the earth and leap over political boundaries! Wind blows across the four directions. Clouds sail in the sky. Colors change. Gardens grow. Just gather the verbs of nature and you and your children will have marvelous times exploring that movement vocabulary!

Choose music from around the world to accompany animal movement dances, dances of seasons, mountains, rivers, forests, and oceans.

### *The Dance and Music of Seasons*

Footprints in snow? Choreography of a snowy day? Seeds sprouting and growing? The opening of flower petals? The falling of autumn leaves? The quiet song of snowflakes? How many ideas can you add to seasonal and cyclical sounds and movement? No end to the list! Gather ideas with the children as you talk about each of the seasons. Write them on the board or on charts. These words and ideas will generate dances, dramas, symphonies! Here are a few components of one of our autumn dances choreographed by a group of kindergarten kids:

> We need sweaters and coats.
> The wind blows harder.
> Squirrels and chipmunks and birds eat a lot of food.
> Leaves start falling, falling, floating from the trees.
> We rake the leaves.
> We jump in the leaves.
> We throw footballs.
> We see huge pumpkins too heavy to pick up.
> It's dark earlier so we run/skip home for a hot chocolate.

The music the children loved for this "story" was Scott Joplin's "The Entertainer." The children danced from one idea to the next. Their movements were very clear. The music bopped them along. It all happened in twenty minutes.

*Note:* In *all* of these suggested integrated activities, children are learning about comparisons, directions, vocabulary, rhythms, counting, comprehension, spatial perceptions, sequential learning, patterning, colors, shapes, and more. Such concepts and skills are built into *every* experience!

### Gather a Collection of Songs and Music Celebrating Nature

Draw on your own memories and experiences to remember and collect the songs and music you know and love that feature themes of our natural world, our environment. You and your students and their families are excellent resources and you already know more than you think you do! Every music maker singing in the education arena has songs honoring topics from nature. Think "Baby Beluga." Think "The Eensy Weensy Spider." Think "You Are My Sunshine." Think "Twinkle, Twinkle, Little Star." Songs about rain, blue skies, mountains, rivers, animals, plants, sunrises, and sunsets are enjoyed across cultures. Sing along. Sing together. If you forget some words, improvise! Write the lyrics in your class song book. Illustrate! Move to the music! Add your own lyrics.

Be prepared to be surprised at the number of songs you know! Share your favorites. With children of all ages, I've sung John Denver's "Sunshine 'Round My Shoulders," the Beatles' "Here Comes the Sun," the old popular tune "You Are My Sunshine," Irving Berlin's "April Showers," and on and on. Check your garage and basement for treasures you may have forgotten you have! Add them to your language-rich song collection! Find city songs! Find country songs!

### Favorite Nature Themes (Magic Vocabulary)

We each have favorite words and ideas that mean the most to us. Certain people, places, animals, objects, and events are held deeply in our hearts. We are very ready to celebrate these ideas in as many ways as we

FIGURE 6–6  *Kids love to draw their favorite trees.*

are given opportunities. Our lists will be unique to ourselves. Which are your animals? What plants and flowers are on your list? What places of the earth are your places? Children have their lists, too. When we surround them with stimulating materials—magazines, posters, pictures, paintings, cards, and books—their lists expand. They fall in love with certain creatures. They are fascinated by specific weather conditions, trees, or land forms. From their Magic Vocabulary list, invite them to choose an idea—draw it, paint it, make it, sing it, write about it, and show it through movement. Turn it into riddles and guess its identity. Choreograph it.

Because of imaginative, creative teachers, children who have never seen the ocean feel ownership of oceans. They turn their rooms into seascapes, read, play, sing, move, talk about the life of an ocean. Children far from trees and forests imagine rain forests inspired by vivid materials, exciting resources, stories shared by enthusiastic teachers. Our Magic Vocabularies are in continuous expansion when we learn together in meaningful, enjoyable ways.

### Honor Dances

Just as all tribal peoples create literature honoring every aspect of nature, so their dances imitate and hallow animals, plants, land, sky, and water forms. I reach to three well-used (probably out of print!) albums in my collection. With all children, I have improvised movement sequences and dances to the offerings on these records. Note the nature titles of the selections: from the album *China: Shantung Folk Music and Traditional Instrumental Pieces:* "Beautiful Spring," "A Happy Evening," "Moonlit Night," "Silent Evening," and "Chirping of a Hundred Birds"; from *Songs of Earth, Water, Fire and Sky (Music of the American Indian):* "Rabbit Dance" (Northern Plains), "Butterfly Dance" (San Juan Pueblo), "Eagle Dance" (Northern Arapaho), and "Alligator Dance" (Seneca); from *Music from the Kabuki (Geza Music of Japan)*, intricate explanations are included to indicate that the *mizuoto* is a drum theme that signifies water, another drum theme signifies waves, the *yamaroshi* drum symbolizes mountains, the *kazoto* is the sound of wind, and the *shinobisanju* is the motif for darkness. Nature is honored in instruments, movement, rituals, dramas, and dances.[17]

Working as a group, in small groups, or individually, children enjoy creating and choreographing their own dances to animals and natural themes they especially love. Add masks, colors, costumes, rhythms, stories, and poems. Or, just "do" them by themselves.

### Prepositions and Directions

Look up! What do you see above you? Clouds, sky, lightning streaks? Look down! What do you notice below you? Stones? Pebbles? Grass? Dirt? Many ancient traditions from Native American to African to Aboriginal throughout history and geography have honored their "sacred directions." Chants from, for example, the Navajo morning and evening songs repeat over and over in many poetry variations like this:

> With beauty above me, I walk.
> With beauty below me, I walk.
> With beauty before me, I walk.
> With beauty behind me, I walk.
> With beauty all around me, I walk.

Imagine how enriched any simple experience becomes when we remind children (and ourselves) to notice what's above us, below us, before us, behind us, and all around us! Our bright lights are *on*! The repetition is powerful and reassures the children as they honor these old connecting ideas.

Numerous peoples also honor the four directions: north, south, east, and west. Invite the children to show all these powerful directions with their bodies, with movement. Most kids will easily reach up, look up, to show "above" and bend to show "below." Honoring these important directions helps the children connect to the greater world of nature that is all around them. Play any steady, rhythmic music from any culture or have the children play their own percussive heartbeat rhythms with homemade or class instruments. Reach toward the sky. Bend toward the earth. Stretch arms before you. Reach back, lean back, to show the idea of "behind us." Circle slowly to demonstrate "all around us." Jump and clap to the north, south, east, and west.

Compose your own chants. Choreograph your own special dances to begin or end or enjoy anytime during the day.

FIGURE 6–7   *With beauty all around us, we dance.*

Because I love these old, simple connections to the world of nature and to the life all around us, I share them with children of all ages. Through the years, I've gathered thousands of original chants, illustrations, poems, stories, sculptures, and dances. Here are two from my vast collections composed by first graders:

| 1 | 2 |
|---|---|
| Above us we see the sky. | Above us we see rooftops. |
| Below us we feel the grass. | Below us we jump on hopscotch. |
| Before us we see birds in the trees. | Before us is a red STOP sign. |
| Behind us we hear a dog barking. | Behind us is a street full of traffic. |
| All around it's sunny. | All around are lots of people. |
| May we walk with friends. | May we play in the playground together. |
| | |
| We wave to the east. | We jump rope to the east. |
| We jump to the west. | We swing to the west. |
| We point to the north. | We rollerblade to the north. |
| We wiggle to the south. | We run to the south. |
| May we dance with friends. | May we wave to each other. |

## Legends, Myths, and Folklore

Our earliest legends were explanations for natural phenomena. Human imagination, over millennia, has created stories about animals, Earth, stars, and the sea: every single aspect of the natural world has been celebrated in stories such as the idea of Mother Nature, Father Time, Father Sky, Sister Moon, and the myriad ways humans played with the awesome world around them. Children love stories from around the world: How did the stars get up to the sky? Why does the moon seem to disappear? Is lightning the thunderbolt of Zeus? Why does the earth freeze during winter?

Children enjoy reading legends, myths, and folktales, improvising on the stories, making up dances, songs, and poems about them as well as making up their own legends and folktales. They are fascinated by the similarity of legends explaining natural phenomena; for example, Turtle is honored by both Native Americans and Chinese people as the animal who dove to the bottom of the sea and brought up land on its shell. The best resource material for original legends about nature comes from the questions and wonderings of your own group of children. The seeds of stories grow from thinking times and talk times. Make time! Time for playing, dancing, improvising, music making, and myth making!

## Celebrations and Special Occasions

Our calendars are a rich resource of events and holidays commemorating themes from nature. Across the planet and through centuries, the human family has celebrated the change of seasons, harvests, new moons, and trees with religious, cultural, and social holidays. Most of these have prescribed activities, songs, games, colors, food, and symbols. In Holland, people celebrate their most popular flower, the tulip. Egyptian families celebrate Sham al-Nessim in mid-March to enjoy the spring. Italian children love St. Joseph's Day on March 19. Flowers and food are in abundance as the new season begins. Even swallows return to San Juan Capistrano in California! All around the world, people celebrate the first of May with cheerful festivals and customs. African American children celebrate the harvest and family unity with candles and special colors and customs for the holiday of Kwanzaa. Jewish children have special songs, prayers, and symbols for the harvest festival of Sukkot (Feast of Booths). Earth Day is a relatively new holiday for children around the world. Sadly, too many children pay attention to concerns about wonders of Earth only once a year! This is an ongoing theme—part of everyday life!

Learn about the special celebrations enjoyed by the children in your class. Share the songs, games, colors, and stories. Go beyond designated holidays. With your children, choose a theme from nature (animals? plants? trees? flowers? fish? stars?) and create your own holiday, with your own colors, songs, games, signs, symbols, and dances. Posters, cards, banners, poems, chants, processions, paintings, and sculptures are delightful ways for you and your children to introduce celebrations to families, friends, and the school community.

### Music and Dances Inspired by Stories and Poems

Nature is a major theme in many of our favorite works of literature. As you read, note those aspects of the material that most easily inspire musical interpretations. When we read the Slovenian folktale *How the Sun Was Brought Back to the Sky*, the children created music, songs, and movements for each of the animals who climbed to the sky to find the sun and bring it back to the cold and dark world. You can imagine that the chick's song and rhythms were very different from the rabbit's song. The children especially loved: "Sun, sun, world's delight. Come out, give us warmth and light." That became their chorus.

There are many examples of literature-related musical experiences, but because of space, we'll include only a few samples. From *The Snowy Day*, the children composed a playful chant to "Down fell the snow—plop! On top of Peter's head. . . ." Many imaginative responses were evoked during our celebration of *The Emperor's Nightingale*, when the children were challenged to create their own song of the nightingale and their own music of the mechanical bird. And what about composing lyrics for the song of the nightingale? How can we show the movement of the nightingale flying? How can we show the contrasting movement of the mechanical bird? What music and rhythms shall we try?

Children love moving, improvising, and making music to such cold places of nature as the Arctic and to such hot islands of color and warmth as tropical islands. Jane Yolen's *Welcome to the Ice House* evokes images of frozen beauty, fabulous animals like moose, bear, and wolf, long winter nights and dark days. Fly across the world to the Caribbean Sea and enjoy the golden sand, shiny blue sparkling water, lush trees, flowers and fruit, and singing birds, as described by Arnold Adoff in *Flamboyan.* How can children *not* move to one of my favorite songs sung by Harry Belafonte, "Island in the Sun"? Reggae and soft calypso music feel like they flowed out of the pages of the book into the children's bodies and pictures! Believe it or not I just found a beautiful book illustrating the lyrics to "Island in the Sun." Sing it as you read it!

One old and dear story beloved by the children is Marie Hall Etts' *Play with Me,* about a child who wants to play with the different animals but in her enthusiasm chases them and scares them away. Alone and lonely, she sits by herself, just listening quietly. One by one, all the animals join her, "Oh now I was happy as happy could be! ALL of them— ALL OF THEM—were playing with me." The kids move, play, and sing the simple story with built-in choreography, lyrics, and an important lesson.

A First Little Golden Book, *Good Morning, Muffin Mouse,* provides delightful greetings to different gifts of nature. As Muffin Mouse wanders through a day, it hails "friends" with greeting such as, "Hi, tall grass," "Hello, cool water!" "Greetings to all you little bugs that crawl and fly." We have a wonderful time greeting our day and its wonders with salutations, imitations, gestures, movements, and songs. The children are eager to express their own greetings, add to the collection of ideas greeted, and turn themselves into the flowers, bugs, and trees.[18]

FIGURE 6–8    *We're happy! All the animals are playing with us!*

When Penni Rubin comes into a classroom, she brings magic with her. In this instance, the kids are deeply fascinated by creepy, crawling creatures. From her collection of STUFF (Stimulating Tools Useful for Fun and Fundamentals), Penni fills her suitcase with rubber snakes, alligators, ants, spiders, cloth creatures, plastic, and string. She's dressed as a bug collector. Under one arm is her guitar. Bug-collecting nets are packed in her bulging suitcase. It's time to play Wonder Lab.[19]

The children dive into the suitcase of insects, lizards, and turtles. Out come empty boxes ready for itemizing and categorizing. The children are "hired" as staff bug collectors, museum curators, and exhibit designers. Together, they decide how to categorize the creatures. They name, count, list, compare, and collect. Labeling and designing, they create excellent exhibits. Penni asks them, "Two legs? No legs? Four legs? Six legs? Thousands of legs?" They invent shadow plays of insects with a sheet, a light, and expressive bodies. They fold paper in half, cut it into bug shapes, drop paint in the middle, press the cut paper together, and string up original bug mobiles to enhance their museum. They act to the Shel Silverstein poem "I'm Being Swallowed by a Boa Constrictor" and "The Eensy Weensy Spider." They celebrate Eric Carle's *Very Hungry Caterpillar*[20] with a puppet show featuring striped knee socks.

Penni describes her approach: "We attach a set of pipe cleaners and pompoms as antennas to both socks, and add two button eyes on both. One of the socks we stuff and make into a butterfly with net wings attached. The other we leave wiggly. As the story goes along, we feed the wiggly caterpillar sock puppet clay and plastic fruit. We let that caterpillar crawl into a dark, cozy bag. As the story unfolds, we push out the other sock puppet, the butterfly one with net wings, and wow—is it magic!"

There's always music and movement in Penni's scientific adventures.

The children love to play scientist, archeologist, and meteorologist. Without you, they sort, collect, and categorize. With your encouragement and guidance they extend those natural, Curious George–like qualities to higher levels of thinking and learning.

Children collect, arrange, improvise, sort, exchange, experiment, infer, and communicate as they "mess with" and play with materials that invite interaction.

Give them time and space, the real stuff of playful learning.

Penni Rubin wanders the country with her Wonder Lab of playful ideas. What's happening with the wonder in your room? I wonder. . . .

### City Sounds, Country Sounds: Music of Our Environment

City children know the cacophony of horns, brakes, sirens, traffic, crowds, airplanes, and subways. Country children know the good morning song of roosters, the comforting clucking of hens, the funny quack quack of ducks, and the gentlest beginning of rain tapping on the roof. With your children, gather a collection of the sounds they hear in their neighborhood or community. Use voices, bodies, instruments, and lyrics to capture the flavor of natural and environmental sounds. Books like the Maestros' *Taxi: A Book of City Words* spark even more urban musical sounds. Play jazzy rhythms, music with pulsing tempos and beats to catch the excitement of city sounds. The children won't have to be prodded to invent their own movement to the music and words catching the flavor of city life. Contrast that experience with the more lyrical, softer music of the sounds of a country environment. Children in more rural settings have more opportunities to celebrate nature. Diane Iverson's *I Celebrate Nature* enriches the children's own gathering of sound images—"the gentle buzz of bees . . . the chatter of birds . . . the skipping, dancing water. . . ." Words, music, rhythms inspire movement and poetry. We were celebrating nature with a group of second graders. One of the children stopped in the middle of his twirling and explained, "Sometimes the wind is noisy and sometimes it just quits!"

Urban environments are electric with fast rhythms, pulsing movement, a special energy that contrasts with more tranquil surroundings. What is the music of city streets? How can we catch the "jazz of our streets" in movement, music, poetry, and drama? In visual images? When children listen to or read along with Fatima Shaik's lively, colorful story *The Jazz of Our Streets*, the text practically choreographs itself! Just move along with the ideas.[21]

### Clothing and Weather and Seasons and Places

We don't wear bathing suits outdoors in the winter. We don't wear snowsuits in July. Children are fascinated by clothing—the colors, styles, patterns, buttons, pockets, zippers, and so on. But our movement possibilities depend on the clothes we are wearing and they are caught in Mother Nature's schemes! One of our favorite movement celebrations is going through the mime/movement sequences of dressing for a snowy, cold day. The children will show you the movement of pulling on snowpants and boots, slipping on sweaters and jackets and hoods and scarves and mittens. With all those layers of heavy clothing, how do we move? We lift our feet heavily as we stomp through the imaginary snow in our imaginary boots. Be careful! We slip on the ice and fall down and up and down and up! (The kids love to fall down and get up again!) We throw snowballs and build snow shapes. We make deep footprints in our imaginary snow. Our boots are heavy and our clothes weight us down. Our movement is more confined and limited. Ah! But spring is coming. A new dance! Off with the hats, scarves, jackets, and boots. Now we can skip and run lightly and freely. Our arms swing and our feet leap through the lovely warm spring days of our imagination.

Find music that moves slowly and heavily for winter. Find light, bouncy music for spring dances. Dance around the seasons! Dance through the seasons! No matter the weather, we dance! Rainy-day dances and sunshiny dances!

## ALL WAYS ART

Kaye Boiarski is an example of an educator with wisdom, practicality, and delightful ideas to share with you.[22] One of her favorite projects was created with a diverse group of preschoolers (medically fragile children with special needs working and playing together with "typically developing" children at the Nisonger Center at Ohio State University). They designed and built an outside playground featuring an undersea theme. On a tall post, they wound soft, cloth-stuffed sculptures of sea plants and sea creatures. Reaching out of the sculptures were tree branches with tufts of heavy nonfilament strings in bright colors. Patricia Wynn Brown wrote about the children's playground:

> A very special playground for children was constructed this past fall. With the theme "Under the Sea," it is both aesthetically pleasing and accessible to kids who rarely get to play outside. . . . A blue canopy covers a structure that shelters children from weather and sunlight. Behind it is a bright interactive sea motif . . . soft sculpture coral, starfish and lobsters. . . . A gently sloping hill allows even the least agile child a chance to climb and roll. And the best way to develop gross motor skills is, of course, to crawl through the play area's giant whale.[23]

Natural materials, kids, and Kaye are the mix that makes for joyful times together. A few of Kaye's numerous adventures using nature as her major focus follow. As you read, imagine the ideas, add on to them, change them to fit your spirit, your children, and your own unique situation.

### *From Kaye's Treasure Chest of Arts Adventures*

**Branched stick-people dancers.** We look for branched sticks on the ground in interesting shapes and bring them back to our table covered with lots of scrounged materials. We decorate the sticks to look like dancing people, dancing for joy to honor nature.

**Wind chimes.** It's so easy to make wind chimes. Gather seashells or small stones, drill holes in them (if they don't already have holes), pull strings through them, and hang them.

**Dream catchers.** From the Native American tradition, we share the idea of the dream catchers. We shape grapevines into a circle, take thin string and design it into a spider web pattern inside the circle, add tiny stones, little feathers, and beads to it, and hang it in our room or over our beds. Only the good dreams are caught; the bad dreams float away. In old traditions, we talk about making gifts for others, always sharing our gifts.

**Nature prints on T-shirts and materials.** We gather dropped flowers, leaves, pebbles, ferns, grass, and stones and arrange them on T-shirts. Then we fill plant-misting bottles with diluted acrylic paint and mist the shirt with the paint. We remove the materials when the paint dries, and we have marvelously designed shirts featuring patterns from nature. Use sheets and mural paper to create larger designs.

**More nature prints.** This kind of print is the reverse. Coat leaves, stones, and pebbles with acrylic paint and press them on paper and materials. They make excellent gifts as well as lively wall hangings and colorful prints.

**Outdoor nature sculptures.** We mix peat moss, sand, and a little cement. This mixture makes weatherproof sculptural material that kids shape into animals and place outside. A variation is to press into the mixture things from the environment like rocks, sticks, leaves, and our own handprints and footprints. After the shapes dry, add them onto and arrange them into three-dimensional bas-reliefs. We think of these as records of what we want to keep, remember, and honor. The children love to create models of their own hands and feet in this soft material.

**Rubbings.** We press sheets of paper against the trunks of trees. As the papers are pressed, we rub them with the sides of crayons to pick up the texture of the bark. The variety of patterns and designs is amazing, especially when they are all displayed together.

**Pinecone necklaces.** The kids love jewelry. Pick small pinecones, string them together, and wear them.

**Assemblages.** On matboard, tagboard, or cardboard, assemble twigs, leaves, stems, and stones. Create original nature scenes.

**Making paper.** We always talk about how trees give us so many materials, so many gifts. We talk about all the products and ideas we get from trees. Making paper is one way of honoring trees and teaching the kids not to waste anything. We gather materials for texture like leaves, flower petals, carrot scrapings, recycled newspapers, and lint from laundry. We mix it all in the blender, then pour the concoction on a framed

FIGURE 6–9 *Children love making masks for their dramas.*

screen. We strain the mixture through the screen, draining the water. Only the pulp remains and dries into a large sheet of paper.

**Bird nests.** When we find abandoned bird nests, we paint little stones and pebbles and put them in the nests. Then we glue together paper strips, party streamers, and dried grass, making our own nests. The kids loves nests!

*Note:* As you enjoy these few samples of visual arts experiences, constantly remind the children that the source of their materials is of great value. Trees provide many of our favorite items like paper, wood, pencils, furniture, floors, and boxes. I ask the children to remember that "a tree was cut down so you could write and draw and paint on the paper made from it. Honor the life of that tree and always try to do your best work! Don't waste the precious materials. Think about your designs, your words, your patterns. Be proud of all your work!"

Because you continually emphasize the importance of saving a large collection of usually tossed materials (like fast-food containers, plastic and Styrofoam, boxes, greeting cards, old magazines, etc.), you are constantly reminding children of the value of recycling, not wasting, usable materials and helping to preserve the environment. These are built-in everyday life lessons!

When children are offered many choices in a free, safe, loving, and encouraging environment, they will experiment with materials, often risking, often returning to their favorites. Give Erin watercolors and she is happy forever. Nick turns any space around him into a construction site. He's a builder, an architect, a sculptor. Be flexible and welcoming of all ideas. Of course, there are times when you will want the children to share a common arts exploration. When our friend Yasue instructs children on creating fabulous origami birds, animals, and insects, everyone participates and learns a new medium.

## Designs and Symbols of Nature

Nature provides a multitude of ideas for patterns, designs, symbols, and color combinations. With your students, always notice and appreciate the stripes, spots, swirls, blends, blotches, and dots found on animals, fish, birds, insects, landscapes, and plants. Children who live in the four seasons can look to, for example, *real* autumn and spring leaves for inspiration to create their own beautiful leaf designs.

Outstanding picture books like Lois Ehlert's *Red Leaf, Yellow Leaf*, Ken Robbins' *Autumn Leaves*, and Zoe Hall's *Fall Leaves Fall!*[24] provide almost firsthand knowledge of one of nature's wonders. They evoke immediate responses in the children to create their own colorful and delightful autumn leaves. Of course, piles of leaves invite jumpers! Leaves falling from trees confetti the air with colors! So many possibilities for extended activities!

I spent a few days with children and teachers in Juneau, Alaska, during a cold, rainy, dark period of time. One of the rooms I visited was very cheery and warm despite the outside gray. The windows of this room were brightened by colorful designs of leaf patterns pressed to the windowpane with clear contact paper, beckoning children to pay attention to and appreciate their lovely designs and patterns. The children loved creating their window leaves!

Artist/educator Jim Arter shares his own deep appreciation of the colors, shapes, patterns, and symbols around us with inner-city children and disadvantaged children in lands far from ours. Wherever he goes, he brings paper, pencils, and colors for the children to enjoy. Wherever he goes, he and his gifts and his loving spirit draw kids to him like a magnet. Even if the spoken languages are different, Jim and the children love and understand the joy of creating the shapes and colors of natural wonders: stars, rainbows, moons, suns, clouds, trees, and the universally recognized symbols of hearts and peace. Immediate and always relevant themes![25]

Since earliest times, images of animals, plants, flowers, as well as stars, sun, moon, mountains, and rainbows, have symbolized qualities such as strength, peace, and harmony. Flags, totems, banners, and coats of arms feature symbols from nature. A challenge to the children is to design their own symbols from their own favorite nature ideas and cre-

FIGURE 6–10   *Nature contains many shapes.*

ate their own banner, flag, or totem. Garden banners and flags are popular now. If you have a class garden (more on that later), hang the children's banners and flags around it to add to the celebration of growing things. I remember first grader Latrice explaining the two animals she painted on her banner. "The kitten is for cuteness and the squirrel is for cuteness, too!"

## *Making Connections, Seeing Relationships*

Old favorite songs like "Green Grass Grew All Around," which begins with "There was a hole in the middle of the ground, the prettiest hole you ever did see . . ." and goes on to add a tree in the hole, a branch on the tree, a nest on the branch, an egg in the nest, and a bird in the egg (that's one variation), are excellent for the pure enjoyment of singing together, moving to every idea in its sequence, and immediately following the song by drawing, painting, or constructing every component of the "plot." I've played with this song with more than a thousand children of diverse ages and never has one child been unable to draw a hole, a tree, a branch, a nest, an egg, and a bird. I always ask, "What else?" Continue with questions such as "What's the weather? What color is the sky? Are there clouds? Is it night or day? Are there any other trees in the picture? Animals? Insects? Butterflies? Birds?" Your entire yearlong celebration of nature could begin with this simple song and the illustrations that describe it with original extensions on every paper! We could go on and on with any idea! Let's add to the above, "What season? What kind of tree? Is this in the city? Country? Rain forest?" It goes on and on. . . .

Michael Joel Rosen's intriguing book *All Eyes on the Pond* encourages children to look at the world through different viewpoints. All the creatures in the pond have their own eyesight and perceptions. *What do the swallows see? What is the view of the snapping turtle?* The lovely progression ends with "If you were here, what would you spy / with your peculiar human eye? / Shh. Come closer. What's your view? / All the creatures watch for you." Think of a pond, a puddle, a field, a forest—what exciting pictures the children create to catch some of the life in those natural scenes. Imagination and observation blend beautifully!

A smorgasbord of nature's miracles is spread before the children in Cynthia Rylant's beautiful book *The Wonderful Happens*. Viera's *Ever-Living Tree: The Life and Times of a Coast Redwood* is an example of a life-affirming wonder of nature. Imagine the children's responses expressed in their own illustrations, constructions, and creations.[26]

### Where Do You Live?

Your immediate environment, your natural surroundings are rooted in your geography. Is yours a desert landscape with strange, mysterious canyon shapes silhouetting a Southwestern sunset? Or do you and your children know the magnificence of sky-high mountain ranges? Are lakes and rivers all around you, or are you landlocked? Do fields, farms, and forests form your designs or do you and your children admire the tree growing in Brooklyn and the lush oasis of Central Park in the middle of bustling Manhattan? These are the familiar images your kids know and love to interpret. Honor the familiar. Books, paintings, posters, films, and videos will help expand their horizons, their landscapes and mindscapes. Marcus has never seen the ocean but he loves to paint oceans. Destiny dreams of mountains. The only mountains she knows are on the pages of books or tacked to bulletin boards. But she is an expert on drawing mountains! Today she is sculpting a mountain out of clay. She's already formed a mountain out of papier-mâché.

### Some More Books to Inspire Works of Art

Animals such as wolves intrigue children, most of whom love to draw, paint, or sculpt animals. Jannie Howker's beautiful and dramatic book *Walk with a Wolf* is exciting to read, look at, and enrich with the children's own visual arts interpretations. Add to the mix Leslie Zak's fantastic "Wolf Song." After the children read and hear the book, study the illustrations, and join Leslie in the "Wolf Song," they are more than ready to create their own powerful images of wolves and their landscapes.

Young children are delighted by foldout flap books that reveal hidden images. Books like Henry Cole's *I Took a Walk* invite the kids to enjoy the woods, ponds, meadows, and all the animals and plants that live in those places. Lots of hidden animals wait to surprise the children. Very original spin-offs from books like these are created with hidden pictures, flaps, and foldouts. One second-grade class created a big book called *We Take a Walk!* It was clear from their pictures and words that it was a great walk![27]

## Collections and Museums

As we noted, kids' pockets are filled with stones, pebbles, dandelions, dirt, and other natural treasures! Children are born collectors, botanists, archeologists, and naturalists. Shoe boxes and boxes of every size and type are excellent for displaying collections. Wrap the boxes in contact paper, wallpaper, or plain white paper that needs the children's touch. When people arrange assortments of materials—like shells, stones, leaves, pinecones—creative energies are in gear. Decisions are made. How do we display our treasures? Do we decorate them? Paint them? Label them? Make patterns? Be sure to invite families and friends to tour the children's museum.

## What's Growing in Your Garden?

I wish every group of kids in the country could grow a garden—even a little garden! How we waste and ignore the possibilities of growing gardens in the too often neglected dirt right outside our buildings!

When we plant gardens with children (and ourselves), we plant seeds of beauty, wonder, and life energy. We plant seeds of connection, cooperation, and appreciation. We help care for the earth. Children learn a great deal of information by heart. They play with colors, shapes, and sizes in their designs. They write journals, sketch, research, talk, sing, plan, and collaborate. Even in the smallest gardens, many seeds

FIGURE 6–11  *Children want to beautify everything!*

are planted. Enrich the beauty of your garden with garden sculptures, mobiles, and banners.

When I visited elementary schools in Taiwan, I noted that just about every class had a designated space to plant a garden! Surround your kids with garden images! The Impressionists spent years painting gardens! Look at paintings by such artists as Monet and Renoir. Can you smell the flowers and hear the songs of birds and the buzz of bees? Folk artists from every culture create images of nature's gifts.

As you have been reading repeatedly throughout this book, so many of our picture books present quality visual arts experiences for our kids. Books about seeds, flowers, plants, planting gardens are unusually beautiful and can't help but inspire the children to create their own real and artistically interpreted gardens in pictures and structures. *Pumpkin Circle: The Story of a Garden* by George Levenson offers readers eye-popping pumpkin-orange photos of a tiny seed to a heap of pumpkins of all sizes. One of the second graders exclaimed after sharing the book, "I never even thought of pumpkin gardens!" He couldn't wait to paint his own ideas of a pumpkin garden. Some of the children created sequential illustrations from seed to roots to stems to leaves and onward to huge pumpkins!

Robert Maass' beautiful book *Garden* takes the children on the journey from finding a spot to dig a garden, to choosing flowers, to planting seeds, and the gorgeous flowering and blossoming. The photos are clear, colorful, and easy to identify with. Besides designing and planting their own small gardens in and outside of your room, children wel-

FIGURE 6–12    *I wish every child could help grow a garden!*

come the opportunity to do their own masterpiece Impressionist paintings of gardens![28]

Of course, you'll need to have a special art show, invite other classes, serve refreshments, and conduct a tour of the "gallery"!

### *Kids Care!*

Throughout the book examples have been shared describing the responsiveness of children to problems and challenges in their classes, communities, and environment. Children are our true caregivers and when they participate in discussions and activities about caring for the earth and community, they immediately answer the call. Pictures, banners, mobiles, posters, illustrated poems and letters, quilts, sculptures, shoe-box scenes, murals, and mosaics are but a few of the creative ways children express their concerns. Fran Avni's beautiful song "Care for the World" and her honor song to trees are excellent stimuli to meaningful talks and extended works. *How can we care for the world?* How can we make our communities and environment more beautiful and in harmony with nature? Air and water pollution, littering, deforestation, shrinking habitats for animals are some topics that evoke strong feelings even in our young children. Greg and Steve's fun song "Don't Throw Your Trash in My Backyard," with its big message, spurs the children on to constant awareness of picking up litter as well as creating imaginative and colorful posters to remind those who may forget!

I have a whole tape of different versions of Woody Guthrie's "This Land Is My Land." Any rendition will be more than a sing-along. It will

FIGURE 6–13   *Kids have great ideas for saving the world!*

remind the children to appreciate the beauty and diversity of this precious land of ours. Play Louis "Satchmo" Armstrong's powerful singing of "What a Wonderful World" and share the beautiful picture book based on the song with the children. The kids will create their own Wonderful World artworks and picture books that will be equally as powerful. Pandell and dePaola's little book *I Love You, Sun, I Love You, Moon* inspires the children to illustrate and write to their loves.

Imagine a class or group book with every page created by a young artist who writes and illustrates such ideas as "I Love You, Stars" or "I Love You, Birds." We take care of the things we love! Encourage more ideas. Ask, "Why?"

Be sure to remember the built-in relationships to movement, drama, creative writing, and improvisation. Show the idea!

Sometimes a tiny book like Rozanne Williams' *Let's Take Care of the Earth* inspires great ideas! This simple, loving book connects children to many parts of the earth—animals, regions, and more. It's so easy to invite the kids to go on with their own suggestions to illustrate, describe, and share.[29]

### Colors! Colors! Colors! Shapes! Shapes! Shapes!

Nature and our environment are rich with colors. Extend your daily inclusions of colors into all topics and talks ("I like your yellow shirt, Landen." "Please find something red in this room, children.") to nature's dazzling bounty of colors and shapes all around us. Help the children see the variations of colors. Encourage them to mix their colors—experiment and explore possibilities. Integrate with all your observations a continuous focus on shapes and hues. Look at the dark brown bark of that tree! Let's describe these houses on this busy street! Children love constructing communities, forests, skylines, silhouettes, mountains, and other scenery. Whether they are working individually, in pairs, or as a group, the theme fascinates them and keeps their attention span *long*! An acclaimed artist well known in the children's literature field, Chris Canyon talked eloquently about the importance of colors. He said, "Do colors belong to poetry, science, math, social studies? I think all subjects. Colors relate to everything. I think of color as a language of communication and my work is that of a visual storyteller who composes with colors and textures instead of words and sounds. . . . The way that colors occur and our reactions are beyond scientific. . . . When I'm with the children, we talk about how they feel about the pictures. I encourage them to really look at the colors around them and the colors in books. . . . Think of nature and colors: how many signs and symbols we understand without the words, just with the colors. . . ."[30]

When young children are constantly aware of and interested in the variety of colors and shapes around them, when they learn to name and recognize them, connections to math concepts, language development, graphing, vocabulary enrichment are obvious!

### Snips and Snaps

On the rare occasion when I draw a blank (did you ever draw a blank?) I think of all the countless areas of interest we left out! Sand, sun, stars, moon, planets, streets, skylines, bridges, tunnels, parks, playgrounds . . . oh, my! We cannot help but have numerous ideas once we begin thinking about our natural world and our environment and ways these worlds can be expressed in the visual arts, in all the arts, in all ways!

But, if time is pressing in on you, reach out, reach up! I climb to my top shelf and pull down two old, well-worn resources: Phyllis Fiarotta's *Snips and Snails and Walnut Whales: Nature Crafts for Children* and her *Sticks and Stones and Ice Cream Cones: Crafts in a Child's World*. I turn to any page and am reminded of yet another idea I'd forgotten, like bird feeders, melon seed necklaces, still-life pictures of arranged fruit, and on and on. . . . If I have time to run to the library, the resources abound.

Maybe an idea-filled book like *Berry Smudges and Leaf Prints: Finding and Making Colors from Nature* will fall from the shelf into your hands! Sparks fly! Ideas are everywhere: quilts, prints, pressings, soft sculptures, mosaics, fabrics, and so on.

Don't despair if visual arts ideas still seem sparse! Thumb through such excellent works as Sandi Henry's *Kids' Art Works: Creating with Color, Design, Texture, and More*. Don't waste a single scrounge resource. Check out *Beautiful Stuff: Learning with Found Materials*. And always keep at your bedside Lillian Katz and Judy Helm's *Young Investigators*. Your only challenge will be time! Stop the clock![31] (And that is why this section is stopping. Time and space limit us!)

## KIDS COUNT

### Taking Inventory

The list on the chalkboard of the nature preserve was rich with information. I took down some of the notes.

1/21/01

10 A.M. 7 deer
12:45 P.M. 12 deer
76 Mallards
8 Easter Gray Squirrels (Eastern)
14 Canada Geese
3 Raccoons
1 Red Fox

Following the above sightings was this list:

| | |
|---|---|
| Cooper's Hawk | Song Sparrow |
| Northern Cardinal | White-Throated Sparrow |
| Mourning Dove | Carolina Wren |
| Downy Woodpecker | House Sparrow |
| House Finch | Sharp-Shinned Hawk |
| White-Breasted Nuthatch | |
| Blue Jay | |
| Tufted Titmouse | |
| American Goldfinch | |

The park ranger explained that records and observations are kept daily. Very often, children make the observation, look up the name and description of the animal in the reference books available, and contribute their discoveries.

I shared this day's observations with my friends in first grade. We talked about the times of sightings in the first list. We compared. We added. How many different kinds of birds were seen that day? From the first list, the children loved figuring out which birds or animals were seen the least. The most. Were more squirrels spotted than mallards? How many different kinds of sparrows were seen?

The natural world and the world of our environment is an amazing resource for counting, collecting, comparing, categorizing, and measuring. *How many trees outside our window? How many buildings? Let's count the number of buses that drive by our school. We can see two traffic lights from our window.* Children are our natural holistic creatures. They don't need prompting to enthusiastically suggest, "Can we make pictures of all those animals and birds, all these buses and traffic lights?" "Can we build it? Construct it? Design it? Graph it? Turn it into a poem or story or song?"

Laughingly, we changed "The Twelve Days of Christmas" into an inventory song using the Nature Preserve's list as our lyrics. The children loved it and not only learned about numbers and counting but language enrichment and vocabulary expansion. "Tufted titmouse" was their favorite even though a few kids with front teeth missing had to lisp that item!

### Gardens Grow

More about gardens, even if it's a classroom garden in a large pot or old tub or blown-up plastic baby pool. Gardens mean planting, designing, patterning, problem solving, decision making, measuring, comprehension, language development, and on and on (too many skills and concepts to list). *Do we plant bulbs? How many for each child? Are the bulbs all the same size? Shall we give everyone one large bulb and one small bulb? Will we have enough for every child? How far apart must they be?*

*What colors shall we choose? All the same colors? One row of whites and another row of oranges? What designs and shapes can we make with our seeds and bulbs? Concentric circles? Ovals?* We can gather little stones and decorate our garden when the plants start growing. *Let's border our plants with squares or ovals or rectangles or circles.* Sing "Inchworm" with the children as you plant. A great way to learn to count starting with two and two and adding and multiplying as you go along.

If a real garden is impossible for you to grow, invite the kids to create their own gardens out of pictures, three-dimensional scenes, murals, and mobiles.

Cut or torn paper, tissue paper, toilet paper rolls, scrounged snips of "treasures" like cotton puffs, beads, bangles, and glitter mixed with glue and paste help grow beautiful images of gardens.

### Constructing a World

I weep for young children who spend time in rooms empty of blocks, sand, water, art materials, hands-on objects easy to manipulate and enjoy as important learning resources. Following talks about the world of nature, our fascinating environment, children want to do something about those areas of interest. Boxes of all sizes are excellent for constructing buildings. Towns and cities develop before your eyes as children use blocks, boxes, plastics, paper, Styrofoam, wood materials in their adventure. *How many buildings? How high? How many windows? Trees? Where in this scene? How many? How tall?* Every idea added helps develop math concepts. Just the adding of ideas enriches comprehension! We start with a blank page, a blank space. We add ideas. If we are constructing a country environment, *What shape barn? House? How many horses, cows, sheep?* Ask thoughtful, relevant questions that evoke decision making and a demonstration of understandings.

A wordless book like J. Baker's *Window* stimulates creativity and imagination. Outside a child's window is a peaceful rural setting. As the child grows older, the scene outside the window changes and finally, bit by bit, adding ideas, the child becomes a grown-up and his environment has grown from a pleasant countryside scene to a city.[32]

Resources like *Window* enrich math comprehension of young children. Ideas are added. There's accumulation. Expansion. More! How do environments change and grow? Valuable experiences for high-order thinking.

When children are actively involved in exploring their own ways of learning, they strengthen skills and develop problem-solving competencies while they continue with their constructions. They ask more complicated questions such as "How come the buildings don't fall down?" and "How do those guys know how many bricks fit?"

They experiment with their own counting, weighing, and measuring and learn about architecture, physics, and their relationships to construction.

Our environment is a language-rich, numbers-rich setting for learning! Numbers of streets, houses, traffic directions ("It says," a first grader reported, "twenty-five miles speed limit!"), gasoline prices, store sale advertisements, time, dates, and so on surround many city and suburban children as they walk through shopping centers, busy streets, malls. One little boy told me he learned his numbers and how to read by looking at license plates! After a while, he said he even learned some states' names! Numbers and letters are around us all the time! Children love to find things! They find the letters of their names in the language of their environment. "That's *my* C!" says Chloe, pointing to a Coca-Cola sign. We find our ages, our lucky numbers, numbers in our telephone code, and our addresses in the numbers surrounding us. Take a walk and listen to the excitement of the children as they recognize their special numbers often blinking to them in neon or calling to them from large signs or billboards. One kindergarten teacher told me she and her children took a walk around the immediate neighborhood. They were looking for numbers from one to twenty. They found them very quickly in the first few minutes of their outing. "Can we go to a hundred?" the kids begged. And they did.

You can count on the natural world to provide experiences in math awareness and concepts. When I told my grandchildren I had counted fifty-four squirrels' nests in a twenty-minute walk around our neighborhood, some of them were inspired to walk around their neighborhoods and see how many squirrels' nests they could spot in twenty minutes! The next highest number was seven! One day Noah reported that he had counted twenty-six birds' nests in his walk through Central Park. Children *love* to count and all kinds of counting count!

If you and your children live near the sea, finding shells and stones is part of that ocean environment. I like the old story of the man walking along the beach, picking up starfish from the countless creatures beached on the sand. He picked up a starfish and threw it back into the ocean. Then another. A passerby stopped him to ask, "There are so many starfish lying here on the beach. What difference is one or two?"

The friend held a small one in his hand and answered, "It makes a big difference to *this* one!"

Even one starfish makes a big difference to young children! They are hunters, gatherers, counters, keepers as they explore their worlds. Count flowers, trees, petals, branches, clouds, birds! Make comparisons. Add them up. Divide them into categories. Make charts and graphs. See how they measure up!

Enrich the children's experiences with some of the outstanding books available. Books like K. Toft and A. Sheather's *One Less Fish*, McMillan's *Counting Wildflowers*, Freymann and Elffers' *One Lonely Sea Horse*, and Eric Carle's *Tiny Seed* are examples of some of our exciting stories and lively illustrations that fill young students' imaginations

FIGURE 6–14 *How much does the puppy weigh? How big will he get?*

with ways the wonders of nature add up, multiplying delight and understanding.[33]

Some children are totally fascinated by statistics. *How fast do cheetahs run? Which animal is faster—a cheetah or an ostrich? How many jumping animals can we think of? Is it true that turtles have thirteen sections on their shells? Which is the biggest animal? Which is the highest mountain? How much do elephants weigh? How tall are giraffes? How old is that redwood tree?* These are questions coming from authentic wonder, interest, and curiosity! When children begin their adventurous journey to finding answers, the ground is hallowed by their wondrous thirst for knowledge.

### It's Time!

Nature provides so many lessons in every subject area, especially math awareness. *How many hours in a day? How many days in a week? How many months in a year?* Learn them. Count them. *How many days till our zoo trip? How many more days until summer vacation?* Calendars, charts, children's illustrations and poems, dances, and songs enrich the learning.

I shared my fascination of day lilies with the second graders. Imagine, only living for one day, twenty-four hours! In that one day the lily blossoms, blooms, beams, and then slowly closes its petals, dries up, and falls. The usually rambunctious group of highly energetic kids was mesmerized by the lily's story. We talked about the twenty-four hours in the lily's life. We turned ourselves into day lilies, opening very slowly, spreading our petals to the sun, beaming and shining, then slowly, slowly pulling ourselves in and slowly falling to the ground. I had very soft, dreamlike music playing (I always have music for every purpose! You never know when it will be needed.) and I gave the kids twenty-four soft beats on my tambourine. By the count of twenty-four, every child was lying on the floor. The lily's day was over. After our session, the children wanted to do time-released sequential pictures of the day of the day lily. They divided their papers into twenty-four sections. Each section had a different illustration following the life of the lily. They added words that described as well as caught the feeling. When our incredible session was over, the principal told me that these were the "worst kids in the school" and she wasn't sure that they would be allowed to participate in my Artists-in-the-Schools program! I only know that to me they were gifted and talented children who expressed their understanding of a very difficult idea to grasp in meaningful and creative ways. I know they will never forget the day of the day lily!

## Counting, Guessing, and Hatching

Count the stars in the Big Dipper. Wish on the first star you see tonight. Fill a jar with sunflower seeds and ask the kids to guesstimate! Keep a record of children and their guesses. Count the seeds together. Who came closest? Marilyn Cohen and her kindergartners spent weeks counting, guessing, measuring, and cooking sunflower seeds. They read sunflower poems and stories, looked at great artworks honoring sunflowers, then created their own sunflower works! Marilyn's kids were the keepers of the hatching eggs. In their incubator, the eggs were the daily (and hourly) subject of attention. The children counted the days until hatching time. They made observations. They knew every egg and watched its every change.

More on beads (art from the earth): Buttons, beads, baubles in designs and jewelry mean counting and decision making. Patterning and sequencing are lessons woven into the activity. Margarette Reid's gorgeous book *A String of Beads* helps reinforce these math components as it presents an array of facts about the history and geography of beads. The narrator has to make choices of how to design her collection, which consists of one face bead, four eye beads, five turquoise beads, seven millefiori beads, and ten silver beads. Shells, beads, buttons, and small stones are some of the most enjoyed materials for children to turn into mosaics, jewelry, constructions, or pictures (kids love glue and paste).[34]

Even though this is the longest theme in our book, it hardly touches on all that's possible for enriched activities and experiences to share with young children. As I close this section (not end it, just close it because of time and space), my mind is running with ideas left out like recipes for meals made from the earth's fruits and vegetables, ways to beautify our environment, looking in our environment and nature for geometrical shapes, saving pennies for good causes, and so on and so forth. This is just a seed! A tiny seed!

### Field Trips and Visitors

Please refer to the long list of suggestions for field trips and class-room visitors at the end of the book. There are enough ideas for these enriched times to cover 365 days a year! You don't have to search in far-off places. The best field trips could be to the local field! The most exciting visitor could be the lady around the corner who loves gardens or the environmental activist who is advocating for "pocket" gardens in inner-city neighborhoods. Keep the fun and joy in these experiences. I spoke to a park ranger/educator in one of our local nature centers. He told me he was taking a group of third graders on a nature walk. One of the kids walked along slowly, never looking at anything, eyes focused on the ground in front of him. Finally, the ranger asked, "What's the matter? Why aren't you noticing all the things we're finding?" The boy answered, "If I see anything I'll have to go back and write about it!" He anticipated the skills-emphasized post-field-trip "lesson." Instead of celebrating such a rich, multilevel adventure with words, visual arts, discussions, and sharings, the child anticipated a formal, structured tension-producing assignment. (Keep the *fun* in fundamentals!)

Through these valuable experiences children learn about people who are helping to improve and beautify our environment—to keep it clean and safe. These are important lessons for our future leaders and caretakers of the world. Despite our many problems in the greater world and the world of nature (mostly human-made problems!), responsible adults are finding ways to solve some of these issues. This is reassuring to our children.

## IT ALL COMES TOGETHER

Of course, it always comes together when you think in a holistic, integrated, connected way. But, in case, just for a minute, you forget that core concept, let me invite you to Squirrel City. I first learned of Squirrel City on the front page of our local newspaper, which boasted a headline reading: "Columbus School for Girls' Kids Make 'Nutty' Idea Work." The article told how this unique outdoor habitat was conceived, designed, and constructed over three years by young students with assistance from teachers, staff, and families.

How did it all begin? When the three- and four-year-olds looked out their window and noticed a squirrel scrounging in the trash for food, their hearts went out to the little guy and they decided to put treats out like walnuts and fruits, which they left in a heart-shaped dish!

This happened a few years ago. The three- and four-year-old children recognized a problem. "Squirrels shouldn't eat trash!" Their concern led them on a three-year journey propelled by numerous problem-solving, brainstorming, research-filled sessions. Their many ideas began to form: sketches, diagrams, pictures, maps, plans. . . . The kids studied the movement of squirrels, their habits and needs. Where to build a city for the squirrels? All of their senses were activated. All opinions listened to and respected. Numerous materials were used for constructions and drawings. Squirrel faces, expressions, bodies were crafted and constructed. Wires, plastic, clay, wood chips, nuts, twigs . . . some of the materials used to honor, decorate, and welcome squirrels were in constant use. The plot thickened. The children, together the next school year, continued to develop Squirrel City. What signs, symbols, pictures, special places, useful spaces should be included? More decision making, cooperative learning, collaboration, problem solving, high-level thinking, imaginative play ("Let's pretend we're squirrels"), songs, stories, dramas, lists, sketches, inventions, contraptions, sculptures, mobiles, a fountain that squirted real water through fake flowers . . . everyone got into the act! Neighbors, families, teachers, other classes. The intensity of the children's interest never wavered. Each idea begot another. Squirrel City was beginning to take shape, a dream becoming a reality.

The official celebration for the grand opening of Squirrel City happened in May of 2001. The children were now in kindergarten, proud tour leaders and guides for the many people who came to witness the excitement.

After reading the newspaper article, I visited Squirrel City. Jeanette Canyon, a treasured enthusiastic art teacher and friend of squirrels and children, was my docent. We saw the three central areas, each devoted to a positive feeling for squirrels. The kids had selected three emotions because they noticed from their relentless observations and research that squirrels are playful and funny. *Silly, Friendly,* and *Happy* were the three specific constructions brightened with sculptures and mobiles for the squirrels to play in and enjoy. Jeanette is a believer in serendipity. The kids wanted to have natural materials for their castle constructions. But, where to find such resources? Jeanette was walking down her street when she noticed a tree had been cut down—a completely hollow tree that was already sectioned! Before anyone else could claim it, she asked for it, hauled it to school, and abracadabra—the wooden hollowed-out sections served as perfect structures for the various buildings of the castle! We don't have time or space to describe the Nut Store, the Squirrel's Diner, the fountain, the pathways, the signs, pictures, and symbols. Too bad you aren't able to listen to the songs the children constantly composed and sang, the squirrel dances and stories they improvised. You'll have to take my word for it—use your imagination. Jeanette and her colleagues documented the entire three-year process in words, il-

FIGURE 6–15    *The squirrels and the kids think it's "super, super, super, super . . . !"*

lustrations, videos, and photos. My favorite quote from one of the children is "We think it looks super, super, super, super, super, super, super, super, super, super, super, super, super, super, super, super, super, super, super, super, super, super, super, super, duper!!!"[35]

## NOTES

1.  Paula Rakestraw is executive director of Partnership for Children, Rockingham County, North Carolina.

2.  Pope, C. Winter 2000. "The Forgotten Family Value: Kids' Inalienable Right to Mess Around Outdoors." *Sierra* 85 (6). pp. 16–18.

3.  Davis, J. Winter 1998. "Young Children, Environmental Education and the Future." *Early Childhood Journal* 26 (2). pp. 117–123.

4.  The Earthworks Group. illus. Monay, M. (and a few kids). 1990. *50 Simple Things Kids Can Do to Save the Earth*. Kansas City, MO: McMeel.
    This is still one of our most practical and accessible resources.

5. Rivkin, M. 1995. *The Great Outdoors: Restoring Children's Right to Play Outside.* Washington, D.C.: NAEYC.

6. Wilson, R. A. Summer 1996. "Healthy Habitats for Children." *Early Childhood Education Journal* 23 (4). pp. 235–238.

7. Liese Milliken wrote a poem called "Arrunning Raway," which was included in a twenty-year retrospective of *Writers in School and an Anthology 1982–1985*, published by the Ohio Arts Council. This line from her poem became the title of the anthology. Liese was in fifth grade when she wrote the poem.

8. Levy, S. 11/1999. "To See the World in a Grain of Sand." *Educational Leadership* 57 (3). pp. 70–75.

9. Wilson, R. Summer 1993. "Nature Education and Science." *Day Care and Early Education.* pp. 15–17.

10. Mary Rivkin coordinates Early Childhood Education at University of Maryland, Baltimore County, Maryland. This interview is based on a conversation with Mary.

11. The late, beloved educator Herb Sandberg, who touched many lives in his years of teaching at the University of Toledo, Toledo, Ohio, was remembered by friends and colleagues. Chuck and Muriel Lee shared this experience in the Memorial Booklet.

12. Carol Highfield and Linda Muzzo work and play with children, animals, and plants in the Early Childhood Program at the Leo Yassenoff Jewish Center, Columbus, Ohio. I highlighted their program in "Schools Kids Run To" included in *Teaching by Heart*, Redleaf Press, 2001.

13. Rylant, C. illus. Goode, D. 1982. *When I Was Young in the Mountains.* New York: Dutton.

McPhail, D. 1985. *Farm Morning.* San Diego, CA: Harcourt Brace.

Soentpiet, C. 1994. *Around Town.* New York: Lothrop, Lee and Shepard.

Polacco, P. 1992. *Mrs. Katz and Tush.* New York: Bantam.

Wyeth, S. D. illus. Soentpiet, C. 1998. *Something Beautiful.* New York: Bantam Doubleday Dell.

DeCoteau Orie, S. illus. Canyon, C. 1995. *Did You Hear Wind Sing Your Name? An Oneida Song of Spring.* New York: Walker and Co.

London, J. illus. Baviera, R. 1998. *Dream Weaver.* San Diego, CA: Silver Whistle Press.

14. Sylvia Wallach Motin is an educator, consultant, and composer based in Chicago and working nationally and internationally. She can be reached at Sylvionics, P.O. Box 60135, Chicago, IL 60660.

15. "Big Thunder, Dark Cloud" can be found on Jack Grunsky's album *Jack Grunsky, Sing and Dance.* 383 Wellesley Street East, Toronto, Ontario, M4X 1H5.

*All* artists in our amazingly talented community of music makers for young children have songs and chants connecting them with nature.

For example, see Tom Chapin's album *This Pretty Planet*. Every song honors a theme from nature. Sundance Music, 100 Cedar Street, Dobbs Ferry, NY 10522-1022. 910-674-0247.

16. Carle, E. 1997. *From Head to Toe*. New York: HarperCollins.
    Walsh, E. S. 1993. *Hop Jump!* San Diego, CA: Harcourt Brace.
    Gomi, T. 1990. *My Friends*. San Francisco, CA: Chronicle.

17. These records are most probably out of print. Perhaps you'll find treasures in garage sales or flea markets! Better still, check the public library for too often unrequested multicultural music. See for yourself how ancient traditional cultures have honored the world of nature in their music, songs, and instruments.

    *China: Shantung Folk Music and Traditional Instrumental Pieces.* Nonesuch Records, New York, NY 10022 <*www.nonesuch.com*>.

    *Songs of Earth, Water, Fire and Sky: Music of the American Indian.* Volume 1. New World Records. Library of Congress Card 75-751053.

    *Music from the Kabuki: Geza Music of Japan*. Nonesuch Records, New York, NY 10022 <*www.nonesuch.com*>.

18. Ginsburg, M. illus. Aruego, J. and A. Dewey. 1975. *How the Sun Was Brought Back to the Sky*. New York: Macmillan.

    Keats, E. J. 1962. *The Snowy Day*. New York: Viking.

    There are numerous adaptations of Hans Christian Andersen's *Emperor's Nightingale*. Pick your favorite.

    Yolen, J. 1998. *Welcome to the Ice House*. New York: G. P. Putnam's Sons.

    Adoff, A. illus. Barbour, K. 1988. *Flamboyan*. San Diego, CA: Harcourt Brace Jovanovich.

    Belafonte, H. and L. Burgess. illus. Ayliffe, A. 1999. *Island in the Sun*. New York: Dial Books for Young Readers.

    Etts, M. H. 1968. *Play with Me*. New York: Viking.

    DiFiori, L. 1989. *Good Morning, Muffin Mouse*. New York: Golden.

19. Penni Rubin is an educational resource specialist, consultant, teacher, performer, and author affiliated with the Cleveland Museum of Natural History and known throughout Ohio. She can be reached at <*www.pennirubin.com*>.

20. Carle, E. 1987. *The Very Hungry Caterpillar*. New York: Philomel.

21. Maestro, B. and G. Maestro. 1989. *Taxis: A Book of City Words*. New York: J and B Communications.

    Iverson, D. 1993. *I Celebrate Nature*. Nevada City, CA: Dawn Publications.

    Shaik, F. illus. Lewis, E. B. 1998. *The Jazz of Our Streets*. New York: Dial Books for Young Readers.

22. Kaye Boiarski has shared arts experiences with thousands of children through Days of Creation Arts for Kids programs in central Ohio. This section features excerpts from long conversations with Kaye.

23. Brown, P. W. Winter 1993. "Playing for Dreams." *OSU Alumni Magazine*. pp. 11–14.

24. Ehlert, L. 1991. *Red Leaf, Yellow Leaf*. San Diego, CA: Harcourt Brace.

    Robbins, K. 1998. *Autumn Leaves*. New York: Scholastic.

    Hall, Z. illus. Halpern, S. 2000. *Fall Leaves Fall!* New York: Scholastic.

25. Artist/educator Jim Arter's work with children in an inner-city neighborhood in Columbus, Ohio, was the inspiration for the outstanding program Children of the Future, sponsored by the Greater Columbus Arts Council with support from Americorps. Children of the Future brings children from disadvantaged communities together with artists in various settings like recreation centers and community centers. Children of the Future is considered one of Americorps' most successful programs! Jim now helps coordinate it for the Greater Columbus Arts Council. For further information:

    Greater Columbus Arts Council
    614-224-4606

26. Rosen, M. J. illus. Leonard, T. 1994. *All Eyes on the Pond*. New York: Hyperion.

    Rylant, C. 2000. *The Wonderful Happens*. New York: Hyperion.

    Viera, L. illus. Canyon, C. 1996. *The Ever-Living Tree: The Life and Times of a Coast Redwood*. New York: Walker.

27. Howker, J. illus. Fox-Davies, S. 1997. *Walk with a Wolf*. Cambridge, MA: Candlewick Press.

    Leslie Zak's "Wolf Song," based on the actual songs of wolves, is on her CD:

    *Walk Dance Talk Sing*
    Zax Trax
    P.O. Box 82361
    Columbus, OH 43202
    Cole, H. 1998. *I Took a Walk*. New York: Greenwillow.

28. Levenson, G. photos Thaler, S. 1999. *Pumpkin Circle: The Story of a Garden*. Berkeley, CA: Tricycle Press.

    Maass, R. 1998. *Garden*. New York: Henry Holt.

29. Fran Avni's album *Daisies and Ducklings: Cheerful Songs and a Story About Our Environment* includes "Care for the World" and "Trees."

    Music for Little People
    P.O. Box 1460
    Redway, CA 95560

    "Don't Throw Your Trash In My Backyard" can be found on Greg and Steve's albums.

    Weiss, D. and B. Thiele. illus. Blanchette, D. 1995. *What a Wonderful World*. Worthington, OH: SA Division of Macmillan/McGraw-Hill School Publishing Co.

Pandell, K. illus. dePaola, T. 1994. *I Love You, Sun, I Love You, Moon.* New York: G. P. Putnam's Sons.

Williams, R. L. illus. Chawla, N. 1994. *Let's Take Care of the Earth.* Cypress, CA: Creative Teaching Press.

30. Christopher Canyon has illustrated numerous children's books. His most recent works are a three-book series:

Lewis, J. P. illus. Canyon, C. 2001. *Earth and Me.* Nevada City, CA: Dawn Publishing Co.

Lewis, J. P. illus. Canyon, C. 2001. *Earth and Us.* Nevada City, CA: Dawn Publishing Co.

Lewis, J. P. illus. Canyon, C. 2001. *Earth and You.* Nevada City, CA: Dawn Publishing Co.

Chris can be reached at:

753 S. Third Street

Columbus, OH 43206

31. Fiarotta, P. 1973. *Sticks and Stones and Ice Cream Cones: Crafts in a Child's World.* New York: Workman Publishers.

Fiarotta, P. with N. Fiarotta. 1975. *Snips and Snails and Walnut Whales: Nature Crafts for Children.* New York: Workman Publishers.

Sensi, E. B. 2001. *Berry Smudges and Leaf Prints: Finding and Making Colors from Nature.* NY: Dutton.

Henry, S. 1999. *Kids' Art Works: Creating with Color, Design, Texture, and More.* Charlotte, VT: Williams Publishing Co.

Topol, C. W. and L. Gandini. 1999. *Beautiful Stuff: Learning with Found Materials.* Worcester, MA: David Publishing Co.

Helm, J. H. and L. Katz. 2001. *Young Investigators: The Project Approach in the Early Years.* New York: Teachers College Press.

32. Baker, J. 1991. *Window.* New York: Greenwillow.

33. Toft, K. and A. Sheather. 1998. *One Less Fish.* Watertown, MA: Charlesbridge.

McMillan, B. 1986. *Counting Wildflowers.* New York: Morrow.

Freymann, S. and J. Elffers. 2000. *One Lonely Sea Horse.* New York: Arthur A. Levine Books (Scholastic).

Carle, E. 1970. *The Tiny Seed.* New York: Crowell.

34. I wrote about Marilyn Cohen's outstanding kindergarten career in:

Chenfeld, M. B. 2001. "Amazed by Chicks." *Teaching by Heart.* St. Paul, MN: Redleaf Press. pp. 60–65.

Reid, M. illus. Wolff, A. 1997. *A String of Beads.* New York: Dutton.

35. John Matuszak wrote the front-page article in the *Eastside Messenger*, May 28, 2001. Squirrel City was conceived, planned, and created by young children over three years beginning in the 1998–1999 school year at the Columbus School for Girls. Their teachers, Devie Hiller and Kate Zutell, assisted the children. Jeanette Canyon of CSG's Art Studio contributed her arts expertise. Barb Acton directed the Program for Young Children for the school.

Thanks for sharing the journey with me as we walk along together playing with simple, practical, joyful ways to be with children so they learn in safe, encouraging, exciting environments with loving, creative teachers (like you). Ohio's 2002 Teacher of the Year, Maureen Reedy, expressed her beliefs eloquently in these words, "With children, the heart is always intertwined with the expansion of the mind and one's abilities. Teaching is a profession which encourages love at its core and captures one's heart many times over in the course of a day. What could be more rewarding than that?"

She believes that there is a place in every class where the hearts and minds of students meet.

May you always live with your children in that special, sacred place. May you always touch the knot in your belt and listen to the song of the real nightingale.

May your students say to you what a child said to Mary Sue Garlinger after a day's residency with an Artists-in-the-Schools program: "Thank you for coming today. You made me happy for the rest of my life."

# APPENDIX

**List One: Ideas for Field Trips and Classroom Visitors**

Actors/Actresses
Airports
Animals/Animal Trainers/Groomers/Rescuers
Anthropologists/Archeologists
Apartment Managers
Aquariums
Arboretums
Architects
Artists/Arts Festivals/Artists' Studios
Astronomers
Athletes/Athletic Teams/Athletic Fields
Authors
Babies
Bakers/Bakeries
Ballet Dancers/Rehearsals/Performances
Barber Shops/Beauticians/Barbers
Beaders (All those bracelets, belts, and necklaces!)
Bikers
Bookmobiles/Bookstores
Botanists
Bus Drivers/Bus Terminals
Cafeterias/Cafeteria Workers
Cake Decorators
Calligraphers
Carpenters
Cashiers
Chimney Sweeps
Circus Workers/Circuses
Clerks
Clothing Mills/Factories/Stores
Clowns

Coin-Operated Laundries
Collectors (of any object)
Community Centers
Construction Workers/Construction Sites
Cooks
Costume Designers/Costume Shops
Craftspersons
Custodians
Dancers/Dance Studios/Dance Schools
Dentists/Dental Hygienists
Doctors
Doll Museums/Doll Shops/Doll Collectors
Dressmakers
Dry Cleaning Shops
Educators
Electricians
Engineers
Environmentalists
Explorers
Fabric Stores
Face Painters
Factories/Factory Workers
Family Businesses/Interests/Skills/Hobbies/Experiences
Family Members
Farms/Farmers
Fast-Food Restaurants/Workers
Festivals
Firefighters/Fire Stations
Fishermen/Fisherwomen/Fisheries
Florists/Floral Shops
Folksingers
Food Stores
Foresters
Friends
Fruit Stands
Furniture Makers/Furniture Shops
Gardeners/Gardens/Garden Shops
Genealogists
Geologists
Glassblowers/Glassblowing Studios
Government Workers
Graphic Artists/Studios
Groundskeepers
Homemakers
Horticulturists
Hospital Workers

Housecleaners/Housekeepers
Houses Under Construction/Renovated/Repaired/Restored
Interior Designers/Studios
Inventors
Janitors
Jewelry Makers/Jewelers/Shops
Joggers
Journalists
Jugglers
Kennel Workers/Kennels
Kitchen Workers/Kitchens
Landscape Workers/Architects
Letter Carriers/Post Offices
Libraries/Librarians
Locksmiths
Lumberyards/Lumber Workers
Magicians/Shows
Maintenance Workers
Marinas
Mayors
Mechanics
Meteorologists
Migrant Workers
Miners
Movers/Moving Companies
Museums/Museum Docents/Museum Guards
Musicians/Musical Instruments/Musical Bands
Naturalists
Neighbors
Newspaper Offices/Deliverers
Nurses
Nutritionists
Occupational Therapists
Oceanographers
Opticians/Optometrists
Orchards
Orchestra Conductors/Rehearsals/Musicians
Ornithologists
Orthopedic Equipment
Parks/Park Rangers
Physical Therapists/Centers
Pizza Parlors/Pizza Makers/Pizza Deliverers
Planetariums
Plumbers
Poets
Police Stations/Police Officers

Potters/Potters' Studios
Puppets/Puppet Shows
Quilters/Quilt Shops
Radio Stations/Radio Announcers
Railroad Stations/Railroad Workers
Ranchers/Ranch Workers
Recreation Centers/Workers
Recycling Centers/Workers
Restaurants/Servers/Cooks
Riggers
Roofers
Sail Makers
Scientists/Labs
Scuba Divers
Sculptors/Studios
Shipbuilders/Sailors
Shoe Repair Shops/Shoe Stores
Sign Language Interpreters
Sign Painters
Skaters/Skating Rinks
Social Workers
Swimmers
Tailors/Tailor Shops
Telephone Operators/Repairpersons
Tool Makers
Translators
Tree Services
Truck Drivers
Veterinarians
Volunteers (community shelters, kitchens, hospitals, etc.)
Weavers
Welders
Window Washers
Wood Carvers
Workers of *All* Kinds
Yoga Teachers
Zoos/Zookeepers/Zoologists

**List Two: Some Starters**
START WITH:
Ages of the Children
An Amazing Observation
Bird's Nest
A Book
Box

Buddies (keep changing and connecting buddy partnerships to new
    ideas and themes)
Celebration
Child of the Week, Day
Classroom Visitor
Clothing
A Color
Comparison
Counting (shoes, fingers, colors, etc.)
Date and Day
Display Table or Shelf
A Doll
An Exercise (connect with all themes)
A "Feeling Word" ("I feel happy today because the sun is shining.
    How do *you* feel today?")
Food
A Game
A Holiday
Humor (such a neglected human resource for all occasions!)
Letter of the Alphabet
Letter Delivered to the Children
Look Around the Room
Loose Tooth
Names/Name Tags
Name-Tagging Everything in the Room
Object
Pantomime
Pet
Photograph/Picture
Pocket Full of . . . ?
Poem
Poll of Opinions
Poster
Puppet
A Question
A Riddle
Scavenger Hunt
Sensory Experience
Search
Serendipity
A Shared Experience
A Shell
Sign on Your Door
Song
Special Snack
A Stone

Story
Stuffed Animal
Surprise
Survey
Take Attendance in a Special Way ("Children, when I call your
    name, can you tell us your favorite color, number, animal, etc.?")
Taste of Something
Treasure Box
Treasure Hunt
T-Shirt (yours or a child's)
Walk Around the School, Street, Neighborhood
Warm-Up Exercise
Weather
Welcome
"What If?"
Wonder
A Word
Work of Art

## SOME EXCELLENT JOURNALS AND
## PROFESSIONAL ORGANIZATIONS

National Association for the Education of Young Children (NAEYC)
    1509 165th Street NW
    Washington, D.C. 20036-1426
    publishes *Young Children*

Association for Childhood Education International
    17904 Georgia Avenue #215
    Olney, MD 20832
    publishes *Childhood Education*

Association for Supervision and Curriculum Development
    1250 N. Pitt Street
    Alexandria, VA 22314-1453
    publishes *Educational Leadership*

*Early Childhood Education Journal*
    Kluwer Academic/Human Sciences Press
    233 Spring Street
    New York, NY 10013-1578

Phi Delta Kappa International
    408 N. Union, P.O. Box 789
    Bloomington, IN 47402
    publishes *Kappan*

Southern Poverty Law Center
    400 Washington Avenue
    Montgomery, AL 36104
    publishes *Teaching Tolerance*

National School-Age Care Alliance
    1137 Washington Street
    Boston, MA 02124
    publishes *School-Age Review*

*Early Childhood News*
    2 Lower Ragsdale #125
    Monterey, CA 93940

National Head Start Association
    1651 Prince Street
    Alexandria, VA 22314
    publishes *Children and Families*

National Council of Teachers of English (NCTE)
    1111 Kenyon Road
    Urbana, IL 61801
    publishes *Primary Voices* and *Language Arts*

International Reading Association (IRA)
    800 Barksdale Road
    P.O. Box 8139
    Newark, DE 19711
    publishes *The Reading Teacher*

*Early Childhood Research Quarterly*
    The Boulevard
    Langford Lane
    Kidlington, OXON OX5 1G UK
    www.elsevier.com/locate/ecresq.

## SOME MUSIC MAKERS

*Note:* This small list is but a sampling of the many outstanding music makers sharing their gifts with children throughout the country and the world.

Mr. Al: 800-487-6725
Peter and Ellen Allard: 508-798-5566
Fran Avni: favi@aol.com
Tom Chapin: 910-674-0247
Debbie Clement: www.rainbowswithinreach.com
Charlotte Diamond: Hug Bug Music, Richmond, British Columbia,
    Canada

Katherine Dines: Hunk-Ta-Bunk-Ta Music: 303-595-8747
Cathy Fink and Marcy Marxer: 800-ROUNDER
Gaia: 800-632187
Gemini: 313-665-0409
Nelson Gill: Etcetera Records: 800-675-0500
Judy Caplan Ginsburgh: 318-442-TUNE
Red Grammer: 800-824-2980
Greg and Steve: 800-548-4063
Jack Grunsky: 800-632187
Arlo Guthrie: 800-ROUNDER
Hugh Hanley: 781-643-6362
Miss Jackie (Silberg): 800-432-6307
Ella Jenkins: Smithsonian: 800-410-9815
Kinderman: 800-944-6246
The Learning Station: 800-789-9990
Thomas Moore: 704-371-4077
Hop Palmer: Educational Activities, Woodland Hills, CA
Raffi: 800-ROUNDER
Mr. Ray: www.mrRAY.com
Ronno: 800-632187
Jim Rule: 312-463-2879
Joe Scruggs: 800-426-4777
Pete Seeger: Smithsonian: 800-410-9815
Sweet Honey in the Rock: 800-ROUNDER
Sylvia Wallach (Motin): Sylvionics, P.O. Box 60135, Chicago, IL
   60660
Leslie Zak: 614-262-4098

(*Note:* For every name listed, ten are left out! Please forgive this sparse list. That gives you an idea of the many superlative music makers enriching the lives of our children.)

For excellent resources and information:

The National Association for Music Education
   1806 Robert Fulton Drive
   Reston, VA 20191
   703-860-4000

The Children's Music Network
   P.O. Box 1341
   Evanston, IL 60204-1341
   877-733-8003

# CHILDREN'S BOOK LIST AND RESOURCE MATERIALS

Adoff, A. illus. Barbour, K. 1988. *Flamboyan*. San Diego, CA: Harcourt Brace Jovanovich.

Aliki. 1989. *My Five Senses*. New York: Crowell.

Ancona, G. 1998. *Let's Dance*. New York: Morrow Jr. Books.

Bahr, M. illus. Jerome, K. 2000. *If Nathan Were Here*. Grand Rapids, MI: Wm. B. Erdmans.

Baker, J. 1991. *Window*. New York: Greenwillow.

Bang, M. 1999. *When Sophie Gets Angry—Really, Really Angry*. New York: Blue Sky Press.

Baylor, B. 1978. *The Way to Start a Day*. New York: Scribners.

Belafonte, H. and L. Burgess, illus. Ayliffe, A. 1999. *Island in the Sun*. New York: Dial Books for Young Readers.

Bertrand, G. D. illus. Howard, R. P. 1999. *Family, Familia*. Houston, TX: Pinata Books.

Boynton, S. 1987. *A Is for Angry*. New York: Workman.

Boynton, S. 2001. *Yay, You! Moving Out, Moving Up, Moving On*. New York: Simon and Schuster.

Carle, E. 1970. *The Tiny Seed*. New York: Crowell.

Carle, E. 1992. *Draw Me a Star*. New York: Philomel.

Carle, E. 1997. *From Head to Toe*. New York: HarperCollins.

Catalnotto, P. 1995. *The Painter*. New York: Orchard Books.

Chenfeld, M. B. 1993. "Stuff." *Teaching in the Key of Life*. Washington, D.C.: NAEYC.

Chenfeld, M. B. 2001. "Snowball." *Teaching by Heart*. St. Paul, MN: Redleaf Press. pp. 90–97.

Cole, H. 1998. *I Took a Walk*. New York: Greenwillow.

Couric, K. illus. Priceman, M. 2001. *The Brand New Kid*. New York: Doubleday.

Daniels, T. illus. Foster, T. 1999. *The Feet in the Gym*. Winslow Press.

Danneberg, J. illus. Love, J. 2000. *First Day Jitters*. Watertown, MA: Whispering Coyote.

DeCoteau Orie, S. illus. Canyon, C. 1995. *Did You Hear Wind Sing Your Name? An Oneida Song of Spring*. New York: Walker and Co.

Demarest, C. L. 2000. *Firefighters from A to Z*. New York: Margaret McEldery Books (Simon and Schuster).

DiFiori, L. 1989. *Good Morning, Muffin Mouse*. New York: Golden.

Dorros, A. illus. Kleven, E. 1991. *Abuela*. New York: Dutton.

Dorros, A. illus. McCully, E. A. 2000. *Ten Go Tango*. New York: HarperCollins.

The Earthworks Group. illus. Monay, M. (and a few kids). 1990. *50 Simple Things Kids Can Do to Save the Earth*. Kansas City, MO: McMeel.

Ehlert, L. 1991. *Red Leaf, Yellow Leaf*. San Diego, CA: Harcourt Brace.

Elya, S. M. illus. Chapman, L. 2000. *Eight Animals on the Town*. New York: G. P. Putnam's Sons.

Etts, Marie H. 1968. *Play with Me*. New York: Viking.

Florian, D. 1993. *A Painter: How We Work*. New York: Greenwillow.

Freymann, S. and J. Elffers. 2000. *One Lonely Seahorse*. New York: Arthur A. Levine Books (Scholastic).

Fujawa, J. 1998. *(Almost) Everything You Need to Know About Early Childhood Education*. Beltsville, MD: Gryphon House.

Gibbons, G. 1998. *The Art Box*. New York: Holiday House.

Ginsburg, M. illus. Aruego, J. and A. Dewey. 1975. *How the Sun Was Brought Back to the Sky*. New York: Macmillan.

Glaser, L. illus. Schmidt, K. L. 1993. *Stop That Garbage Truck*. Morton Grove, IL: Albert Whitman.

Goldstone, B. illus. Cahoon, H. 2001. *Ten Friends*. New York: Henry Holt.

Gomi, T. 1990. *My Friends*. San Francisco, CA: Chronicle.

Hall, Z. illus. Halpern, S. 2000. *Fall Leaves Fall!* New York: Scholastic.

Hausherr, R. 1997. *Celebrating Families*. New York: Scholastic.

Hausman, B. photos Fellman, S. 1999. *A to Z—Do You Ever Feel Like Me?* New York: Dutton.

Henkes, K. 2000. *Wemberly Worried*. New York: Greenwillow.

Hindley, J. illus. Grastrom, B. 1999. *Eyes, Nose, Fingers, Toes*. Cambridge, MA: Candlewick Press.

Howker, J. illus. Fox-Davies, S. 1997. *Walk with a Wolf*. Cambridge, MA: Candlewick Press.

Hubbard, W. M. 2000. *All That You Are*. New York: G. P. Putnam's Sons.

Hubbell, P. illus. Sweet, M. 2000. *Bouncing Time*. New York: HarperCollins.

Hughes, L. 1987. "Hope." *Selected Poems of Langston Hughes*. New York: Vintage.

Hutchins, P. 1986. *The Doorbell Rang*. New York: Greenwillow.

Iverson, D. 1993. *I Celebrate Nature*. Nevada City, CA: Dawn Publications.

Kalman, B. 1998. *Community Helpers from A–Z*. New York: Crabtree Publishing.

Keats, E. J. first printed 1962. *The Snowy Day*. New York: Viking.

Kraus, R. illus. Aruego, J. 1971. *Leo the Late Bloomer*. New York: E. P. Dutton.

Kroll, S. illus. Appleby, E. 1987. *I'd Like to Be*. New York: Parents Magazine Press.

Laskey, K. illus. McCarthy, S. 1992. *The Tantrums*. New York: Macmillan.

Lester, A. 2000. *Ernie Dances to the Didgeridoo*. Boston: Houghton Mifflin.

Lester, H. illus. Munsinger, L. 1998. *Tacky the Penguin*. Boston: Houghton Mifflin.

Levenson, G. photos. Thaler, S. 1999. *Pumpkin Circle: The Story of a Garden*. Berkeley, CA: Tricycle Press.

Lewis, J. P. illus. Canyon, C. 2001. *Earth and Me*. Nevada City, CA: Dawn Publishing Co.

Lewis, J. P. illus. Canyon, C. 2001. *Earth and Us*. Nevada City, CA: Dawn Publishing Co.

Lewis, J. P. illus. Canyon, C. 2001. *Earth and You*. Nevada City, CA: Dawn Publishing Co.

Lionni, L. 1973. *Frederick*. New York: Pinwheel.

London, J. illus. Baviera, R. 1998. *Dream Weaver*. San Diego, CA: Silver Whistle Press.

Look, L. illus. Heo, Y. 2001. *Henry's First Moon Birthday*. New York: Anne Schwartz Books (Atheneum).

Maass, R. 1998. *Garden*. New York: Henry Holt.

Maestro, B. and G. Maestro. 1989. *Taxis: A Book of City Words*. New York: J and B Communications.

Martin, B. Jr. 1983. *Brown Bear, Brown Bear, What Do You See?* New York: Holt, Rinehart and Winston.

Maynard, Christopher. 1997. *Jobs People Do*. New York: Dorling Kindersley.

McBratney, S. illus. Beachus, J. 2000. *I'm Sorry*. New York: HarperCollins.

McMillan, B. 1986. *Counting Wildflowers*. New York: Morrow.

McPhail, D. 1985. *Farm Morning*. San Diego, CA: Harcourt Brace.

Merriam, Eve. 1964. "Thumbprint." *It Doesn't Always Have to Rhyme*. New York: Atheneum. p. 63.

Merriam, E. 1992. "Mean Song." *The Singing Green*. New York: Morrow.

Merriam, E. illus. Gorton, J. 1999. *Ten Rosy Roses*. New York: Harper-Collins.

Millman, I. 1998. *Moses Goes to a Concert*. New York: Frances Foster Books (Farrar, Straus and Giroux).

Millman, I. 2000. *Moses Goes to School*. New York: Frances Foster Books (Farrar, Straus and Giroux).

Milne, A. A. 1957. "Expedition to the North Pole." *The World of Pooh*. New York: Dutton. p. 104.

Moon, N. illus. Ayliffe, A. 1995. *Lucy's Picture*. New York: Dial.

Moore, T. *Thomas Moore Sings the Family*. Thomas Moore Enterprises, Inc. 3710 Monroe #2, Charlotte, NC 28205. 704-371-4077.

Murphy, S. J. illus. Karos, G. B. 1997. *Elevator Magic*. New York: Harper-Collins.

Murphy, Stuart J. illus. O'Malley, K. 1999. *Jump, Kangaroo, Jump!* New York: HarperCollins.

Murphy, S. illus. Floca, B. 2000. *Let's Fly a Kite*. New York: HarperCollins.

Myers, S. illus. Frazee, M. 2001. *Everywhere Babies*. San Diego, CA: Harcourt Brace.

Newcome, Z. 1996. *Toddlerobics*. Cambridge, MA: Candlewick.

Nikola-Lisa, W. illus. Bryant, M. 1994. *Bein' with You This Way*. New York: Lee and Low Books.

Older Effin. illus. Hayashi, N. 2000. *My Two Grandmothers*. San Diego, CA: Harcourt.

Oram, H. and S. Varley. 1998. *Badger's Bad Day*. New York: Arthur A. Levine.

Osofka, A. 1992. *My Buddy*. New York: Henry Holt.

Pandell, K. illus. dePaola, T. 1994. *I Love You, Sun, I Love You, Moon*. New York: G. P. Putnam's Sons.

Paul, A. W. illus. Wescott, N. B. 1998. *Hello Toes! Hello Feet!* New York: DK Ink.

Paulsen, G. illus. Paulsen, R. W. 1997. *Work Song*. San Diego, CA: Harcourt Brace.

Pollaco, P. 1992. *Mrs. Katz and Tush*. New York: Bantam.

Poydar, N. 1999. *First Day, Hooray!* New York: Holiday House.

Raschka, C. 1993. *Yo! Yes?* New York: Scholastic.

Ratner, S. and S. Calcagnno. 2000. *The Body Book*. New York: Orchard.

Reid, M. illus. Wolff, A. 1997. *A String of Beads*. New York: Dutton.

Rickert, J. E. photos McGahan, P. 2000. *Brian's Bird*. Morton Grove, IL: Albert Whitman and Company.

Rickert, J. E. photos McGahan, P. 2000. *Russ and the Almost Perfect Day*. Bethesda, MD: Woodbine House.

Ringgold, F. 1991. *Tar Beach*. New York: Crown.

Robbins, K. 1998. *Autumn Leaves*. New York: Scholastic.

Rockwell, A. illus. Rockwell, L. 2000. *Career Day*. New York: Harper-Collins.

Rosen, M. J. illus. Leonard, T. 1994. *All Eyes on the Pond*. New York: Hyperion.

Rosen, M. J. illus. Rand, T. 2000. *With a Dog Like That, a Kid Like Me*. New York: Dial.

Rylant, C. illus. Goode, D. 1982. *When I Was Young in the Mountains*. New York: Dutton.

Rylant, C. 1993. *The Relatives Came*. New York: Aladdin.

Rylant, C. 2000. *The Wonderful Happens*. New York: Hyperion.

Sachs, M. 1976. *The Bears' House*. New York: Dell-Yearling.

Say, A. illus. Dorrow, A. 1997. *Allison*. Boston: Houghton Mifflin.

Say, A. 2000. *The Sign Painter*. Boston: Houghton Mifflin.

Schwartz, D. illus. Kellogg, S. 1985. *How Much Is a Million?* New York: Lothrop, Lee and Shepard.

Sesame Street. 1974. *Grover and the Everything in the Whole Wide World Museum*. New York: Random House.

Seuss, Dr. illus. Johnson, S. and L. Foucher. 1996. *My Many Colored Days*. New York: Alfred Knopf.

Shaik, F. illus. Lewis, E. B. 1998. *The Jazz of Our Streets*. New York: Dial Books for Young Readers.

Shower, P. illus. Aliki. 1991. *The Listening Walk*. New York: HarperCollins.

Silverstein, S. 1974. "Invitation" and "Orchestra." *Where the Sidewalk Ends*. New York: Harper and Row.

Smith, C. 2000. *Jingle Dancer*. New York: William Morrow.

Soentpiet, C. 1994. *Around Town*. New York: Lothrop, Lee and Shepard.

Steig, W. 1969. *Sylvester and the Magic Pebble*. New York: Simon and Schuster.

Steig, W. illus. Euvremer, T. 2001. *Toby, What Are You?* New York: HarperCollins.

Stevenson, J. illus. Stevenson, H. 1998. *Sam the Zamboni Man*. New York: Greenwillow Books.

Sweeten, S. 1990. *Freckly Feet and Itchy Knees*. New York: Doubleday.

Tapahonso, L. and E. Schick. illus. Schick, E. 1995. *Navajo ABC: A Dine Alphabet Book*. New York: Simon and Schuster.

Toft, K. and A. Sheather. 1998. *One Less Fish*. Watertown, MA: Charlesbridge.

Viera, L. illus. Canyon, C. 1996. *The Ever-Living Tree: The Life and Times of a Coast Redwood*. New York: Walker.

Viorst, J. 1972. *Alexander and the Terrible, Horrible, No Good, Very Bad Day*. New York: Atheneum.

Waber, B. 1972. *Ira Sleeps Over*. Boston: Houghton Mifflin.

Walsh, E. S. 1993. *Hop Jump!* San Diego, CA: Voyage Books (Harcourt Brace).

Weiss, D. and B. Thiele. illus. Blanchette, D. 1995. *What a Wonderful World*. Worthington, OH: SA Division of Macmillan/McGraw-Hill School Publishing Co.

Weiss, N. 2000. *The World Turns Round and Round*. New York: Greenwillow.

Williams, K. L. illus. Cooper, F. 1991. *When Africa Was Home*. New York: Orchard Books.

Williams, R. L. illus. Chawla, N. 1994. *Let's Take Care of the Earth*. Cypress, CA: Creative Teaching Press.

Wittman, S. C. illus. Gundersheimer, K. 1978. *A Special Trade*. New York: Harper and Row.

Wyeth, S. D. illus. Soentpiet, C. 1998. *Something Beautiful*. New York: Bantam Doubleday Dell.

Yolen, J. 1998. *Welcome to the Ice House*. New York: G. P. Putnam's Sons.

# BOOK LIST FOR ADULTS

Acredolo, L. and S. Goodwyn. 1996. *Baby Signs*. Chicago, IL: Contemporary Books.

Armstrong, T. 1994. *Multiple Intelligences in the Classroom*. Alexandria, VA: Association for Supervision and Curriculum Development (ASCD).

Baily, B. 1997. *There's Gotta Be a Better Way: Discipline That Works!* Oveido, FL: Loving Guidance, Inc.

Banks, J. A. 1994. *An Introduction to Multicultural Education*. Boston: Allyn and Bacon.

Beaty, J. J. 1997. *Building Bridges with Multicultural Picture Books for Children 3–5*. Upper Saddle River, NJ: Prentice Hall.

Benson, P. L. 1997. *All Kids Are Our Kids*. San Francisco, CA: Jossey-Bass.

Benzwie, T. 1998. *A Moving Experience: Dance for Lovers of Children and the Child Within*. Tucson, AZ: Zephyr Press.

Berger, E. H. 1995. *Parents as Partners in Education: Families and Schools Working Together*. Englewood Cliffs, NJ: Prentice Hall.

Blecher, S. and K. Jaffee. 1998. *Weaving in the Arts: Widening the Learning Circle*. Portsmouth, NH: Heinemann.

Boone, E. and K. Barclay. 1995. *Building a Three Way Partnership: The Leader's Role in Linking School, Family and Community*. New York: Scholastic.

Bredekamp, S. and C. Copple. (editors). 1997. *Developmentally Appropriate Practice in Early Childhood Programs*. (rev. ed.). Washington, D.C.: NAEYC.

Carnes, J. (project director). 1997. *Starting Small: Teaching Tolerance in Preschool and the Early Grades*. Montgomery, AL: Southern Poverty Law Center.

Carpenter, T. P. and E. Fennema. 1999. *Children's Mathematics: Cognitively Guided Instruction*. Portsmouth, NH: Heinemann.

Chen, J. (editor). H. Gardner, D. H. Feldman, and M. Kreschevsky. (series editors). 1998. *Project Spectrum: Early Learning Activities.* Washington, D.C.: NAEYC.

Chenfeld, M. B. 1993. *Teaching in the Key of Life.* Washington, D.C.: NAEYC.

Chenfeld, M. B. 2001. *Teaching by Heart.* St. Paul, MN: Redleaf Press.

Copley, J. V. 2000. *The Young Child and Mathematics.* Washington, D.C.: NAEYC.

Council on Physical Education for Children. 1994. *Developmentally Appropriate Physical Education Practices for Young Children.* Reston, VA: American Alliance for Health, Physical Education, Recreation and Dance.

Denham, S. S. 1998. *Emotional Development in Young Children.* New York: Guilford.

Derman-Sparks, L. 1993. *Anti-Bias Curriculum: Tools for Empowering Young Children.* Washington, D.C.: NAEYC.

Duckworth, E. 1987. *The Having of Wonderful Ideas and Other Essays on Teaching and Learning.* New York: Teachers College Press.

Edwards, C., L. Gandini, and G. Forman. (editors). 1993. *The Hundred Languages of Children: The Reggio Emilia Approach to Early Childhood Education.* Norwood, NJ: Ablex.

Edwards, P. A., A. Pleasants, and S. Franklin. 1999. *A Path to Follow: Learning to Listen to Parents.* Portsmouth, NH: Heinemann.

Fiarotta, P. 1973. *Sticks and Stones and Ice Cream Cones: Crafts in a Child's World.* New York: Workman Publishers.

Fiarotta, P. with N. Fiarotta. 1975. *Snips and Snails and Walnut Whales: Nature Crafts for Children.* New York: Workman Publishers.

Fisher, B. 1995. *Thinking and Learning Together: Curriculum and Community in a Primary Classroom.* Portsmouth, NH: Heinemann.

Fisher, B. 1998. *Joyful Learning in Kindergarten.* (Rev. ed.). Portsmouth, NH: Heinemann.

Forest, H. (compiler). 1995. *Wonder Tales from Around the World.* Little Rock, AR: August House.

Gallas, K. 1994. *The Language of Learning: How Children Talk, Write, Dance, Draw and Sing Their Understanding of the World.* New York: Teachers College Press.

Garcia, J. 1999. *Sign with Your Baby* (book, video, and laminated signing card). Northlight Communications. <www.handspeak.com>

Gardner, H. 1983. *Frames of Mind: The Theory of Multiple Intelligences.* New York: Basic Books.

Gardner, H. 1993. *Multiple Intelligences: The Theory in Practice.* New York: Basic Books.

Gardner, H. 1996. "Are There Additional Intelligences? The Case for Naturalist, Spiritual, and Existential Intelligences." *Education Informa-*

*tion and Transformation*, ed. by J. Kane. Englewood Cliffs, NJ : Prentice Hall.

Goleman, D. 1995. *Emotional Intelligence.* New York: Bantam Books.

Gordon, A. M. and K. Williams-Browne. 2000. *Beginnings and Beyond.* (5th ed.). Albany, NY: Delmar.

Helm, J. and L. Katz. 2000. *Young Investigators: The Project Approach in the Early Years.* New York: Teachers College Press.

Henry, S. 1999. *Kids' Art Works: Creating with Color, Design, Texture and More.* Charlotte, VT: Williams Publishing Co.

Holt, J. 1970. *What Do I Do Monday?* New York: Dutton.

Hughes, L. 1995. *The Book of Rhythms.* New York: Oxford University Press.

Isenberg, J. and M. Jalango. 2000. *Creative Expression and Play in Early Childhood.* (3rd ed.). Upper Saddle River, NJ: Merrill/Prentice Hall.

Jones, E. and J. Nimmo. 1994. *Emergent Curriculum.* Washington, D.C.: NAEYC.

Katz, L. and S. Chard. 1989. *Engaging Children's Minds: The Project Approach.* (2nd ed.). Stamford, CT: Albex Publishing.

Kessler, R. *The Soul of Education.* 2000. Alexandria, VA: Association for Supervision and Curriculum Development (ASCD).

Kiefer, B. Z. 1995. *The Potential of Picture Books: From Visual Literacy to Aesthetic Understanding.* Upper Saddle River, NJ: Merrill/Prentice Hall.

King, E. W., M. Chapman, and M. Cruz-Janzen. 1994. *Educating Young Children in a Diverse Society.* Boston: Allyn and Bacon.

Kriete, R. 1999. *The Morning Meeting Book.* Greenfield, MA: Northeast Foundation for Children.

Lankford, M. illus. Milone, K. 1992. *Hopscotch Around the World.* New York: Morrow.

Levin, D. E. 1994. *Teaching Young Children in Violent Times: Building a Peaceable Classroom.* Philadelphia, PA: New Society.

Levy, S. 1996. *Starting from Scratch: One Classroom Builds Its Own Curriculum.* Portsmouth, NH: Heinemann.

McCracken, J. B. 1993. *Valuing Diversity: The Primary Years.* Washington, D.C.: NAEYC.

McIntyre, E., A. Rosebery, and N. Gonzalez. 2001. *Classroom Diversity: Connecting Curriculum to Students' Lives.* Portsmouth, NH: Heinemann.

Moorman, C. 1985. *Talk Sense to Yourself: The Language of Personal Power.* Portage, MI: Personal Power Press. pp. 104–113.

Moorman, C. 1998. *Parent Talk: Words That Empower, Words That Wound.* Merrill, MI: Personal Power Press.

Neugebauer, B. (editor). 1992. *Alike and Different: Exploring Our Humanity with Young Children.* Washington, D.C.: NAEYC.

Owocki, G. 1999. *Literacy Through Play.* Portsmouth, NH: Heinemann.

Paley, V. G. 1981. *Wally's Stories: Conversations in the Kindergarten*. Cambridge, MA: Harvard University Press.

Paley, V. G. 1986. *Mollie Is Three: Growing Up in School*. Chicago, IL: University of Chicago Press.

Paley, V. G. 1999. *The Kindness of Children*. Cambridge, MA: Harvard University Press.

Ramsey, P. 1998. *Teaching and Learning in a Diverse World: Multicultural Education for Young Children*. (2nd ed.). New York: Teachers College Press.

Rivkin, M. 1995. *The Great Outdoors: Restoring Children's Right to Play Outside*. Washington, D.C.: NAEYC.

Roethke, T. 1974. *Straw for the Fire*. New York: Doubleday.

Saldana, J. 2000. *Drama of Color: Improvisation with Multiethnic Folklore*. Portsmouth, NH: Heinemann.

Sensi, E. B. 2001. *Berry Smudges and Leaf Prints: Finding and Making Colors from Nature*. New York: Dutton.

Snoufe, L. A. 1997. *Emotional Development: The Organization of Emotional Life in the Early Years*. Cambridge, UK: Cambridge University Press.

Sornson, R. and J. Scott. (editors). 1997. *Teaching and Joy*. Alexandria, VA: ASCD.

Sullivan, M. 1996. *Feeling Strong, Feeling Free: Movement Exploration for Young Children*. (2nd ed.). Washington, D.C.: NAEYC.

Tomlinson, C. A. 1999. *The Differentiated Classroom: Responding to the Needs of All Learners*. Alexandria, VA: ASCD.

Topol, C. W. and L. Gandini. 1999. *Beautiful Stuff: Learning with Found Materials*. Worcester, MA: David Publishing Co.

Wardle, F. 1999. *Tomorrow's Children: Meeting the Needs of Multiracial and Multiethnic Children at Home, in Early Childhood Programs and at School*. Denver, CO: Center for the Study of Biracial Children.

Wolery, M. and J. W. Wilbers. (editors). 1994. *Including Children with Special Needs in Early Childhood Programs*. Washington, D.C.: NAEYC.

Yakota, J. (editor). 2001. *Kaleidoscope: A Multicultural Booklist for Grades K–8*. (3rd ed.). Urbana, IL: NCTE.

Yolen, J. 1992. *Street Rhymes Around the World*. New York: Boyds Mill.

York, S. 1992. *Developing Roots and Wings: A Trainer's Guide to Affirming Culture in Early Childhood Programs*. St. Paul, MN: Redleaf.

Zaslavsky, C. 1985. *The Multicultural Math Classroom: Bringing in the World*. Portsmouth, NH: Heinemann.

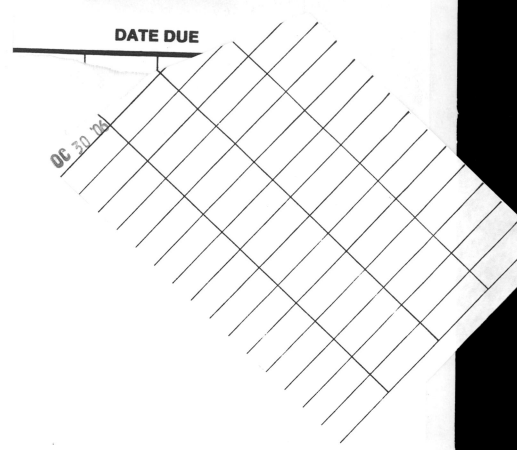